The Hidden Wisdom of the Goddess

The Hidden Wisdom of the Goddess

DEVADATTA KALI

MOTILAL BANARSIDASS PUBLISHERS
PRIVATE LIMITED • DELHI

First Indian Edition: Delhi, 2010
First Published in 2006 by Nicolas-Hays, Inc. Lake Worth, Florida, USA under the title *Veiling Brilliance: A Journey to the Goddess*

ISBN: 978-81-208-3425-5 (Cloth)
ISBN: 978-81-208-3466-8 (Paper)

MOTILAL BANARSIDASS
41 U.A. Bungalow Road, Jawahar Nagar, Delhi 110 007
8 Mahalaxmi Chamber, 22 Bhulabhai Desai Road, Mumbai 400 026
203 Royapettah High Road, Mylapore, Chennai 600 004
236, 9th Main III Block, Jayanagar, Bangalore 560 011
Sanas Plaza, 1302 Baji Rao Road, Pune 411 002
8 Camac Street, Kolkata 700 017
Ashok Rajpath, Patna 800 004
Chowk, Varanasi 221 001

For Sale in India Only

Printed in India

By Jainendra Prakash Jain at Shri Jainendra Press,
A-45 Naraina, Phase-I, New Delhi 110 028
and Published by Narendra Prakash Jain for
Motilal Banarsidass Publishers Private Limited,
Bungalow Road, Delhi 110 007

CONTENTS

Offered at the lotus feet of
Ma Dakshineswari

Preface

Most likely, any created thing has a moment of conception, and whether that moment slips by unnoticed or proclaims itself with fanfare, something has been set in motion. Something was set in motion on the evening of March 23, 2002, at Kali Mandir in Laguna Beach, California. Usha Harding had invited me to speak at the Kali temple about my recent translation of the Devimahatmya, published the following year as *In Praise of the Goddess*. Beyond speaking to the devotees, I had no idea of what else was to happen that night.

The evening began with devotional singing, led by Swami Bhajanananda, and soon the music rose to a heady intensity. I wondered if this fervent outpouring of love for Ma Kali was anything like the scenes of ecstatic devotion at Dakshineswar during Sri Ramakrishna's lifetime. When the singing ended, I arose and headed across the room to the speaker's seat, stopping on the way in front of the shrine to offer salutations to Ma Dakshineswari, the Laguna Beach Kali. In an instant the image's sparkling dark eyes wiped my mind blank of the talk I had planned to give. I sat down not knowing what to say.

Still, without hesitating, I began to retell the story of the Devimahatmya in my own words. In places where the text could speak better than I, the bound copy of my manuscript opened again and again to exactly the right place. For an hour and a quarter, reading, narrative, and spontaneous commentary flowed in an unbroken current, and the listeners' delight indicated that something special was happening.

Recently Usha confirmed this: "We remember that night. There was something in the air. I think Ma had her special blessing on you, because we all felt it; it was magic. I think the best talk you've ever given, you probably gave that night, because something happened between Ma and you. There was something going on. It was so magical. You were shining that night. I remember it clearly."

Two mornings later, while I meditated in my shrine at home, the idea crystallized for a second book. Taking the Devimahatmya as its point of departure, it would capture the simplicity, spontaneity, and joy of the evening at Kali Mandir. It would be a book for seekers of direct, simple answers to life's perennial questions and a book for those who approach the Divine Mother purely out of love. That morning the beginning pages wrote themselves.

The Veiling Brilliance: A Journey to the Goddess is an extended meditation in the form of a novel that follows the Devimahatmya's basic outline, condensed here and expanded there in freely imaginative ways. In the Devimahatmya the seer Medhas teaches through the language of myth, which cries out for interpretation, because little is spelled out. *The Veiling Brilliance* communicates the hidden wisdom of the holy man's teachings simply, directly, and eloquently.

Most of the book consists of newly invented scenes, incidents, and conversations between Medhas and his two disciples, the king Suratha and the merchant Samadhi. As the book progresses, the main characters become fleshed out and take on a life of their own. All the while, the writing probes ever deeper into the mysterious heart of human existence.

Each chapter belongs to the overall, unfolding narrative but focuses on a particular set of philosophical, psychological, or spiritual topics, presented in a natural, practical, and easy-to-understand way. The teachings derive from the vast body of Hindu wisdom found in the Rigveda Samhita, the Upanishads, the Bhagavadgita, Patanjali's Yogasutra, the Puranas, and the Tantras. Through the eloquent voice of the seer Medhas, these teachings convey the wisdom and grace I received personally from my own guru, Swami Prabhavananda, a spiritual grandson of Sri Ramakrishna Paramahamsa in the lineage of the Ramakrishna Order. This book represents also my own gathering of wisdom over four decades from many other revered teachers of the Ramakrishna-Vedanta lineage and from holy men and women of other traditions as well.

The Veiling Brilliance is a deliberately provocative title. In the course of Medhas's teaching, we learn that the Divine Mother, Shakti, projects the rich diversity of our human experience by veiling her own pure, undivided oneness. Reveling in her own divine play through the self-imposed limitations of time and space, she simultaneously and ever remains the self-luminous brilliance of infinite consciousness-bliss. The title aims to capture that seeming paradox.

■ ■ ■

Acknowledgement

I would like to thank everyone who directly or indirectly played a part in the creation of this book. Deepest gratitude to my guru, Swami Prabhavananda, and to my revered Ma Jaya Sati Bhagavati. Gratitude also to Usha Harding and Swami Bhajanananda of Kali Mandir for providing the circumstances that set the creative process in motion. Thanks to Swami Bhavatarini and Yogacharya Laxman Das Jaya of Kashi Ashram, Los Angeles for allowing me to read the book chapter by chapter as it took shape, and to the devotees who came to listen. Thanks to Valerie Cooper for her wise and caring oversight throughout the production of this book. Most of all, thanks to Kalishyam DeVito.

CHAPTER 1

The King, the Merchant, and the Seer

Ever so long ago, when the world was young, a king named Suratha ruled over a vast realm. He ruled justly and wisely and treated his subjects as though they were his own children. Throughout his kingdom, peace and prosperity reigned.

But human nature being what it is, ideal conditions rarely last for long. Envious of Suratha's power, some petty chieftains banded together and one day attacked the hill tribes who lived under the king's protection. Suratha had no choice but to go to war, and despite his superior forces and firm resolve, he was defeated in battle. With the taste of defeat bitter in his mouth, he retreated hastily through his lost lands to the safety of his capital.

There, weakened by his losses, the good king faced new adversaries. His ministers, now emboldened, grew corrupt and disposed to evil. They seized control of the city and plundered the treasury. Uncertainty and chaos spread through the streets and marketplaces, and the citizens, depending on their loyalties, lived either in fear or in wanton revelry.

Suratha should have fought to restore order. As a monarch and warrior he was duty-bound by the rules of his caste to uphold the eternal *dharma*, the proper order of things. Instead he let cowardice overwhelm him. He arranged for his wife and children to be spirited away to safety, and when the tumult threatened to reach the palace gates, Suratha, now fearing for his life, mounted his horse and slipped away.

He rode furiously into the early morning, glancing over his shoulder now and again to make sure he was not being followed. Desperately he urged his horse onward until the city had vanished over the horizon. Even then, with no sign of pursuit, horse and rider, welded by a singleness of purpose, galloped on and on into the accelerating heat, a solitary speck moving across the empty plain, trailing clouds of dust.

Suratha slackened the pace only when he felt his mighty steed faltering. Stopping now and then for rest and water where nature afforded it, he continued to flee southward away from the capital and toward what he knew not. One day passed in this way and then another. All through the second day he rode across the grasslands until nightfall, when fatigue overrode his fear and forced him to take shelter in a small ravine.

At the first sign of daylight he resumed his journey, and before the sun had reached its zenith, he forded a broad, shallow river. Then turning to the east, he came by late afternoon to the edge of a dense forest. The king cautiously directed his mount into the leafy coolness and pressed on. Had he not been so lost in despair, he might have noticed a quiet presence in the wilderness. Aranyani, the elusive mother and guardian of beasts and all sylvan things, moved gently amid the leaves with the sound of tinkling bells. But Suratha was as oblivious to the forest goddess's sweet sounds and scents as to the abundant foods she gave forth, all without the tilling of any field. With his mind gripped by the grief of loss, he made his way deeper and deeper into the dense wood until daylight faded and the moon's soft glow guided his slow journey through the long night.

Soon after daybreak, in the pale light of early morning, the king came upon the wall of an enclosure and followed it to an entrance. His first impulse was to ride grandly through the open gate—after all, he was the king, or had been until recently—but exhausted in body and spirit, he could not muster the strength for such grandness. No sooner had he entered the compound than there approached a young man with close-cropped hair. He wore a simple white cloth secured around his waist and sandals on his feet. After greeting the king, he asked him to dismount, and Suratha, too tired to object, complied and watched his horse being led away by a second young man of similar appearance. On the verge of collapse, the monarch allowed himself to be taken to a nearby hut, where he soon fell into a deep, troubled sleep.

When he opened his eyes, Suratha felt a dull ache in his head and fever coursing through his body. For a while he lay motionless, staring up through the dimness at a thatched ceiling, knowing neither where he was nor how long he had been there. As his eyes began to penetrate the gloom, he recalled having been brought to a hut—this hut, which he now surveyed. It was remarkably clean; even in the dim light its white-washed walls looked spotless. Raising himself on one elbow, Suratha saw that the hut was sparsely furnished. On the opposite side stood a cot similar to the one he lay on. Each cot claimed a small table, a shelf on the wall above, and nothing more.

The king arose, his head spinning, and went to the door on unsteady feet. Bracing himself against the door frame and the pale light outdoors, he peered through his feverish haze, unable to tell whether it was dawn or dusk. The hut stood in a small clearing, and directly ahead a path snaked its way through a tangle of lush foliage and towering trees. Just then an amazing sight met the king's eyes: a tiger approached, ambling peacefully along the path in the company of two fawns. Suratha blinked, not trusting what he saw, but the unlikely vision persisted. He blinked again, harder. No, it would not go away.

Then he heard a voice inquire, "Did you have a good rest?" Suratha turned and saw the young man who had met him at the gate.

"Where am I?" he asked.

"At the *ashrama* of Sri Medhas. He's a holy man, and we who live here follow his teachings."

"They too?" the king inquired, nodding toward the unlikely trio of tiger and fawns. His question veered between sarcasm and incredulity.

The young man laughed politely. "Yes, they too have been touched by our teacher's grace. Even the wild beasts become pacified here in the holy atmosphere." Despite the strangeness of his utterance, his smile was reassuring.

"How long have I been here?" the king asked, shifting the conversation back to himself and still hoping he was only dreaming and would soon wake up.

"You arrived just after sunrise, and since then the sun has set and risen again."

"I slept for a whole day?"

"It would seem so."

Again the king took the initiative. "I am King Suratha, the lord of this vast realm. I would like to meet this Sri Medhas."

"You shall," the young man replied, "in due time. But for now you must bathe and put on clean clothes, be properly fed, and allow yourself to enjoy the peace of our forest retreat, away from the cares of the world. When he thinks you are ready to see him, our master will receive you."

"But I am the king!"

"Your protestations will be of no avail here, my friend. Sri Medhas is the master, and as he wills, so shall it be. By the way," he added, "my name is Krishanu."

■ ■ ■

Certainly in this tranquil setting Suratha expected to find peace. For some days he wandered about the compound, exploring first in one direction and then in another. The ashrama was exactly as Krishanu had described it. To the north a swift-flowing river formed a natural boundary. The enclosure wall, made of vertical logs, ran southward from the river bank, then stretched eastward for a long distance until the land began to rise steeply and form a second natural boundary. The lush vegetation of the surrounding forest filled most of the compound as well, except for a series of clearings and a network of paths connecting them. In most of the clearings Suratha discovered one or two huts like the one he occupied. A larger clearing held a structure that housed a kitchen and dining hall, and beyond that lay a cluster of vegetable gardens and a pasture for the ashrama's few cows.

Suratha explored many of the paths, but there was one on which he did not venture. That was the path running eastward from a central point where most of the other paths converged. Set apart by a gate, it led to the dwelling-place of the holy man, Sri Medhas. Often the king would stand gazing at the gate, curious to know what lay beyond—a destination obscured by the luxuriant greenery that bordered the curving trail.

The king should have reveled in the natural beauty of his surroundings. He should have delighted in the multicolored birds and jewel-like butterflies, the fragrant flowers bursting into bloom, the rushing river's babble, and the sunlight glinting off its waves. He should have been soothed by the rustling of the tall trees overhead and the caress of the breeze. He should have felt at one with the glory of it all, but surprisingly he found neither joy nor peace. Instead, his mind churned with the recurring thoughts of the beloved city his ancestors had built and governed before him, now under the rule of despots. Was his family safe, his dear queen Malati and the children he doted on? How would his prized elephant fare in the hands of his enemies? His retainers, ever eager for favor and feasting, surely submitted now to other lords, who would squander the wealth he had amassed. Soon the treasury would be depleted, and hard times would fall upon the land. Clearly he had failed in his duty as a king.

The days wore on in solitary grief, until one day found him seated on a log just inside the ashrama's gate, sunk in despondency and idly tracing patterns in the dirt with a stick, as if to give shape to his sorrow, anger, worry, and regret. So lost was he in the thought of all his losses that he failed to notice a stranger approach until the man stood directly before him. Sensing his presence, the king looked up and asked, "Who are you, and what brings you here?"

Even before the stranger could reply, his dejected demeanor spoke loudly. His words only confirmed this appearance. "My name is Samadhi," he began haltingly. "I'm a merchant." He paused. "I was a merchant." Another silence. "But now I'm just a wanderer. It's not my choice. I come from a line of traders—in textiles—and used to be well off. My business prospered, and I gave my family everything they needed and more. Life was good. But as my sons grew up, they got greedy and plotted with my wife to seize control of my fortune. They threw me out. It hurts me to talk about this—it's embarrassing—but it's been a long while since I've had anybody to talk to. Strangers aren't that interested in hearing about my troubles. Maybe they have enough of their own. So, I just wander around from place to place with nothing to call my own. Except my sorrow," he sighed, "and the constant thought of my wife and children at home—my betrayers. And you know, I still worry about them and how they are."

"Why should you care?" the king exclaimed, more annoyed than sympathetic. The newcomer's plight had touched a raw nerve. "How can you still hold such thoughts for those who dispossessed you?"

"I know. It makes no sense. It's interesting that you ask, though, because I wonder too. I can't say I feel bitter even after what they did. I still feel affection for them, even though I know they don't deserve my love. The pain, awful as it is, hasn't hardened my heart. Why is that, and what can I do about it?"

The deposed monarch was hardly the one to answer that question, nor did he have to try.

Just then Krishanu approached and announced, "Sri Medhas will see you now—both of you."

The two men followed him eastward through the compound to the gate beyond which the king had not yet ventured. By now Suratha felt his anticipation melt into perplexity and resentment. This was not how he had imagined it would be. Why should this newly arrived stranger, who was clearly beneath his caste, intrude on his audience with the holy man? Suratha had imagined the meeting with Medhas as a meeting between equals, of one powerful man with another. Now he felt cheated, but he would not let it show. He may have been forced to give up his throne, but he would not surrender his dignity. Glancing sideways at the sorry figure who accompanied him up the path, he had a sudden change of heart. Pity tempered his resentment for this newcomer who walked along so innocent and unquestioning, not knowing in the least what lay ahead.

The path ended at a spacious clearing. On the far side stood a hut similar to all the others but four times larger. Behind it the hillside rose steeply. Just to the right and slightly forward grew a large *kadamba* tree with a canopy of dark, shiny leaves and globes of fragrant, orange flowers.

The king and the merchant caught their first sight of the sage, Sri Medhas, sitting crossed-legged on a low platform in the tree's cool shade. He wore the same plain attire as his disciples—a white cloth covering his body from the waist down. A second cloth, neatly folded, was draped over his left shoulder. The white sacred thread that crossed his bare chest identified him as a man of the priestly caste. Medhas wore his pure white hair in a topknot, and his smooth, lean face was clean-shaven. He had a golden complexion and a youthful radiance that belied his advanced age. Because of the simplicity of his appearance, the only thing that set him apart from his disciples was his aura of holiness and spiritual authority.

When the king and the merchant reached the platform, Medhas motioned for them to sit down and instructed Krishanu to bring refreshments for the guests. Suratha and Samadhi bowed with all the deference due the holy man and took their places where he had indicated.

Medhas's attitude was welcoming, and for a while the three men exchanged pleasantries. Soon Krishanu reappeared, bearing a tray with pottery cups of green coconut water and leaf-bowls containing fruits and sweets. Suratha and Samadhi partook of the food and drink with polite formality while Medhas intently regarded them. For Samadhi, who was ravenous, it was difficult to maintain any semblance of propriety, but he dared not commit a breach of manners before his host. When they had finished, Medhas asked the king and the merchant what had brought them to the forest.

First the king related in great detail all that he had suffered. When there was nothing more to tell, he grew thoughtful and said, "Revered sir, may I ask you one thing? Even here in this tranquil place, I'm coming to grief. I feel strongly possessive toward my lost kingdom as if it were still mine. Even though I know that others now rule in my place, my mind gives me no rest.

"And this poor fellow—" He indicated the merchant, who seemed too weary or perhaps too overawed by the holy man to speak for himself. The king told what he knew of the wanderer's plight. "I think you'll agree that he seems a good-hearted man, but he was robbed and humiliated by his wife and sons, forsaken by his own people and cast out with nothing but the clothes he wears." The soiled and tattered remnants of the merchant's once fine clothing now hung loosely on his body as a sorry reminder of his former affluence. The king winced at this wreck of a man and continued, "Still, his feelings of love toward his treacherous family persist. He and I—we're both caught in the grips of despair over our betrayal and loss, even though we should know better. I think you can say we're both men of knowledge, but we act as perplexed as those who are blind to right understanding."

At this the seer smiled, not in amusement, but out of compassion. His eyes sparkled with an inner light. Then, unexpectedly he arose and announced, "We're going for a walk." He chose a path that ran to the north along the base of the steep hillside and ascended gradually. After the men had walked for a while in silence, they arrived at a promontory overlooking the river. In the rapids below, the current frothed white before flowing swiftly but smoothly on downstream, a silver ribbon cutting through a sea of green. Beyond the far bank a grand vista opened up: the thick forest stretched northward toward a broad expanse of distant hills that rose to meet the cloudless sky.

Medhas stood for a while in contemplation before turning toward his guests. He pointed into the distance and asked unexpectedly, "What color are those hills?"

"Purple," the king replied.

"If I ask you to go there and bring back some foliage, what color will it be?"

"Green, of course, just like the foliage here."

"And not purple? Then why are the hills purple?"

"They're not—they only look that way."

"But that is what your eyes tell you, is it not—that the hills are purple?"

"Well, yes, but they're not, not really."

"Illustrious king, not long ago you told me that you are a man of knowledge, and now you cannot even tell me the color of the hills! How then do you expect to understand something as complex as your feelings of betrayal and loss? You say you should know better, being a man of knowledge, but of what knowledge do you speak?"

The king could speak of nothing at this point, let alone knowledge, so Medhas pressed on. "Do you know that knowledge is of two kinds, the lower and the higher?"

The king mutely shook his head.

"Then let me explain. Through the five senses—sight, hearing, smell, taste, and touch—living creatures have knowledge of the world. But the objects of the senses reveal themselves in different ways, depending on the creature that perceives them and the conditions under which they are perceived. The bat is blind by day but sees well at night, other creatures see better by day, and some see equally well by day or night. In the same way, the other senses also are differently attuned according to the creature that possesses them. Like other living beings, humans also gain knowledge of the world through the five senses. But in the case of humans there is much more to consider."

Medhas walked to a nearby tree and pointed toward a nest in the upper branches. "Look at those birds. Even though they feel the pangs of hunger, see how they busy themselves feeding their young! Why do you think that is? Are they expecting some favor in return, as humans expect gratitude from their offspring?" He paused while Suratha and Samadhi looked on expectantly. It was clear they had no idea where this conversation was headed.

Suratha ventured a guess. "Do you mean that birds are nobler than people?"

The holy man smiled. "Nothing of the sort. I mean that birds and animals have a different level of awareness than human beings. When birds ignore their own hunger but feed their young, they act out of instinct. Their behavior is inborn. But with people, matters are not so simple. People have the additional faculties of will and reason and the ability to make conscious choices. Often those choices arise from selfish motives and the hope of personal gain.

"But know for certain—and this is important," Medhas emphasized, "all these forms of awareness—sense perception, instinct, will, and reason—belong to the category of lower knowledge. And so, illustrious king, when you say that you and this merchant are men of knowledge, this is the knowledge of which you speak. Hear me well: this lower knowledge is subject to the delusion inherent in the world."

"Delusion?" the king queried. "How can you speak of knowledge and delusion in the same breath?"

"Are the hills green or purple?"

"I'm confused."

"Precisely!" The seer clasped his hands in obvious delight. "And so is everyone else. Not even the wise escape this delusion."

From the blankness that crossed the king's and the merchant's faces, Medhas knew he would have to explain a great deal more. Walking to the edge of the promontory, he pointed across the river to the opposite bank. "Do you see that elephant over there, taking a drink?"

"Yes."

"Now hold up your hand at arm's length and then move it to cover the elephant. Tell me, which is larger, your hand or the elephant?"

"Everyone *knows* the elephant is larger!" Suratha exclaimed, barely managing to conceal his annoyance. What a silly question.

"But is your hand not large enough to cover it?" Medhas asked.

"Well, my hand *looks* larger, but that's only because of its nearness. If I were over there with that noble beast, it would not be so."

"And so you see," Medhas said, "knowledge gained through the senses is relative. In every way, time and space distort our perceptions, and we know the world not as it is but only as we experience it from our own vantage point and according to our own capacity.

"If our senses deceive us so, how much more confused we become over our personal feelings, memories, reason, and will. For example, if I ask you tomorrow about the meal you will share tonight, will each of you remember it in the same way? Perhaps one of you likes eggplant or pulses and the other does not. You, a king, already know that our simple fare does not compare with the sumptuous feasts of your royal palace. And you, Samadhi, who are so hungry now, will you not remember that same simple food with delight? But will you not also grieve as you remember the meals taken at home with your wife and children while tonight you eat in the company of strangers? Do you see how feelings and memories affect what we experience?"

Medhas gave his visitors time to reflect. Then he resumed.

"Now, let us consider reason. If one is given faulty information to start with, reason will not lead to truth; and even with correct information, who is to say that logic will not take two people along separate paths to entirely different conclusions? If you have ever listened to philosophers debating, you will know exactly what I mean.

"And then there is will. That colors everything, because more often than not it is driven by desire, self-interest, and expectation. Moreover, as we journey from infancy to youth and from adulthood to old age, our desires change as everything steadily changes around us. What we wanted as children no longer appeals when we are grown up, and at every stage of life we view ourselves and the world in a different way.

"Since all these forms of knowing—or experiencing—are imperfect, knowledge as you understand it is thus confounded. How can you or anyone else not be subject to delusion and its attendant woes? Listen well: *nothing in this world is as it appears to be.*"

This was something neither the king nor the merchant had ever thought about before. They were intrigued but at the same time unsettled.

Then Medhas said something truly astonishing. "It is the blessed Mahamaya who seizes the minds of even the wise and hurls them into the whirlpool of attachment, the pit of delusion. She, the Divine Mother, creates all this universe, moving and unmoving. She, the Mahadevi—the Great Goddess—is the sovereign of all sovereigns. Even as she is the cause of bondage to this worldly existence, she graciously bestows liberation on humanity. You see, she is the supreme deluder and the supreme knowledge that dispels all delusion. That supreme knowledge is called the higher knowledge."

After some moments the king asked, "Revered sir, who is this Mahamaya? Where did she come from? What does she look like? How does she act? All this I wish to learn from you."

Medhas replied, "She is the possessor of great *maya*—that is what her name means—but then again it means that she *is* the great maya."

"Which is correct?" the king asked.

"What is the difference?" the holy man shrugged enigmatically. "One day you will understand."

The merchant, having no inkling of what the seer was talking about and wondering if the king did, felt compelled to ask, "What is maya?"

Medhas smiled gently. "There is much to tell, but the day's heat grows oppressive. In the morning I shall tell you more."

CHAPTER 2

MAHAMAYA

The soft light of Ushas, Goddess of the Dawn, began filtering into the hut where Suratha had lain awake for some time, his mind a swirling sea of thoughts and memories. Soon, in the wake of the goddess's heralding light, Surya, the sun god, would raise his fiery orb above the eastern horizon and cast his warmth-giving radiance on the new day. Across the room the merchant, who now occupied the other cot, slept fitfully, turning now and then and emitting an emphatic sigh, while the king reflected on the events of the day before.

His thoughts arose in no particular order, one memory or idea somehow prompting the next. Suratha glanced over at Samadhi. How different the merchant appeared now from when the king first saw him. Neatly groomed and dressed in the same clean garments as the ashrama's other residents, Samadhi looked entirely presentable.

Appearances—how deceptive they could be. Were the distant hills really green? The land that lay beyond them and in everv direction had until recently been the king's domain. Now look at me, Suratha thought. In the absence of other clothing, he too had little choice but to don the simple white garments of the ashrama, but on one point he remained adamant: he would not relinquish the narrow gold headband that still adorned his long, regal locks. It was a reminder, albeit a painful one, of his former glory. Were it not for that sign of kingship, would he be taken for anything but a commoner?

Samadhi was a commoner, and he had allowed his hair to be cut short, the king mused as his attention drifted back to the merchant. Samadhi stood at least half a head shorter than the king and was of slighter build. His finely formed features were softly contoured, not angular like the king's, and overall his face gave the impression of boyish innocence. He couldn't be as guileless as he looks, Suratha thought. After all he *is* a merchant. It's interesting, though, that he bears none of the aggressiveness typical of people whose livelihood depends on selling things. For this the king was thankful. This poor merchant, whose fine features were darkened with an unrelenting sadness—how unjust it had been for the king to resent his presence the afternoon before. He would apologize, except that doing so would reveal the pettiness that had briefly seized his mind. There was no need to embarrass himself.

The thatched roof overhead momentarily claimed the king's attention, stirring up mental images of the evening before—the thatched roof of the open-air dining hall, its wooden supporting pillars, the reed mats that covered the floor, the twenty-or-so residents of the ashrama seated in two facing rows amid murmurs of conversation. Suratha recalled himself and Samadhi sitting at the end of one row while two of Medhas's disciples ladled helpings of fish, vegetables, pulses, and boiled barley onto the leaf plates. Was it true what Medhas had said that afternoon—that the merchant would recall with sorrow the meals taken with his family in happier times? Samadhi had said little but seemed to eat with great pleasure. To the king's own royal palate the food was lamentably bland, owing to the prevailing idea at the ashrama that highly spiced fare increased the mind's restlessness and that onions and garlic, in particular, incited lust. Was that what Medhas taught—Medhas, who otherwise seemed so wise?

That thought prompted the return of a prickling question to the king's mind. Medhas had kept him waiting for several days before granting an audience. Then why, when Krishanu finally came with the summons, did he say, "The master will see you now—both of you"? How did

Medhas know of Samadhi's arrival? He could not have known. Krishanu must have taken it upon himself to include the merchant. No, he would not have assumed that authority for himself. There had to be another explanation. Just then the sound of the merchant emerging from his uneasy sleep brought Suratha out of his reverie.

An hour later, having bathed, dressed, and eaten the morning meal of barley porridge, curd, and fruit, Suratha and Samadhi set out for Medhas's hut. By now a shroud of milky gray had spread over the sun god's brilliance and drained the world of color, adding to the king's desolation. Suratha wondered about his companion's frame of mind but, not being a man to share his own feelings, he did not ask. And so, the two men moved along the forested path, together but separate, each encased in his own private suffering.

Yet behind those walls of silence there was anything but quietude. Each man recalled in his own way the previous day's conversation with the seer. Medhas had goaded them into thinking. Now curious, they approached his abode, eager for further instruction.

"So, you have come back," the holy man said by way of greeting. "Please, friends, sit down." He directed them to the platform under the kadamba tree, its dense shade now weighted with the gloom of the cloud cover overhead.

At first Medhas said nothing, but regarded the king and then the merchant intently. A proud bearing, the king's, he observed, but beneath it a burden of grief, anger, and self-doubt. Still, he made for an imposing figure beside the slighter merchant, who wore his grief openly. Tragedy beclouded Samadhi's face, but behind the sadness Medhas detected a glimmer of inquisitiveness in his dark eyes.

"What I am about to tell you," he began, "is not given to everyone to hear. Of the few who hear, fewer still comprehend. Rare indeed is he who speaks of it, fortunate are they who learn of it, but blessed are they who truly understand." A momentous pause ensued. Then Medhas continued, "I shall accept both of you as my disciples. The formalities can wait until later, but now let us begin the instruction."

Not knowing the proper response for such a situation, if indeed there was one, Suratha and Samadhi remained quiet.

"Ever since the world began, men and women have tried to make sense of their lives. The basic questions are three: Where do we come from? Why are we here? Where are we going? Not everyone likes to think about these matters. The more deeply one questions, the more questions arise. It can be disconcerting. Do you see the danger? Except for those few who are naturally inclined toward such inquiry, people are happier keeping themselves occupied with their day-to-day living than giving any thought to the bigger questions. Do you follow me?"

The two disciples nodded.

"Those bigger questions arise only when something goes dreadfully wrong. We all experience ups and downs, but we do not question the good times. Why am I so fortunate? Who asks that? One simply enjoys the good fortune. Why am I so miserable? Ah, that is another story! When misfortune arises—an accident, an injustice, an illness, a death—suddenly there are many questions. Why did this happen? Why was I wronged in this terrible way? Why was I deposed?" Medhas looked knowingly at the king, then shifted his glance to the merchant. "Why was I robbed and betrayed by those I love?" He added, "What will happen to me? Is there anything I can hold onto? What law governs us, whose lives run their course through happiness and misery? Does anything make sense here and now? Does anything have any ultimate meaning?"

Turning to the king, Medhas said, "You asked yesterday, 'Who is this goddess called Mahamaya, and what is her origin?' Now I shall tell you. She is the Devi, the Divine Mother. She has no origin, because she is self-existent. You asked what she looks like. She is formless, yet all forms are hers. Indeed, it is she herself who has become all this." Medhas emphasized "all this" with a graceful, sweeping gesture, as if to encompass the whole of creation. "She pervades all that is. Though eternal and everywhere present, she also comes forth in specific ways to accomplish the purpose of the gods, and then she is said to be born in the world."

"The purpose of the gods?" Suratha interrupted.

"Yes. Their purpose is to defend the cosmic order against the chaos wrought by demonic forces. To the gods it is given to see that day follows night and night follows day, that the rains fall in the appointed season, that the earth blossoms and brings forth abundance, that prosperity graces every home, and that humankind abides in peace. Whenever the gods fail and wickedness spreads over the earth, the Devi herself, who is more powerful than all the gods together, intervenes to restore order and righteousness.

"These are the answers to your questions, illustrious king, yet I see by your face that they fail to satisfy you. Allow me to relate the story of how the blessed Mahamaya overcame a pair of demons named Madhu and Kaitabha. Listen while I tell exactly how it happened."

BEFORE THE PRESENT CREATION, when the previous universe was dissolved into an endless cosmic sea, the blessed Lord Vishnu lay slumbering on the thousand-headed serpent, Shesha, who drifted on the primordial waters. From Vishnu's navel grew a lotus stalk as radiant as sunlight. It swayed gently in the breeze, and in the blossom that crowned it sat Brahma, the Lord of Creation, gazing in the four directions at once.

Suddenly two demons—the *asuras* named Madhu and Kaitabha—sprang forth from the wax in Vishnu's ears. When these monsters saw Brahma, their first and only impulse was to kill and devour him. Repeatedly they shook the lotus stalk, attempting to dislodge him from his place of safety. Desperately Brahma tried to awaken Vishnu—who could not be awakened, for the sleep that had settled over his eyes was the Great Goddess Mahamaya herself. Finally Brahma had no recourse but to appeal to the goddess with a hymn of praise and ask her to release Vishnu from her spell. Adoringly he sang:

You are the mantras of consecration to the gods and the ancestors. At your bidding they are uttered, and they are your very embodiment. You are the nectar of immortality, O imperishable, eternal one. Truly you abide as the transcendent being.

Yet in every moment you abide, inseparable and inexpressible, as the eternal source of all becoming. Indeed you are she, Savitri, the source of all purity and protection; you are the supreme mother of the gods.

By you is this universe supported, of you is this world born, by you is it protected, O Devi, and you always consume it at the end.

You are the creative force at the world's birth and its sustenance for as long as it endures. So even at the end of this world, you appear as its dissolution, you who encompass it all.

You are the great knowledge and the great illusion, the great intelligence, the great memory and the great delusion, the great goddess and the great demoness.

You are primordial matter, differentiating into the threefold qualities of everything. You are the dark night of periodic dissolution, the great night of final dissolution, and the terrifying night of delusion.

You are radiant splendor; you reign supreme yet are unassuming; you are the light of understanding. Modesty are you, and prosperity, contentment, tranquility, and forbearance.

Armed with sword and spear, and with club and discus, waging war with conch, bow and arrows, sling and iron mace, you inspire dread.

Yet, you are pleasing, more pleasing than all else that is pleasing, and exceedingly beautiful. Transcending both highest and lowest, you are indeed the supreme sovereign.

Whatever exists, true or untrue, and wherever it may be, O soul of everything, you are the power of all that. How can I praise you?

By you, even he who creates, protects, and devours the world is subdued with sleep. Who here can praise you?

You have caused even Vishnu, Shiva, and me to assume our embodied forms. Who then can truly praise you?

Thus extolled, O Devi, may you with your exalted powers confound those unassailable asuras, Madhu and Kaitabha.

Let Vishnu, the lord of the world, be quickly awakened from his slumber and be roused to slay the two great asuras.[1]

Hearing this hymn, the dark goddess emerged from Vishnu's eyes, mouth, nostrils, and heart and appeared before Brahma. Sparkling like a deep blue sapphire, she was infinite as the night sky, and her ten hands, betokening omnipresence, revealed the range of her powers from the dark destructiveness of ever-turning time to the penetrating brilliance of the knowledge that dispels all unknowing.

Vishnu awoke and beheld the raging asuras, still shaking the lotus stalk though without much success. Ugly brutes, he thought, all brawn and no brain, no doubt. And he rose up and fought with them, hand-to-hand. But Madhu and Kaitabha, exceedingly strong and courageous and seeing red with anger, kept up the fight for five thousand years. With no end to the battle in sight, the dark goddess once again intervened and caused the undefeated asuras to grow intoxicated with their own might.

Huffing and puffing in the heat of battle and confounded by Mahamaya, they exclaimed breathlessly to Vishnu, "Your valor so pleases us that—we have decided—to offer you—a boon. Ask what you will, and—it shall be granted."

Without hesitating, Vishnu replied, "Since you are pleased with me, so be it. I can think of only one boon. Let me slay both of you here and now."

That was not what Madhu and Kaitabha had in mind, if they had anything in mind at all beyond their own self-aggrandizement, and too late they realized their folly. About to be done in by their own arrogant stupidity, they made a final, desperate effort to save themselves. Looking about at the endless expanse of water, they exclaimed, "Very well, but slay us only where water does not flood the earth."

Again Vishnu was too clever for them, for in their language the words for *earth* and *thigh* sounded almost alike. And so, the blessed Lord Vishnu lifted Madhu and Kaitabha to his thighs and lopped off their heads.

Medhas laughed heartily. "It is said that a pun is the lowest form of humor and this is fitting because Madhu and Kaitabha represent the lowest form of humanity. Their awareness is densely shrouded in ignorance. Does their unprovoked attack on Brahma not remind us of the senseless violence in this world? Madhu and Kaitabha are intent on gratifying their base instincts, usually through brute force. Indeed, they thrive on the thrill of intimidation. You see in this story how through physical strength they grow exceedingly vainglorious."

With Medhas regarding him earnestly now, the king thought he should say something. He cleared his throat and observed, "Of course, pride goes before a fall." Uncomfortable in the ensuing silence, he added, "There is danger in taking oneself too seriously, isn't there?"

"By all means, but I urge you to look more deeply. As you say, the story of Madhu and Kaitabha is a cautionary tale, but you have only scratched the surface. Those two demons represent the most brutish aspects of human nature. People of such unevolved character live barely above the level of beasts. That is why a person of this nature is referred to as a *pashu*, literally a creature that is fettered."

"Fettered by what?" the king inquired.

"By the bonds of ignorance, of course! Unawakened as such people are to human decency and the higher virtues, they understand only violence, anger, and brute force. They know neither generosity nor kindness. Overblown ideas of their own importance delude them. They seek only their own satisfaction without regard for others."

"Surely you are not implying that either I or the merchant here are men of such character?"

"Of course not, but should you ever recognize even a trace of such cruelty or arrogance in yourselves, you must call on the Devi to help you overcome those faults."

"I would not allow such thoughts to enter my mind," the king protested.

"You are missing an important point. The great Lord Vishnu, the sovereign of the gods, was powerless to defeat the demons without the Mother's help. Only when she exposed Madhu and Kaitabha's vulnerability was it possible for Lord Vishnu to accomplish their destruction. As you said, pride goes before a fall."

The merchant, sensing tension, broke through his reticence to change the subject. "Revered sir, the hymn that Brahma sang—it's beautiful, but there is much I don't understand. Can you tell us what it means?"

Medhas beamed, recognizing in Samadhi a quiet disposition that eventually would be drawn to a contemplative life. "I told you yesterday that nothing in this world is as it seems to be. Do you remember?"

It was a startling utterance that neither Samadhi nor the king could have forgotten.

"The hymn is all about appearance and reality. It contains many matters for philosophical discussion, but for now you need not concern yourself with the details. What you need to know is that Brahma's words of praise reveal the nature of the Divine Mother, the world, and human existence.

"Have you ever witnessed offerings being made to the gods—how the priests chant mantras when pouring oblations into the sacrificial fire? Brahma says that those sacred mantras are the Divine Mother's actual embodiment. Their sounds express her presence and power—they *are* her presence and power. You see, she herself directs our actions and makes them efficacious.

"Through her power, called maya, the Divine Mother gives birth to everything and fills it with her presence. She is the mother of the gods and men and every living creature, from the exalted to the lowly. Everything emerges from her and has its being in her. Everything returns to her in the end, for hers alone is the power to create, sustain, and dissolve.

"But beyond that—," Medhas trailed off, regarding his two listeners thoughtfully. How to express the inexpressible? "Beyond this world of matter and the senses, beyond this world of appearances, there is a greater reality. The Divine Mother is that reality. *She is the pure oneness that is the essence of all this.*" With a start Medhas raised his hands to chest level, palms outward, as if in a gesture of wonder at what he had just expressed. Then, clasping his hands over his heart, he smiled, joyful and satisfied.

"How can we name that which is beyond name and form?" he continued. "Some call her Adyashakti, the primordial power. Others say she is *anuttara*—that beyond which there is nothing else. Some call her Brahman—the infinite, ever-blissful consciousness."

Suratha and Samadhi tried to wrap their minds around this, but it was too big.

Medhas paused, thinking about how to proceed. He knew by heart the philosophy that explained these matters but needed to transform the abstract words into the luminous reality they sought to describe. It would not be easy. King Suratha was a man of action and the world, not given to high-flown thought, but Samadhi, he could see, would come to follow the path of inquiry and dispassion in his quest for knowledge.

The seer continued, "You have both known the pleasure and the pain of existence in this world. You, Suratha, enjoyed the power of kingship, even while honoring its responsibility. You knew the respect and affection of your subjects and lived an opulent life with every comfort your heart could desire. Yet you saw every delight slip through your fingers and turn to dust. Where is that pleasure now? The memories of your former happiness bring only bitterness and grief." He eyed the gold diadem the king had refused to give up.

"And you, Samadhi, enjoyed material comfort and the love of family. Your betrayal is more bitter than the king's, coming from those dearest to you—your wife and sons—yet you still cherish them in your heart. But what pain is greater than that of lost love? You cannot bear to let go, nor can you endure much longer the agony of holding on. You are being torn apart.

"I say this to both of you. Only by understanding the nature of the world can you rise above it and its sorrow. There is no joy without misery, and no misery without joy. This pattern is woven into the very fabric of the universe. Hear me out, because we must start at the very beginning."

Suratha and Samadhi shifted positions and settled in for what promised to be a long but intriguing lesson.

"There are some who say that God the Mother is the impersonal Brahman without form—that it is neither male nor female nor neuter. Nothing can be said about it. Having experienced it in the deepest states of meditation, its knowers call it *sat-chit-ananda*, pure being-consciousness-bliss. Even this is only an approximation, bound by language and the smallness of our understanding. This supreme reality is One without a second. Truly, there is nothing else.

"What, then, can we say of our realm of manyness? Do you never look around and wonder how this wide world and the vast, vaulted sky came into existence? The fiery sun and softly glowing moon? The plants and all living creatures? What manner of being created the radiant beauty and awesome power of all this? It is all the Divine Mother's doing. She said, 'I am one; let me become many.' Just as the tiny seed contains, invisible within itself, the mature tree with its leaves and branches, trunk and roots, and all the rest, the entire universe exists within the seed that philosophers call the *bindu*. And what is this bindu? It is the Mother's creative power concentrated into a single point and ready to expand into the whole of creation."

The merchant sat unmoving but moved, his mouth slightly open at the wonder of what he was hearing. As for Suratha, his impassivity revealed nothing of what he thought.

"To sum up thus far, when the Mother is inactive and abides as the pure formlessness of being-consciousness-bliss, she is called Brahman. When she is active and manifests herself through her power of creation, she is called maya or Shakti. Imagine a vast ocean endlessly stretching without movement, so calm that its surface is like a mirror and its depths are perfectly clear. Now imagine that same ocean during a tempest, lashed into waves that rise up, take form, and subside. No reflectivity remains on the surface, and the clarity of the depths is obscured. The Mother herself declares, 'I breathe forth like the wind, setting all the worlds in motion.' Yet in either state, what is the ocean but water? Do you understand how Brahman and Shakti are one and the same, though appearing different?"

Here the merchant interjected somewhat shyly, "Yesterday you said that Mahamaya meant either 'She whose maya is great' or 'she who is the great maya.' When the king asked which was correct, you asked, 'What is the difference?' I think I understand now."

The guru clasped his hands in delight. "Yes! You see, it is not a matter of either this one or that one being true; both are true. There is no difference between power—Shakti—and the possessor of power!"

Along with his joy at the merchant's quickness to grasp this idea, Medhas sensed that he was losing the king's attention. That would not do. Lest Suratha's mind glaze over and the lesson be lost on him, the holy man urged, "The matters we are talking about now may seem remote and abstract and of no immediate value. These are impersonal expressions of the Divine, but the Mother also assumes personal forms, which are more easily approached. Then she is called by other names, such as Chandika, Ambika, Durga, or Kali, depending on how she reveals herself. You see, there are many different ways to reach her. Later we shall discuss the practical matters, such as how to live in this world, how to cope with its constant flux of enjoyment and misery, how to make moral choices, and how to find lasting peace and satisfaction. But for now, please bear with me."

With the king's renewed attention, the philosophy lesson continued. "Before the beginning, when not even time and space exist, Shakti is one. She is also called *prakriti*, which means 'primordial matter' or 'nature,' but remember that this is pure, unexpressed energy in itself. Next this energy expresses itself in three different ways as the three basic forces of the universe. They are called *gunas*, or 'threads.' You may think of the gunas as the threads from which the Divine Mother weaves the fabric of creation. A nice image."

Medhas seemed pleased to have presented a difficult abstraction in a way that the king and the merchant could easily grasp. "*Guna* also means 'quality,'" he continued. "The gunas are *sattva*, *rajas*, and *tamas*. Tamas is the Mother's power to conceal. It manifests as darkness, heaviness, inertia, dullness, and stupidity. Sattva is the revealing power. We experience it as light, calmness, purity, goodness, and wisdom. Tamas and sattva are like opposite poles and between them is rajas, the energy by which they act on each other. Rajas manifests as restlessness, impurity, urgency, and passion.

"As the universe evolves, the gunas combine and recombine into ever more complex patterns. Their interplay forms all created things from physical matter to human thoughts and feelings. Everything in the universe is nothing but the vibrating energy of the gunas, which in turn is the vibrating energy of consciousness.

"Take, for example, that stone." Medhas pointed to a half-buried rock at the other side of the clearing. He laughed. "Just imagine! A lesson from a stone! Which guna do you think predominates in it? Remember, all three are present in every created thing although the patterns and proportions differ in every case."

"That's easy," the king answered. "Tamas. The stone is not active; it just sits there. It's heavy and would resist being moved, but if it were rolled down a hill, its own weight would make it unstoppable. And it's very dense—no light can shine through it."

"Excellent!" This was more than Medhas had hoped for.

Next as an example of something rajasic the seer mentioned a fierce tiger—not one from his holy ground, of course, but a wild one from the surrounding forest. Then he asked if either of his listeners could think of something sattvic.

"The moon," Suratha suggested confidently, "because its light soothes the earth."

Medhas concurred, then asked his disciples to consider their own moods. When they were content, which guna ruled?

"Sattva."

And which guna prevailed in states of anger or agitation?

"Rajas."

In states of despondency or exhaustion?

"Tamas."

Medhas went on, "Just consider this. If you observe your moods as the play of the gunas, will they still toss you around so violently as they have until now? Will you not cultivate dispassion by knowing that it is not you who are fearful or sad or restless or angry, but merely the gunas that are at play in your mind? With this understanding, will you not cease to identify with those passing moods and claim them as your own?"

At last, here was a teaching that Suratha and Samadhi could put to practical use.

"In the hymn," Medhas reminded them, "Brahma calls the Devi 'the great knowledge and the great illusion, the great intelligence, and the great delusion.' He points out that the Divine Mother is everything, whatever its quality. Do you understand?"

Suratha and Samadhi hesitated. The implications were troubling.

"There is nothing in creation that is not the Mother. She is everything, whether she uses her power to reveal or conceal, to enlighten or confound. Why, Brahma even says she is the Great Goddess and the Great Demoness!"

Yes, the implications were indeed troubling. The disciples were confused at this revelation. Perhaps they wanted to be confused; after all, it was better than being disconcerted.

Medhas knew what he had to say. "Think of dark and light, heat and cold, good and evil, happiness and misery, endless pairs of opposites. This is called duality. This is what you experience. You must consider that the Mother controls everything, positive and negative alike, for she is the supreme power of the universe. But you must remember also that she is the *only* power in the universe. Through her play of the gunas, all this arises." Again Medhas punctuated "all this" with a sweeping gesture.

"We cannot dispute that good and evil exist, because we experience them in our own lives. Can you deny that? Of course not! But good and evil exist only in a relative sense—that is, relative to each other. Without the concept of good, there could be no idea of evil, and the reverse is also true. Neither is possible without the other to define it. This is a profound truth: The Mother is the source of both, yet she is beyond both. She encompasses and transcends all."

Silence descended while the king and the merchant considered the holy man's words. After a while Samadhi began to fidget. He obviously wanted to ask a question, but his natural reticence held him back. Finally, with an assenting nod from Medhas, he spoke.

"Revered sir, Brahma mentioned three different kinds of night and said that the Mother was all of them. What did he mean?"

"Ah, you are referring to 'the dark night of periodic dissolution, the great night of final dissolution, and the terrifying night of delusion.' You see, everything goes in cycles, just as day alternates with night. When the universe is manifest, that period is called a day of Brahma, and the Lord of Creation is said to be awake. He remains awake for four billion, three hundred twenty million human years. When the universe dissolves back into seed form, Brahma is said to sleep for an equal length of time and that is called the dark night of periodic dissolution. Three hundred sixty such days and nights make one year of Brahma. After one hundred such years everything dissolves completely into the Absolute for an equal time, and that is called the great night of final dissolution. Then the cycle of creation begins anew."

Suratha and Samadhi struggled to imagine such numbers, but the magnitude was well beyond their grasp.

"Now, the terrifying night of delusion is something quite different. This is the darkness of duality, the condition in which the vast majority of men and women the world over live day by day, bound by desires and attachments and fears, completely unaware of anything beyond their petty concerns and—even worse—completely unaware of their own limited understanding. Even in our benighted state we all live in the Mother; we just do not know it.

"But notice that in the next breath Brahma praises the Devi as radiant splendor and the light of understanding. The philosophers teach that Mahamaya is both *avidyamaya*, the deluding power that binds us to worldly existence, and *vidyamaya*, the liberating power of divine knowledge.

"What a spectacle she parades before our eyes! Everywhere we look, we see limitless possibility, breathtaking beauty, and appalling horror. How easily we go from success to failure, from elation to despair, as you two well know. In this way we are deluded by the Great Goddess Mahamaya, whose dark aspect veils her infinite perfection and creates this imperfect world. In such a world torn between apparent good and apparent evil, questions naturally arise. How do we conduct our lives? In virtue or in vice, or does it matter?"

Medhas thought that would be a good place to leave off. "Now go and reflect on what I have told you," he instructed. "Surely you have much to think about for the next few days."

CHAPTER 3

DURGA

"No philosophy today," Medhas laughed while motioning for his disciples to sit down. "Not much, anyway—but many, many more demons. More than you can count!"

Suratha wrinkled his brow. "Like Madhu and Kaitabha?"

"We have finished with them for now. But who knows? Maybe those two dimwits will have something more to teach us later on. There are many other demons far more clever than they, and you must watch out for all of them!

"We call the demons asuras, *daityas*, or *danavas*, and there are reasons for these names. Do you remember how we talked earlier about duality, the pairs of opposites that account for so much of human misery? Now think about this: the word *sura* means 'god,' and the word *asura* means the opposite, 'demon.' The gods bring blessings and the demons create strife. That is simple enough.

"So that you will have more insight, I shall tell you about another pair of opposites. One of the most ancient names of the Great Mother is Aditi, which means 'undivided boundlessness.' Aditi's dark opposite is Diti, restriction, and her sons are the daityas. As for the danavas, they are the sons of Danu, whose name, like Diti's, refers to cutting off or division. What do these words teach us about good and evil? They teach that the divine qualities are infinitude, wholeness, freedom, and light, and that the demonic qualities are limitation, separation, bondage, and darkness.

"You have already learned how the Divine Mother used her tamasic power to confound and defeat the brutish Madhu and Kaitabha. Admittedly, the world-creating goddess, Mahamaya, seems abstract and remote. Now I shall tell you about the Mother in a more personal form and about a far more clever demon whom she slew through the power of rajas. You see, the Divine Mother acts in this world. Listen well, great king. This story is meant especially for you."

LONG AGO, WHEN THE GOLDEN, thunder-armed Indra ruled the celestial kingdom, order and harmony prevailed in the three worlds of heaven, atmosphere, and earth. Under the rule of this mighty protector and doer of fair deeds, the gods—the shining *devas*—attended to the natural order of things, each to his own duty, and there was neither strife nor misfortune in the world. As wide as the heavens' reach Indra's power extended, and the people on earth enjoyed prosperity and peace.

But there arose a fierce demon named Mahishasura. He was called the buffalo demon, for he had assumed the powerful form of a buffalo in order to conquer the other asuras and become their chief. But the mystery of such power is that it fails to satisfy, and under its spell Mahisha craved only one thing: still more power. And so it happened that he marshaled his demonic hordes and stormed the gates of heaven. Although Indra's celestial forces fought bravely for a full hundred years, in the end Mahisha was victorious. He expelled the gods from their dwelling place and proclaimed himself the lord of heaven.

The hosts of celestial gods beyond number sank into the despondency of the dispossessed. Following Brahma's lead into exile, they went off in search of Vishnu and Shiva. Finding them, they related in detail how Mahishasura had wrought their defeat.

Together they lamented, "He has flung the sun god, Surya, from his resplendent throne and usurped the authority of Indra, our glorious chief. Great Agni, the god of fire, the messenger between heaven and earth, no longer attends the sacrifices of men, no longer carries their offerings skyward to us. This Mahisha has seized the wind god Vayu's gentle breezes, and the earth now suffers in scorching heat. None of us can fulfill our natural functions, not even Yama, the lord of death, who causes everything to pass in its season. Chaos reigns while demons rule, and we, cast out from heaven, wander over the earth as mere mortals.

"We appeal to you, Lord Vishnu and Lord Shiva. Great gods, can you not devise a means for this evil Mahishasura's destruction?"

When Vishnu and Shiva heard these pitiful pleas, they knit their brows in fury. A breathless silence ensued, and then a great radiance shone forth from Vishnu's rage-contorted face and from the faces of Shiva and Brahma.

And then from Indra's body and the bodies of all the other gods, that same great light streamed forth, united, and became one. The gods saw in their midst a blazing mountain of light pervading the sky in every direction. Within its unformed radiance features began to take shape.

In the light that streamed from Shiva's face, the Devi's own lovely face appeared. Vishnu's radiance formed her graceful, yet powerful arms. The moon god's soft luster took shape as her rounded breasts, and Agni's flaming brilliance, her three eyes. In the same way, each god's resplendence was revealed as part of her body. One by one her features emerged until the auspicious Devi Durga, fully revealed, stood before them in all her glory, and they rejoiced.

Then awestruck and humbled, they recognized that the great Durga was not their creation at all. The light that emerged from them was not their own, but the splendor of her indwelling presence, fragmented among the many gods and now reuniting at its source. They were but the agents of her power. How could they have forgotten? Had she herself not said as much when she proclaimed: "I move through the gods of storm and light, through the gods of the heavens, through all the gods. I uphold the lords of day and night, the sovereign of the atmosphere, the god of fire, and the benevolent celestial guardians. I am the sovereign in whom all the auspicious gods are united. Shining with consciousness, I am foremost among those worthy of worship. The gods diffuse me in every direction, my presence abiding in many places and revealed in manifold ways."

Each deva thought of his individual power and knew that it was ultimately the Devi's own merely working through him. To acknowledge the truth of this, each god in turn approached the resplendent Durga and knelt reverently before her.

Shiva drew out a trident from the one he bore and placed it in her hand, saying, "This trident is the essence of your threefold power over time, space, and causation. Through you alone I wield this power, which truly belongs to you."

Then Vishnu spun out a flaming discus from the one he held, saying, "This solar wheel of ever-turning time holds the power of life and death. Through you alone I wield this power, which in truth belongs to you, the supreme Shakti."

Agni presented a spear that flamed with the piercing light of knowledge, and Indra held out the thunderbolt of invincibility and illumination. Brahma offered prayer beads, symbolizing devotion, and an ascetic's water pot brimming with the purifying water of self-restraint. Still more the Devi received in recognition of her omnipotence, as one by one the gods acknowledged her as the true possessor of all power and themselves as her agents.

In the same way, they recognized in the Devi Durga all that was gentle and lovely. Kubera, the lord of wealth, brought forth a drinking vessel ever-brimming with the wine of bliss. Other gods presented the ever-renewing garments of nature's seasonal array and jewelry beyond compare, set with every kind of precious gem and sparkling indescribably. As if such beauty were not enough, they decked the Devi with garlands of unfading lotuses, the mark of eternal purity.

Finally, Himalaya, the Lord of Mountains, stepped forth with a lion to ride upon, magnificent of body and all-conquering in strength. "This lion," he said, "is the whole and mighty dharma, for in righteousness and truth you move through the world. Hence you will be known as Simhavahini, the lion-mounted goddess. Hail to you, and victory!"

"*Jai Ma*—victory to the Mother!" the gods exclaimed joyfully while the sages who witnessed this scene bowed in devotion.

Then the Devi laughed defiantly, filling the sky with her thunderous roar. From the immeasurable din a great echo resounded and shook all the worlds. The oceans churned, the earth quaked, and the mountains heaved as if their massiveness weighed no more than a cloud. When the enemies of the gods saw the three worlds in disarray, they rose up as one and hastened to their leader.

"What is this?" Mahishasura bellowed in fury. He commanded all the asuras to prepare for battle. Quickly they formed an army around him—a vast ocean of weapons and armor glinting in the light. Thus readied, Mahisha rushed headlong toward the source of the commotion and there beheld the awesome Durga, who is called Chandika because of her fierce glory. He saw her penetrating every direction with her arms, bending the earth under her tread, piercing the sky with her crown, and sending shock waves through the nether regions with the terrifying resonance of her bowstring. What manner of woman was this?

Dumbfounded but enraged still more, Mahisha prepared to attack, and at his signal the battle between his demonic forces and the Devi Chandika began. Swords and missiles, hurled in every direction, thickened the air. The light reflecting off them lit up the quarters of the sky until swallowed in the billowing dust clouds of the advancing cavalry, chariots, elephants, and footsoldiers. Led by the great general Chikshura, they advanced in deadly, graceful waves—demons coarse and belligerent and foul in every conceivable way. Multitudes of elephants and horses streamed around Parivarita, the demon of encircling gloom and confusion, who seizes the mind and imprisons it in despondency.

Amid the din of battle stood the evil Mahishasura, reveling in the power he commanded—lances and javelins, spears and clubs, swords and axes in uncountable numbers, all aimed at the Devi. Surely she had no hope of survival.

But while the asuras swarmed about, grimly determined to assault her, she showered them with weapons as if in play. She remained serene, hearing through the din of battle the sweet praises of the gods and seers who looked on.

Next the Devi's heaving sighs became her legions by the hundreds and thousands, borne on the current of her breath to destroy the daitya hordes. They reveled in the zest of battle while the Devi brought down multitudes of demons, leaving gory trails in their wake. Under the crushing blows of her mace, some asuras vomited forth blood. The Devi's arrows flew so thick that the daityas they struck lay on the ground like bristling porcupines, breathing their last. Shrieks of agony rent the dense, dusty air, the sounds of horror unimaginable. Asuras, their legs cut from under them, toppled heavily to the blood-soaked ground, while others fell in two, severed lengthwise by the Devi's slashing sword. While the battle drums throbbed and the conches blared their raucous notes, decapitated asuras fell and rose again, irresistibly drawn into the dance of destruction—headless bodies dancing, still grasping weapons in hand.

Where that battle raged, the earth became impassable with fallen chariots, elephants, horses, and corpses. Torrents of blood gushed like mighty, frothing rivers, and there the Devi's lion-mount, shaking its mane in fury, prowled among the demon throngs in search of any life-breath still issuing from the enemies' nostrils.

As quickly as fire consumes a heap of straw and wood, the Devi brought the vast legions of the gods' foes to destruction. When the battle was over, she stood victorious amid the carnage, while in praise the gods showered her with flowers.

"Well, Suratha, what do you think?" Medhas asked. "Do you know why this story was intended for you?"

Darkness draped the king's motionless face. While the moments throbbed on, he could feel the seer's expectation and also the fullness of Samadhi's attention. In the merchant's eyes the king was certain he detected sympathy.

After a deep breath he spoke. "I am a king without a kingdom. All my lands, my palace, my wealth, my sovereignty, and everything I held dear were wrested from me by enemies, just as Indra and the other gods were deposed and cast out of heaven by the asuras. My situation is very much like theirs. They wander the earth in exile, bereft of their former glory. I sit before you an outcast who suffers the pangs of separation and loss." The king struggled to hide his anger.

"You say," Medhas queried, "that what happened to Indra and the gods is what happened to you?"

"The circumstances are similar. Or do I presume too much, comparing myself to the gods?"

"You are a king and a warrior. You know from the sacred law that royal power is an earthly reflection of divine power and that your duty is to uphold the dharma. As a king you rule by divine right and are obliged to preserve justice and order. What happens in heaven reverberates in earthly affairs. So, you see, you are not at all presumptuous in comparing your situation to that of the unfortunate gods."

Suratha was relieved not to have overstepped an invisible boundary. Embarrassment was something he feared. But now something else troubled him. He was a mortal who had fought against mortal enemies. He had known every sight, sound, taste, and sensation of war in full force, but the fierce battle between the Devi and the asuras was like nothing in his experience. It seemed like fantasy, and he voiced that concern. "All this talk of monstrous demons that look like no creatures I've ever seen, and armies in the billions, and the Divine Mother riding a lion and hurling weapons from multiple arms! This is more than I can imagine—or accept."

Suratha's frankness did not perturb the holy man. Medhas merely responded, "The story is a myth. So was the story of Madhu and Kaitabha. Did that one bother you?"

"You didn't ask me to identify with that one," the king commented, "and it didn't arouse strong feelings the way this one does. If it's only a myth, as you say, why should it perturb me so?"

"*Only* a myth? A myth is not fiction, good king. A myth tells of things that never happened but always *are*. Some truths are elusive and difficult to talk about in ordinary ways. By their very subtlety they get tangled in the thicket of words. More readily are they revealed by the language of symbols, which speaks directly to the deeper levels of our understanding. We experience those subtle truths in a way that awakens and inspires us to new possibilities.

"Take, for example, the battlegrounds. Do you think they are actual places on a map and that you can mount your horse and ride there? Of course not. The battleground exists within your own heart and mind. And what of the asuras that battle there? The asuras are every selfish, evil, harmful, or unhappy impulse that arises within you and plagues your existence. The clashes on the battleground are the internal struggles that you and everyone else face every day."

"You'll have to excuse me," the king broke in. "My head is spinning—too many ideas all at once—and I need a minute by myself. Sorry," he added, standing up and turning away.

You'll have to excuse me? Samadhi thought. He would not have phrased it that way, but would have said something like, May I be excused? If the king's imperious manner was not lost on him, a mere commoner untrained in proper comportment, how must it look to the venerable holy man?

"Do what you must," Medhas replied, dismissing the king with an upward flick of the wrist. "We shall resume when you come back."

Suratha headed down the path with Medhas's teaching echoing behind him. He did not like what he had heard, because it pointed to his own shortcomings, which he was not yet ready to acknowledge. All that talk of demons and cosmic battles was just fine as long as it did not reflect on him personally. He was a good man, a wise and just ruler. Why should he admit to harboring the darkness of ordinary men?

Reaching the low gate that set off the guru's private domain, he stopped and drew a deep breath. Now what? He remembered the times he had stood on the other side of this gate, wondering what lay at the far end of the path, what mystery it concealed from him. Now he knew, or at least he thought he did, and now the gate stood as a barrier of another kind, this time keeping him inside while he gazed out toward the place where so many of the ashrama's paths converged.

After staring ahead for a while, he noticed two figures in the distance coming his way and struggling with a heavy load of firewood—too heavy, he thought, for Hiranya, the slight, flat-chested young man on the left. It was he who had taken charge of the king's horse on that first morning. The other lad—fair, curly-haired, and sturdy—was known to the king as Dhataki. From where Suratha stood, he could not make out their conversation, but the distance that swallowed their words failed to hold back the smiles and ringing laughter that made light of their ponderous burden.

They approached ever so slowly and with considerable effort. Then Hiranya, catching sight of the king, waved a hearty greeting with his right arm while his side of the firewood, too heavy for his left arm alone, went crashing to the ground, almost taking him with it. More laughter and a winning smile from Dhataki. The king waved back and looked on while the boys resumed their burden and disappeared onto the path that led to the dining hall, their laughter trailing behind them.

Suratha figured it was time to rejoin the conversation with Medhas and Samadhi. He took his seat nonchalantly, unaware of his apparent rudeness but still brooding over what had troubled him.

"Well?" Medhas asked, resuming the discussion.

Suratha cringed inwardly at the thought of his next question but had to ask it regardless of how Medhas might react. "We were talking about the various demons as symbols in a myth and how they stand for what is inside us. Does that mean that the Devi also is only a character out of a myth or a creation of my own mind?"

Medhas saw this coming and brought fire to his words. "Are your personal demons only characters out of a myth? By the same token, are your feelings of love and goodness to be denied? They are the devas of the myth: nobility, goodness, compassion, and wisdom. And the Devi? She dwells within you as the soul of your soul. And know this:

she exists outside of you as an external reality, without form and with many forms. She who created all this universe is more real than anything you think is real, more real than you can possibly imagine. Some day you will understand, but for now it is enough to let these stories be a reminder that there is a greater reality beyond this world of your ordinary experience."

Somewhat mollified, the king posed another question. This one seemed safer, and he spoke without misgiving. "When you first told us of the Devi, you called her Mahamaya. Now you call her Durga, Chandika, and Ambika. Can you explain why she has so many names?"

Medhas cupped his chin in his hand for a moment, then said, "Tell me, Suratha, when you occupied the throne, what were you called? Did your subjects and courtiers not address you as king or Lord of Men or Lord of the Earth?"

"Yes, all those and more they called me out of respect for my position."

"And your closest friends—what did they call you?"

"Suratha."

"And your wife?"

"In public she addressed me as lord, at home as Suratha, in private by terms of endearment that she alone used."

"And your children?"

"According to their age, either father or something more affectionate."

Each of these names, Medhas pointed out, reflected a certain role and the circumstances at the time. The king was sovereign to his subjects, master to his servants, friend to his friends, son to his parents, husband to his wife, father to his children, and so on. Yet whatever he was called, he was still himself and not someone else.

"In the same way," Medhas continued, "the Mother has many names, according to her roles and depending on how she chooses to reveal herself. Yet in every aspect she is still the Divine Mother, whether she is called Durga, Chandika, Ambika, or anything else.

"Of all her names, Durga is the one that is dearest to her, the name by which she is most widely known and worshiped. It means 'difficult of access or approach.' Durga is like an unassailable fortress—in her we find protection. She grants us refuge from *durga*, a word that means 'rough going.' That is to say, she rescues us from every kind of worldly adversity. In her all the powers of the gods reside, for she is the supreme Shakti. Yet beyond her awesome strength she is all tenderness and unconditional love.

"Durga grants fearlessness and victory in our spiritual battles, both in the external world when we oppose unrighteousness and evil and within our own minds and hearts when we struggle against the inner demons of fear, anger, pride, lust, hatred, and countless others. She, the great protector, turns our minds away from those evil tendencies and draws us back toward her infinite goodness. Much more can be said of her, and you will hear it in due course."

"And Chandika?" the king prompted.

"Chandika is the name given to Durga when she appeared in the world to slay the buffalo demon. This name means 'the violent and impetuous one.' Because Mahishasura was so ill-tempered, so under the spell of rajas in its destructive form, the Mother had to counter his fury with her own fierce passion. But as you will see, Chandika's and Mahisha's rajas are of an entirely different sort, because Chandika's purpose is to subdue wickedness and to defend the dharma. Because her wrath is directed at destroying evil, she appears to her devotees as benevolent."

Speaking to both disciples, Medhas continued, "Ambika is a name that each of you have uttered many times to address your own mother out of respectful affection. So it is that we call upon the Devi as our very own mother. Do you not remember your own mother sometimes stern and sometimes gentle and caressing? When you misbehaved as children, did you not sense the love even in your mother's scolding, knowing that she was merely trying to correct your waywardness? In the same way the Divine Mother, Ambika, acts purely out of love, whether stern or gentle. You must never forget that her nature is always maternal.

"Now that is quite enough for one day," Medhas concluded. "I have yet to tell you how the Devi Durga slew Mahishasura, the fierce buffalo demon, but that is a story for another day."

CHAPTER 4

CRISIS

Suratha regarded the copper ax that gleamed in his hands, a fine and costly tool that gave him no pleasure in holding. Although it conferred power, enabling a man to accomplish things he could not do with his hands alone, for the king on this morning, it was a symbol of humiliation.

Earlier, just after he and Samadhi had returned from the morning meal, two white-clad disciples appeared in the doorway of their hut. One of them was Hiranya. Seeing him now at close range, the monarch took note of his quiet, dark eyes and slightly receding chin. Hiranya was not the sort of fellow to draw attention to himself. In fact, his presence prompted Suratha to think of the horse he had entrusted to the young man and to hope that it was being properly cared for. The other disciple could not help drawing attention to himself. Lambana—tall, heavy-set, and shaven-headed—cut a dour but imposing figure.

Hiranya announced that Suratha was to spend the day in the forest with Lambana, gathering and chopping wood for the ashrama's cooking fires. Samadhi would assist Hiranya in the garden plots.

"I suppose we have to earn our keep," was Samadhi's departing remark, made almost lightheartedly. It was true, Suratha thought. Still, the king was anything but amused.

Lambana gestured with his large, bald head to indicate that he was ready to leave. Suratha followed, all the while fighting an impulse to resist. When they had passed through the gate of the compound, Lambana turned left onto a well-worn trail that hugged the enclosure wall for some distance before plunging southward into the forest's depths. They walked for some time, and the king's growing discomfort over his abortive attempts at conversation made the journey seem much longer than it probably was. Barely acquainted with his massive companion, he did not know that Lambana was a man who spoke no more than he had to and hardly ever initiated a conversation. When addressed, he grunted a wordless answer if that would suffice. On those rare occasions when this giant of a man had to articulate his thoughts, he did so with the fewest words possible.

Feeling slighted by Lambana's unwillingness to communicate and dwarfed by the forest's engulfing green immensity, Suratha retreated into as black a mood as he had known since coming to the ashrama. So taken up was he by his companion's imagined affront and his own sensation of smallness that when Lambana stopped at an open space in the forest, the king failed to notice and collided with his bulky form. Momentarily jolted out of his private turmoil, he apologized begrudgingly. Then, more embarrassed than sorry, he surveyed the scene. At the center of the glade stood a large, flat stump that served as a chopping block. At the periphery were neat stacks of firewood covered with palm-frond matting as protection against the rain. Specks of brilliant hue flashed here and there as birds flitted from branch to branch of the encircling trees, but their presence failed to lighten the king's worsening mood. Saying very little, Lambana demonstrated the best technique for chopping the firewood and then went off in search of more fallen trees to fuel the ashrama's fires.

Suratha stared at the pile of broken logs and reluctantly chose a piece from the top. Its musty coolness insulted his flesh. He positioned it upright on the chopping block and struck it with the ax, as if to retaliate for the affront. Thwack! It split cleanly down the middle. He repeated the process with each half and now had four pieces of firewood. He picked up the next log, and the next. Piece by piece the wood yielded to his blows, releasing its inner fragrance. Still, this was a task beneath his dignity and with each fall of the ax his annoyance grew. Why should he have to engage in this menial work? Lambana's a burly fellow, perfectly capable of chopping wood by himself. He doesn't need me, the king thought. And how surly he is! A burly, surly fellow! Burly, surly—the words punctuated the rhythm of the ax. He doesn't need me. What was Medhas thinking? Asking me to do this demeaning labor! Between one leader and another, he ought to know better. Maybe he's less wise than he'd have me think.

Suratha placed another log on the chopping block. Thwack! It did not yield. Thwack! This time the ax barely made a dent. Thwack! Thwack! The log was impervious to his blows. Insolent, the king thought. He'd show it! Yes, he would! And then: quick, heavy breathing—explosive anger, rising unstoppable, feeding on itself, fury. The weapon came down, glanced off the recalcitrant log, and hacked away repeatedly at the chopping block, sending up a flurry of chips. Whole wedges of wood went flying. His anger still not spent, Suratha raised the ax over his head with both hands and rushed blindly across the clearing. Thud! The ax found its mark in a small tree, which shuddered from the impact.

All went silent except for the king's panting. He clung with both hands to the immobile haft of the ax. The blade was buried deep in the heart of the tree. He tried to dislodge it, but it would not yield.

Something moved at his feet and his downward glance rested on a birds' nest and two not-yet-fledglings, gray against the brown of the forest floor. One was already dead. The other was struggling to lift its tiny head and was about to expire against the king's right foot. Only then did Suratha hear the frantic squawking in the branches overhead.

Again, but in vain, he tried to remove the ax that clung resolutely to the wound it had inflicted—*he* had inflicted. Without warning a larger hand than his closed over the haft and extracted the ax from the tree.

Lambana regarded him reproachfully. Suratha did not have to say a word. The scene said it all: the devastated chopping block, the fallen nest, the lifeless baby birds, the tree's oozing gash. And the broken blade of the gleaming copper ax.

Lambana motioned with his head, a quick jerk open to interpretation, and the two began their silent walk back to the ashrama. If the walk to the wood-chopping site had been uncomfortable, the walk back was made excruciating by the king's remorse. He fully expected to be led into Medhas's presence, where he would have to account for his actions. They were indefensible, of course, and his best defense would be to say he did not know how it all happened. Something had come over him; he wasn't himself, not for those few destructive moments.

Instead Lambana, more dour than ever, conducted him back to his hut and left him there without a word. That made it all the worse. Suratha did not know what to expect next. He sat down on his cot, alone but for his restless fear and disorientation, not his companions of choice. Maybe he should slip away before word of his misbehavior became common knowledge. His horse—where was it? A plan began to take shape. He would comb the ashrama until he found where his steed was kept, and then he would leave, never to return.

Suratha stepped to the doorway of the hut and looked furtively to either side. With no one in sight, he crept toward the place where most of the paths intersected, constantly on guard. From there he struck out first along one path and then another and another, hoping each time that this one would lead to his goal. He came to a place where one path forked, and while he stood there speculating over the advantages of left or right, he became aware of approaching footfalls. Instinctively the king vanished into the sheltering greenery and crouched there, waiting until it was safe to come out and continue on his quest.

A second figure approached from the opposite direction and met the first one. The two greeted each other and chatted within earshot of the king, who felt a wave of shame sweep over him. Suratha, glorious monarch and lord of men, found himself in the unintended and despicable role of eavesdropper.

From the conversation he learned what food would be prepared for the evening meal. He would be gone by then, so the eggplants and chick peas didn't concern him. The discussion of the menu went on and on in excruciating detail. When would it end? When would those two cease their idle chatter and go about their business? Just when the king thought he could stand no more, the talk shifted to a subject that was of utmost interest. His horse had just been groomed and was enjoying some freshly cut fodder.

As soon as the way was clear, Suratha emerged from hiding and made his way along the path to where he now knew his horse was being kept. What a stroke of good fortune! His shame at eavesdropping evaporated in the excitement of anticipated departure as he hastened along. Finding his horse at last, he regarded the animal with admiration and pride. Admiration, yes; it was a magnificent horse. But pride? What did he have to feel proud about? Like a tidal wave the morning's events came crashing down on him. He patted the horse, reassured by its placidity and strength. And then he sat down to think.

To leave or to stay? He had already fled once before—twice if you counted his temporary absence from yesterday's conversation—and even here in this blessed place he could not leave his grief, shame, and fear behind. If he fled again, it would not be any different. That much he knew. His feelings would accompany him wherever he went. And where would he go? His life had lost all purpose. Maybe he had better remain here and accept the consequences of his actions. But what if he was asked to leave? Could he face the humiliation—he, a king? None of his forebears had ever dishonored the family name. Would he be the first to bring disgrace upon his line? For an hour or more he vacillated between fleeing and staying, and in the end he thought he would stay. Patting his horse affectionately, Suratha turned and retraced his steps and then headed toward the river.

He proceeded upriver along the bank until the land began to rise steeply. There he stepped into the swift current, as close to the rapids as he dared to go, and let the purifying water bubble around him. He washed his cloth of every trace of the day's events. In the bracing, cold water, with the benevolent warmth of the sunlight on his face, Suratha breathed deeply and tried to let go of every impulse that sullied his mind and every memory that sat heavy on his heart. After some time he emerged from the river and spread his cloth on a large, flat rock. When it was dry, he dressed and headed back.

When he reached the customary bathing place, where the current flowed gently beside the broad, grassy bank, he saw Samadhi approaching. Looking less melancholy than usual, or so the king thought, the merchant asked, "How was your day?" Not waiting for a response, he added, "I've just finished in the garden and need a bath."

"I've just finished mine," Suratha replied. "Chopping wood raises a sweat too." He tried to say this as if nothing were amiss.

"Pulling weeds is backbreaking but, you know, I kind of enjoyed it. Coming from a long line of tradesmen, I can honestly say that this was something new to me. I learned a lot about farming. Oh, and I learned something else. Hiranya told me that Sri Medhas says that the field is like our mind and for it to yield good results, we have to cultivate it. If we neglect it, weeds will pop up all over and crowd out the crops. Or if we leave it unfenced, animals will walk through and trample it and then what are we left with? You know, while I was pulling the weeds, I imagined this one to be one of my faults and that one another. It got me to thinking about my life in a way I hadn't before—to be more aware, I guess, and more discerning. Farming—who would have thought?" Pausing, he asked, "What about you? Are there any lessons in wood chopping?"

"I didn't think about it," the king replied.

Samadhi entered the river, performed his ablutions, and then sat down next to the king on the grassy bank. No sooner had he settled down comfortably than Krishanu joined them.

"A glorious afternoon, isn't it?" he smiled in his usual, affable way.

"Yes," Samadhi agreed. "I was just telling Suratha about my day in the garden." Again he related the lesson, concluding, "When I started out this morning, I thought this would be a wasted day, but it wasn't, not at all. I guess a lot depends on attitude."

This last remark only deepened the king's remorse. As a member of the ruling caste, he had been trained to act nobly in all circumstances and did so all the while he occupied the throne. But now he had betrayed his dharma and for what?

In the soft afternoon breeze and the warm sunshine, the day reached its peak of fulfillment there at the river's edge. The water's soothing murmur added to the magic while the three companions sat in friendly conversation. For the king it should have been a moment of rare contentment—except for that awful thing he had done.

If Krishanu knew, he gave no sign of it. Responding to Samadhi's remark, he said, "Yes, attitude means a lot, because much of life is what we make of it." He gazed at the river. "Sri Medhas teaches that the river of life does not always flow smoothly. Up there at the rapids, the steep descent accelerates the flow, and the water tumbles down all frothy and white. Then when the riverbed levels off again, the agitation subsides and the water flows calm and clear. It's important to know how to navigate in order to avoid a wreck. The master has taught me a lot more about life and my own nature through the symbolism of the river. It goes very deep, but I don't think it's my place to be sharing that with you. These are teachings given in private from guru to disciple."

"What brought you here?" the king asked, changing the subject.

Krishanu flashed a smile and continued in his friendly way. "Oh, there's not a lot to tell, not really. I was a foundling. Someone left me at the side of a road, and someone else discovered me and took me to the nearest village. A childless potter and his wife took me in and raised me as their own."

"You have no idea of your lineage?" the king interrupted. The idea was disquieting, especially in regard to such a handsome, well-bred young man.

"None at all. Anyway, it doesn't matter. I couldn't have had more loving parents than those who gave me a home. They didn't care who I was either, or where I came from. I became the son they nurtured and watched grow up. That's all the sense of belonging any of us needs.

"Not knowing the time of my birth, the village astrologer couldn't even draw up my horoscope, and for a while the question of my destiny was up in the air. No one could say where I'd come from or where I was headed."

"As the potter's adopted son," Samadhi interrupted, "wouldn't it be natural for you to follow in his footsteps?"

"We tried that." Here Krishanu knitted his wide, dark brows into a mock frown. "I was terrible at it!" he laughed. "Every pot I made was either lopsided or leaky. My father just couldn't impart his skills. Don't think he didn't try, but I was a lost cause.

"The astrologer was also the village schoolmaster. He taught us boys how to read and write and do mathematics. He schooled us in the scriptures and that was the part I liked best. I used to linger on after the lessons when all the other boys ran off to play, and we would talk about religion.

"My mother said I was attracted to spiritual things from an early age. Ours was a devout household. We had an image of Durga in the family shrine, and my mother worshiped her every day with incense, flowers, and food, usually followed by a devotional song or two.

"It was the schoolmaster who recognized that I was destined for a holy life—even without a horoscope." Again Krishanu flashed his winning smile. "He said that the name I had been given was prophetic. Krishanu—he carefully accented the second syllable—it means 'bending the bow.' It's usually applied to a good archer, someone who will hit the mark right on. The schoolmaster saw it as a metaphor for my spiritual destiny.

"So how did I come here? To get back to your question, Suratha, the schoolmaster knew of this ashrama. The reputation of Sri Medhas had spread far and wide, and when I was deemed old enough, I was brought here. That was six years ago."

"Do you ever regret it?" the king inquired.

"Why? This is my dharma. I'm very happy here." Krishanu spoke without a hint of pretense. Laughing, he added, "It's a better life than making wretched pots that are of no use to anyone."

Suratha and Samadhi laughed also, and then the king asked gravely, "Do you think some day you'll regret having missed the joys of marriage and raising a family of your own?" As soon as he had posed the question, he wished he could take it back. Maybe it was insensitive to broach the subject of marriage and family in front of the merchant, who was suffering so terribly on their account. Before Krishanu could reply, Suratha quickly added, "And what about the future? Will you ever leave here?"

"Sri Medhas says, 'There is no profit in regretting the past or worrying about the future.' Will I ever leave here? I don't know, and I don't think it's for me to say. My life is dedicated to the Divine Mother, and I'm happy to do whatever she wills. I may not be able to tell you the name of the man who fathered me or the name of the woman who gave birth nine months later, but I know this: I am a child of the Mother. That is my true parentage, and that is all I need to know."

About to take his leave, Krishanu added, "By the way, Sri Medhas would like to see both of you in the morning."

CHAPTER 5

MAHISHASURAMARDINI

The heavens rumbled overhead while Suratha and Samadhi advanced along the path toward Medhas's hut. In the landscape of the sky, dark clouds loomed like mountainous fortresses where Vritra, the drought demon, hoarded the celestial waters. When breached by the great god Indra's thunderbolts, the clouds would release the rain, causing the rivers to swell and Prithivi, the earth mother, to yield forth her abundance. But if Indra's thunderbolts missed their mark, or if Vritra's defenses proved too strong, the rains would not come. Then famine, starvation, and death would stalk the earth, and chaos would reign all around. One could never be sure.

The two disciples hurried along, less concerned with what was happening above them than with what the new day would hold. Samadhi, with a growing hunger for knowledge, was eager for whatever new teaching the seer would impart. Suratha's feelings, though no less strong, were of a different sort altogether; today his every footfall along the path thudded with dread.

They found Medhas sitting outside his hut, more aware than they of the weather. It was he, in fact, who called their attention to the gathering storm. For the first time Suratha took note that the seer's dark eyes seemed to gaze outward and deep within at the same time. How extraordinary, he thought. Truly this guru is not like other men.

"I shall tell you today," Medhas began, "how Durga came to be called Mahishasuramardini, 'the slayer of the buffalo demon.' Another of her names is Vrikshamadhyanivasini, 'she who dwells within the tree.'" He shot the king a knowing glance and when their eyes met, Suratha braced himself for the worst.

But, as if nothing had transpired, the holy man continued, "I told you the last time we met that the battleground of this story is your heart and mind, indeed the whole field of your awareness. The conflict between the Devi and the asuras is the struggle within your own consciousness between your higher and lower impulses. Hear now how the Devi Durga slew Mahishasura. I shall continue from where I left off."

CHIKSHURA SURVEYED THE DEVASTATION all around. The battlefield lay as if swept by a tempest, thick with the debris of broken chariots and weapons and spread with the limbs and bodies of asuras. The stench of death summoned scavengers to feed their hunger on the rotting demon corpses beyond number.

Chikshura's gaze, dark with anger, revealed also the color of fear. As Mahishasura's general, he would shoulder blame for the overwhelming defeat. All too well he knew Mahisha's temper and the countless times that his master had flown into an uncontrollable rage over far less provocation than this. What would be a worse fate, he wondered—to face Mahisha's wrath or the Devi Durga's?

Having rallied the remaining daitya forces, Chikshura rode forth in desperation to face the Devi. He found her standing serenely on the battlefield, the Devi Bhadrakali—at once the fierce warrior and the benevolent Mother pleased by the worship of her devotees. She stood amid the flowers that the adoring gods had showered upon her. Where the circle of fragrant red blossoms ended, the red of the blood-soaked battleground began and stretched across the silent plain. Not long before, the screams of the dying had rent the air. Now unnatural quiet hung heavy, a portent of worse to come.

The uneasy lull ceased with Chikshura's swift and determined attack, but his arrows rained down on the Devi as harmlessly as the gentle showers that caress the summit of Meru, the holy mountain at the center of the world.

Not so invulnerable was he. Durga, advancing like lightning on her noble lion, slashed through the asura general's bow and high-flying banner and destroyed his driver, steeds, and chariot. Enraged, he rushed at the Devi, but when his sharp-edged sword struck her graceful arm, it shattered, its fragments dispersing in a silvery mist.

His eyes red with rage, Chikshura seized his blazing lance and flung it at the Devi as though he were hurling the very sun from the sky. Such was the force of his fury. Still the auspicious Durga remained serene, while her own lance split the fiery missile in mid air, then sped onward to cut Mahisha's mighty general into a hundred pieces. With a single, effortless throw she wrought his destruction.

Udagra, arrayed in glorious armor, came swaggering toward the Devi, and she crushed his arrogance with the simple weapons of boulders and uprooted trees. Next she rushed at the cruel Uddhata and reduced him to a pulp with the blows of her humbling mace. Next her volleys of arrows killed Tamra, the oppressor, and Andhaka, the demon of moral blindness. When Durdhara, the bearer of evil, and the foul-mouthed Durmukha rushed at her, she loosed her arrows once again and sent both to the abode of death. One by one the asuras met their destruction.

Then Mahishasura rushed forward to slay the Mother's noble lion, but Durga stood firm. She, the Great Goddess, and he, the maddened buffalo demon, came face to face, Mahisha with his nostrils flaring, the Mother calm of gaze. The chief of asuras struck the earth with his hooves and bellowed frightfully. Who was this woman to stand in his way? Under his frenzied wheeling the trampled earth broke apart and mountains, flung skyward by his horns, came crashing to the ground, scattering their debris all around. Lashed by his tail, the ocean overflowed, and lacerated by his horns, the gentle clouds fragmented and dispersed. Mahisha's fury knew no bounds.

He advanced and Durga, arousing her own rage, resolved to slay him. She threw her noose over his body and bound him tightly. Shaking convulsively, he assumed the shape of a lion and slipped out of his fetters. He lunged at the Devi, and she severed his head with her sharp-edged sword. But in an instant the evil Mahisha reappeared as a man with sword in hand, mighty and fierce to look upon. Before he could move against her, she cut him to shreds with a volley of arrows. Then taking the form of an elephant, huge and menacing, he grasped her noble lion with his trunk and dragged it along the ground, trumpeting wildly. In a flash Durga's shining sword descended and severed his trunk.

Once more Mahisha assumed his buffalo form and caused the three worlds to tremble. Durga, angered, drank a divine potion distilled from pure rajas, and her eyes reddened. Her wild hair blew over her face like the bank of a cloud, her expression grew frightful, and peals of bone-chilling laughter rolled off her lips.

Mahisha bellowed in return, intoxicated by his own might. Durga, flushed with inebriation, exclaimed, "Bellow, you fool, bellow for now. After I have slain you, the gods will cheer in this very place!"

She leaped upon the buffalo demon and pinned his neck underfoot and pierced him through with her spear. Trapped and crushed by her might, Mahisha emerged halfway from his buffalo's mouth, his true form hideous to behold. Thus exposed and fighting still, he fell to the Devi Durga, beheaded by her great sword.

At his destruction the divine hosts exulted in dancing and singing. The devas rejoiced, and the great seers praised the Devi.

Suratha reflected for a while on the scenes of struggle and carnage, then said, "All those asuras that were felled in battle, all those horrible creatures—I recognize them in my own thoughts and feelings. Even though I was known as a just ruler, I'm hardly free of imperfection. I know my own haughtiness, anger, rudeness, and aggression, and even if I don't express them openly, they are there to trouble my mind. Sometimes I feel my despair hovering overhead like a dark cloud or surging up in waves. I grieve over my lost kingdom, you know, and my resentment shows no sign of lessening. Each reminder of my loss reignites the pain, and then the desire for vengeance flares up all over again."

"All the same," Medhas observed, "you admit to ruling wisely and well. Surely you recognize the presence of the lion of dharma within you and the Devi's own hosts of warriors—all your excellent impulses of kindness, truthfulness, generosity, and compassion. And also your resolve to overcome your torment—do not forget that."

The king had to admit to a glimmer of hope, although with some effort. Maybe there was a way out of his despondency after all. He just didn't know what it was.

Medhas pressed on. "Now consider who this Mahishasura is and what his destruction at the hands of the Devi Durga really means."

"He doesn't seem all that different from Madhu and Kaitabha. He comes across as another nasty brute."

"You are correct, Suratha. His nature is indeed steeped in tamas," Medhas agreed, "and his violent behavior shows all the signs of a beast. In fact, the form he assumes is that of a water buffalo. Earlier, when discussing Madhu and Kaitabha's bestial nature, I told you that a man of such disposition is called a pashu, which means a 'fettered creature.' What do you suppose are the fetters that bind such a man?"

Suratha could not answer. A large part of his mind was preoccupied with the events of the day before, the fact that they had not been resolved, and the fear that they would be.

"We speak of eight fetters," the holy man explained. "One is hate. It causes a person to act horribly toward others, creating nothing but grief. Can you tell me something else about hate?"

The king knew he should reply, but words failed him.

"Hatred is the blackest of forces," Medhas continued, "and it poisons the mind of the one who hates. No matter how much destruction it can bring to others, hate destroys the hater as well. Of that you can be sure."

Regaining his voice, Suratha asked, "Sir, if hatred is so dangerous—and I am not suggesting that it is not—then why do people allow themselves to indulge in it?"

Medhas smiled affectionately. "You see, it is not a question of thinking things out, to indulge or not to indulge. Hatred is a purely brutish instinct, bereft of reason. Moreover, we hate what we fear."

Here the king objected, "Well, what about those fears? Are they always bad or unfounded? Suppose I came across a cobra in the field."

"What would be your reaction?"

"Fear, of course. Its bite could kill me."

"Yes. You see, some fears are legitimate. They are about survival—instinctual and self-protective. You do not have to stop and think; if you did, it might be too late. But the kind of fear that fetters is another matter altogether. That fear has no real basis although we delude ourselves into believing it does."

Recalling his travels through his vast kingdom, Suratha asked, "Do you mean the kind of fear that causes us to hate people of a different tribe, who speak a different language, who look different from ourselves and follow unfamiliar customs?"

"Yes. Your example shows how closely these two fetters—hate and fear—are intertwined."

"In maintaining peace throughout my kingdom, now and then I came face to face with troublemakers who spread the poison of fear and hatred to serve their own ends."

"So much of human trouble is unnecessary," Medhas sighed. "Do you not think so?" he asked, turning to the merchant.

Samadhi, who had been silent for some time, nodded his forlorn agreement. If he had anything to say, it remained unspoken.

The holy man continued, "The goal of men and women living in the world should be harmonious peace. With our many differences, that can only be achieved through a sense of unity in diversity, not of unity in uniformity. Hah! How boring *that* would be! You see, *diversity is the whole point of the creation*. The Divine Mother creates all this out of her fertile imagination and for her own delight. Who are we to stand in her way?"

"Yet we do," the king insisted. "As long as some people feel they are better than others, that their ways are better than others' ways, won't this conflict go on and on without end?"

"Yes, and here you have identified another fetter: the pride of birth. By this I mean thinking oneself superior because of caste or tribe or station in life. I am a *brahmana*; to my caste it is given to preserve the sacred knowledge. You are a *kshatriya*; the duty of your caste is to uphold the dharma through wise rule. Our friend Samadhi here is a *vaishya*; the task of his caste is to create material prosperity for society as a whole. You see, it is not a matter of superiority and inferiority, but of balance in difference. Spiritual, political, and economic power are not to be concentrated in any one place. The point is that pride of birth is pointless! Only those who are insecure about themselves indulge in such foolishness. Yes, I say 'foolishness,' because such pride negates the true wisdom that we are all children of the Divine Mother.

"And the same can be said for the next fetter: pride of family. Your lineage, good king, does not make you superior to our merchant friend, whose family is less illustrious than yours. And do not think yourself superior to Krishanu, who has no knowledge whatever of his lineage. The only lineage that matters is the one that teaches that we are all brothers and sisters—children of the Mother and heirs to immortal bliss."

What the holy man said contradicted the king's deeply held opinions, yet he could not dispute the nobility and rightness of Medhas's teaching. He struggled to hide his conflicted emotions even while thinking that this conversation with the guru touched on too many of his recent experiences to be coincidental.

"Another fetter," he heard Medhas say, "is the concern over always presenting the right image, always acting in what will be seen as the proper way. This has nothing to do with true right conduct, of course; it is all about convention and appearance. Surely in your court you must have noticed the superficiality of some of your retainers whose actions were probably more appropriate to the stage than to real life. You yourself may have engaged in such play-acting in your role as king. You may be doing that now, but is that really living? Why let your life be ruled by what others expect? Or what they think?"

A defensive redness surged and warmed Suratha's face. Had he no secrets from this holy man?

"Do you understand how much effort goes into keeping up appearances, in sustaining a deception?" Medhas continued. Hear me, Suratha. Secrecy is a terrible fetter. It consumes a vast amount of energy. Always having to keep on one's guard! Always wondering who knows what. How easy it is to slip up with a casual comment or something said in jest. On the other hand, when there is nothing to hide, there is openness to life—spontaneity and freedom."

Looking down, the king said nothing.

"We tend to think that others think and act as we do. If we are secretive, we believe that others harbor secrets as well, and then what happens? We become distrustful, and there you have another fetter—suspicion. And finally, when there *is* something to hide, it follows that what is being hidden is shameful, and shame is a most dreadful fetter! There you have all eight: hatred, fear, pride of birth, pride of family, concern over appearances, secrecy, suspicion, and shame. They are all tied together in one way or another like a mass of knots."

"Sometimes—much too often lately—I feel that I am all tied in knots," the king confided.

Only seeming to change the subject, Medhas pressed on. "To return to the matter of Mahisha, what you said is true. He shares many of the beastly qualities with Madhu and Kaitabha, but you must remember that he is far more clever and dangerous than the two of them put together."

Suratha felt an important revelation was on the way. "Go on," he urged.

"In one sense Mahishasura represents anger—fiery, rajasic rage. Look at the harm this anger unleashes—how the trampled earth broke apart under his hooves, how even the gentle clouds were torn asunder by the fury of his horns. Suratha, have you never smashed some object out of rage or struck a living being or inflicted anguish with a harsh word? Have the innocent ones around you not also been affected by the power of anger, just like the clouds that drifted too close to Mahisha's thrashing horns? Keep in mind that anger comes in many degrees, from mild, unexpressed annoyance to wrathful fury."

Suratha felt his words surge forth despite himself, like a torrent rushing through a broken dam. "I'm so ashamed!" He spoke emphatically but barely above a whisper. His voice rasping, he poured out the whole account of the day before, detail by detail: the annoyance that he had let grow—had consciously fed—until it erupted, the damaged ax, the injured tree, the dead birds, the shame he had brought on himself, and the hours of private torture that followed. Perhaps, he said, choking back his sobs, he was not fit to remain at the ashrama; perhaps the holy man would order him to leave.

"What more can I do to you that your mind has not already done?" Medhas asked gently. "Do you want me to inflict further punishment? Punishment is not the answer. The answer is for you to be kind to yourself, Suratha."

Looking on with concern and compassion, the holy man asked, "Do you know where anger comes from?"

A moment or two passed before Suratha replied. "The way you described Mahishasura's rage reminds me not only of myself yesterday but also of my youngest son, Taraka, and the tantrums he throws whenever he doesn't get his way. You should see him screaming and hollering, red in the face and pounding his little fists! All because of something he wants." Suddenly the king's face lit up. "Why, anger arises when desire goes unfulfilled!"

"Yes, Suratha. You have discovered something true. Now about this anger: if it has no healthy outlet or is repressed, it turns to despondency. Look at your own state of mind. Plagued by grief, you admit to the anger you feel. Let us go one step deeper. Do you know the cause of your anger?"

"Isn't it unfulfilled desire?" the king queried.

"Can you be more specific?"

The king thought of his tiny son's tantrums and Mahisha's colossal rage and his own rage over his lost kingdom. His desire to rule and all the other desires that went with it had been thwarted.

Medhas pressed ahead. "Do you recall saying that you still feel possessive over your kingdom even though you know it is no longer yours?"

"I might have said something like that, and yes, I do feel that way."

"You see, the answer was there all along, only you did not notice. That sense of attachment, that 'my-ness,' is the cause of your anger and the underlying cause of your grief."

Suratha's brow wrinkled as if he were considering this possibility for the first time. Then understanding, he blushed. Could he really have been so foolish?

"You see, Suratha, beneath all his raging passions Mahishasura is in the grip of that sense of attachment. There is no need for you to be embarrassed, because that same Mahishasura dwells in everyone, along with his hosts of lesser demons.

"At the beginning of the struggle, Chandika fought effortlessly, as if in play, against Mahisha's grimly determined forces. At the beginning of the spiritual struggle, it is the same way. Some faults and shortcomings are more easily conquered than others. A sharp tongue, for example, can be tamed without too much difficulty if we learn to think before we speak and then practice the proper restraint. One by one our lesser faults must be overcome first.

"But later the Devi faces Mahisha himself and that requires greater resolve. Then she arouses her own rage."

Suratha interrupted, "Divine rage seems like a contradiction in terms."

"Very well. When you went to war to defend the hill tribes under your protection, did you do so out of wrath or out of resolve to right a wrong?"

Suratha answered that he acted to defend the moral order.

"When the Devi Durga arouses her anger," Medhas continued, "she is doing the same. Her anger is something like righteous indignation. It is fiery, rajasic energy, no doubt, but rajas directed to a noble purpose. Look at the difference: Mahisha's destructive fury arises from his selfish desires, then it overwhelms and controls him. But the Devi's benevolent anger is at all times completely under her control.

"The buffalo demon's anger stems from the dissatisfaction of unfulfilled desires—desires rooted in the sense of attachment, or 'my-ness.' Still deeper, that 'my-ness' is rooted in the sense of 'I-ness' that is fundamental to the experience of the world."

"I-ness?"

"Ask yourself, Who am I? Do you know your true nature? No, you know yourself only as the 'I-ness,' the ego sense that arises from the blessed Mahamaya's deluding power. The 'I,' or self, that you understand is only your sense of individuality. It depends on limitation for its very existence—on being identified with mind, senses, and body, and on being distinct from every other creature.

"This 'I' even claims external objects as its own and then falls prey to attachment and fear of loss. And where there is attachment, there is also its opposite—aversion. This 'I' spends all its time either running after things or trying to avoid them, depending on whether they bring pleasure or pain. You see, Suratha, by holding on to the thoughts of your lost kingdom, you are holding on to more than its remembered pleasures. You are holding on to your pain as well."

Medhas explained that Mahisha's shape-shifting symbolized what happens in the mind whenever the sense of selfhood feels threatened. As long as Mahisha kept changing from one form to another, he could not readily be slain.

"Do you understand," the seer asked, "that when the small self feels threatened, it disguises the thoughts and tendencies that it feels are under attack? They seem to disappear, hoping to elude destruction, but they merely come back in different forms. And for a while it works. The lion slipped out of the noose, but the Mother assailed him again. He became a man, but the Mother destroyed his defensive sword and shield. In the same way, we cannot keep hiding our true motives and defending our faults forever.

"Next Mahisha became an elephant, seized the Mother's lion in its trunk, and dragged it along the ground. In our desperate attempts at self-preservation, we try to destroy the very truth that threatens to expose us, all the while trumpeting loudly in our own defense. Is this behavior not something you recognize?"

"In others certainly. And in myself too," the king agreed.

Medhas explained to the two disciples that after Durga sliced through the elephant's trunk, disabling him from twisting the truth any longer, Mahisha saw his defenses exhausted. The only recourse left was plain, unadorned force. Believing that might makes right, Mahisha returned to his powerful buffalo form. Then Durga resolutely pinned down his neck under her foot. "To pin down" means to find out, ascertain, or determine. From this point on there would be no more evasion. The Mother pierced Mahisha's shoulder with her spear, as she pierces the mind with the penetrating light of right knowledge. Only then was Mahisha's true demon form revealed in all its vulnerability.

"Listen," Medhas said, "in this internal struggle, as long as you allow the source of your misery to hide behind the protection of one disguise after another, it remains elusive and unconquerable. How can you overcome your turmoil unless you recognize it for what it is and know its causes? As long as you are ruled by attraction and aversion, attachment and fear, personal demons will bedevil you in one form or another."

The seer's pause signaled a change of direction. "Do you see, both of you, that this struggle we have talked about is intimately connected to the idea of good and evil?"

The king's response was so slow in coming that Medhas proceeded without waiting. "Through Mahamaya's delusion we perceive the limitless wholeness of reality as finite and fragmented. From this multiplicity arises the appearance of good and evil. They coexist as a pair, a 'package deal,' as our friend the merchant might say. 'Two for the price of one!'" Medhas laughed. The king and the merchant could not help laughing either.

"You see, good and evil are relative, and neither can exist without the other to define it. Practically speaking—and all this teaching is worthless if it is not practical—we can call evil that which distances us from the divine wholeness, that which causes separation and strife. And we can call good that which leads us toward the Divine, toward unity and peace.

"When the Devi, who is whole and infinite, enters into her creation and experiences it as her divine play, her *lila*, she seemingly fragments her single awareness into countless separate centers of consciousness that all clamor 'I-me-mine!' and cause no end of trouble. Inevitably the desires and interests of one clash with those of another and in the confusion arises the need for moral choices. How are we to act—out of selfishness or compassion? Are we to create strife or peace in the world? Hatred or love?

"We celebrate the story of Durga's slaying of Mahishasura as the victory of good over evil. Whenever evil prevails, the Devi—the universal mother, protector, and savior—intervenes in worldly affairs. She who upholds the dharma destroys wickedness and reestablishes righteousness and virtue. But the story is more than that. There is one last point, and this is a wonderful secret. The moment before Durga slays Mahishasura, there dawns on his face a look of recognition. He regards her raptly, because at last he has understood that she is the blissful Mother who dwells within himself and all beings. What need is there to resist any more? The individual soul meets the Divine face to face. No longer enslaved by passion, it feels its former anger and fear slip away. It knows itself only as a child of the Mother, and from this time on the Devi herself guides the inner events of the heart and mind."

Medhas regarded both disciples and then stood up, saying, "Suratha, what I shall say next is for your ears alone." He dismissed the merchant and motioned for the king to follow him into the hut.

Inside, Suratha looked around. The area to the right of the entrance was sparsely furnished with no more than a cot and a small chest. To the left was empty space save for the reed matting on the floor and a pile of cushions leaning into the corner. Suratha surmised correctly that Medhas's disciples would gather here for spiritual instruction.

A heavy, ochre-colored drape stretched nearly across the room's expanse, screening the back half of the hut from the front. Suratha followed Medhas behind this curtain and watched him sink to his knees and bow reverently, his forehead touching the deerskin that rested on the floor. The king followed his example. Before them on an altar of dark, polished marble stood a stone image of the goddess Durga, exactly as Medhas's myth had portrayed her. In the light of a single oil lamp and amid the gleaming brass of worship vessels and the delicate splendor of flowers, she radiated a gentle beauty and a compassion that the king would have thought impossible to convey in stone. Surely it was a miracle and not a mere sculptor that had fashioned this image. The intense quiet of holiness pervaded the shrine, and Suratha looked on in reverence.

At last Medhas spoke quietly but intently. "When you pray to the Mother, to Mahishasuramardini, ask her to move through your heart in all her glory and to destroy the disquiet arising from attachment, malice, and fear. If you worship her who rides upon the lion of dharma, what enemies can touch you? If you care not for worldly gains, your mind will be free to rest at the Mother's feet, and all pain will be healed. Know that you were born of the radiance of her pure intelligence and bliss. Pray to her, 'May you, Durga, who alone can destroy the enemies of the gods, ever conquer. May I always meditate upon you in the surrender of pure love.'"

Suratha gazed downward through half-closed eyes. The quiet filling the air had seeped through his pores and into his heart. It was the first peace he had felt in many days, in many weeks. No, longer. This was something entirely new, never before experienced, not to be thought about or figured out, but simply allowed to happen.

Without warning a loud thunderclap pierced the silence, and the heavens rumbled above. In his inner silence Suratha remained unmoved, even as the first raindrops fell on the thatched roof overhead.

"Ah!" Medhas exclaimed in delight. "Indra's thunderbolt has found its mark, and Vritra is vanquished once again! The earth will prosper, and we will not go hungry in the coming year."

CHAPTER 6

PRAISE

Suratha and Samadhi plunged through the gray half-light of the new day, hastening through the driving rain, their gait punctuated by occasional thunderclaps and the relentless drum of raindrops on the forest leaves. Where only days before the sun's heat had blasted down, dense clouds now darkened the way through the dripping woods. Giant puddles with a thousand rippling points dancing on their surface obscured the path. Under pandanus-leaf umbrellas, the two disciples found scant protection from the storm and arrived at their teacher's hut soaking wet. They were surprised to find other disciples assembled there. About half the ashrama's residents mingled in the front part of Medhas's dwelling, conversing among themselves.

"A good day to stay indoors," Medhas greeted them cheerfully, emerging from behind the partition and proceeding to the cot, where he took his seat. He ordered Lambana to draw the curtain aside, and the shrine was revealed, ablaze with votive lamps and bedecked with flowers. In its midst stood the image of Durga, radiating a living presence while the fragrant smoke of incense curled before her in graceful arabesques. The disciples touched palms and foreheads to the floor in heartfelt *pranams*. Then facing the guru, they looked on expectantly—gentle Hiranya, fun-loving Dhataki, confident Krishanu, solemn Lambana, and half a dozen others. One of them readied a large drum while Lambana tuned the droning strings of a *tambura* and Dhataki toyed with a pair of small cymbals. Then all fell silent, waiting for Medhas to speak.

"After the Devi Durga struck down the wicked Mahishasura and his demon hosts, Indra and the other gods assembled before her and reverently bowed their heads. Then Brahma, Vishnu, the moon-crowned Shiva, and all the other shining gods of heaven followed Indra and lifted their voices in a chorus of praise."

Under Lambana's fingers the strings of the tambura sprang to life, emitting a steady, bronze-hued wash of sound. Medhas began to chant a sinuous melody that for each verse rose and subsided over a span of fifty-six syllables. One by one the others joined in, their song riding on the drum's gentle pulse, here and there punctuated by cymbals ringing brightly. Voices of all registers—deep-chested bass, full-throated baritone, and floating tenor—together sang the Mother's praise:

> *To the Devi, who spreads out this world through her own power and who embodies herself as all the powers of the hosts of gods; to Ambika, who is worthy of worship by all the gods and great seers, we bow down in devotion. May she grant us that which is auspicious.*
>
> *May she whose unequalled might and splendor even the blessed Vishnu, Brahma, and Shiva are powerless to describe, may she, Chandika, be intent on protecting all the world and on destroying the fear of misfortune.*
>
> *O Devi, we bow before you who are yourself good fortune in the dwellings of the virtuous and misfortune in the abodes of the wicked, intelligence in the hearts of the learned, faith in the hearts of the good, and modesty in the hearts of the high-born. May you protect the universe!*

How can we describe this form of yours, which surpasses thought? And your abundant, exceeding valor that destroys evil? And your deeds in battle, O Devi, among all the throngs of gods and demons?

You are the cause of all the worlds. Though containing the triple forces of creation within yourself, you are untouched by any imperfection. You are unfathomable even to Vishnu, Shiva, and the other gods. You are the refuge of all. You are this entire, manifold world and you are primordial matter, supreme and untransformed.

O Devi, you are the mantra of consecration whose utterance in all sacrifices brings satisfaction to the whole assemblage of gods, and you are the mantra which humans proclaim as the cause of satisfaction to the hosts of ancestral spirits.

O Devi, who are the cause of liberation and great, inconceivable austerities: sages yearning for liberation contemplate you with senses restrained, intent upon truth, with all faults cast off, for you are the blessed, supreme knowledge.

With sound as your essence, you are the treasury that holds the taintless Vedic hymns, sung to resound joyfully with your holy name. You are the blessed Devi, who embodies the three Vedas. Intent on conferring well-being, you are the supreme destroyer of pain in all the worlds.

O Devi, you are the intelligence by which the essence of all scriptures is understood. You are Durga, the vessel free of attachments that takes one across life's difficult ocean. You are Shri, the radiant splendor that abides in the heart of Vishnu. You are Gauri, the shining goddess who abides with the moon-crowned Shiva.

Gently smiling, your shining face resembles the full moon's orb and is as pleasing as the luster of the finest gold. Beholding it, how could Mahishasura, even though enraged, be moved to strike it?

Still stranger was it, O Devi, that Mahisha did not perish the instant he beheld your wrathful face, reddened like the rising moon and scowling frightfully. For who can behold the enraged face of death and still live?

O Devi, who are supreme, be gracious to all creation, for when angered you can annihilate multitudes. We saw this the moment you brought Mahishasura's vast power to an end.

Those to whom you are bounteous are honored among peoples, theirs are riches, theirs are glories, and their righteous acts know no limit. They indeed are blessed with devoted children, attendants, and wives.

One who is virtuous and ever mindful performs daily all righteous deeds, O Devi, and by your grace attains to heaven. Are you not then the giver of rewards in all the three worlds?

Remembered in distress, you remove fear from every creature. Remembered by the untroubled, you confer even greater serenity of mind. Dispeller of poverty, suffering, and fear, who other than you is ever intent on benevolence toward all?

The world attains happiness when you slay its foes, and though they may have committed enough evil to keep them long in torment, even as you strike down our enemies, O Devi, you think, May they reach heaven through death in battle with me.

Why does your mere glance not reduce all asuras to ashes? Because when assailed by your weapons and thus purified, even those adversaries may attain the higher worlds. Even toward them your intentions are most gracious.

If the intense light flashing frightfully from your sword or the glaring brilliance of your spear point did not blind the asuras' eyes, it was because you made them behold the moonlike radiance beaming from your face.

O Devi, your nature is to subdue the misconduct of the wicked. Others cannot equal your inconceivable grace, for even while your might destroys those who have wrested power from the gods, you show compassion toward those very foes.

To what may your prowess be compared? Where else is there beauty so ravishing, yet striking fear into enemies? Where in the three worlds are compassion in heart and resolve in battle seen as they are in you, O beneficent Devi?

Destroying all foes, you have saved the three worlds. Slaying them at the battle front, you led even those frenzied, hostile throngs to heaven, even while dispelling our fear of them. Salutations to you!

Protect us with your spear, O Devi, and protect us with your sword, O Ambika. Protect us with the clangor of your bell and the resonance of your bowstring.

Guard us in the east and in the west, O Chandika. Guard us in the south and also in the north, O Ishvari, by brandishing your spear.

With your gentle forms that move through the three worlds and with your surpassingly terrible ones, protect us and also the earth.

O Ambika, with sword, spear, mace, and whatever other weapons your tender hands have touched, protect us on all sides.[2]

After the last tones had faded away, Medhas asked Lambana to draw the curtain, and Krishanu, disappearing in the back, returned a few moments later with a tray of sweets.

"*Prasad*," Medhas explained for Suratha's and Samadhi's benefit. "Food that has been offered to the Mother and thus consecrated." Each disciple received his share with due solemnity and then departed until only the king, the merchant, and the seer remained.

Outside the rain streamed down from the broken clouds; within the hut the warm light of oil lamps dispelled the gloom. Medhas took his seat on a cushion before the curtain and signaled for the disciples to sit down near him. Suratha faced the seer in awe and anticipation. Now and then he felt a gust of moist air enter from the doorway, bearing on its coolness the green fragrance from outside. Causing the lamps to flicker, it was a comforting reminder of the shelter overhead.

Something in that atmosphere captivated the king. In a quiet, self-contained way, he had never felt so alive. Since the day before he had sensed an indefinable openness that made him eager for whatever Medhas would reveal next. He glanced to his left at Samadhi and wondered if the merchant shared this delicious expectancy.

"Shall we begin?" Medhas asked, his dark eyes sparkling in the lamplight. "The hymn you heard is the very one with which Indra and the gods praised the Devi. They worshiped her with rare flowers from Indra's paradise and anointed her with perfumes. They rang bells and waved sparkling lights that illuminated the clouds of incense that rose up before her. Do you know what happened next?"

Suratha and Samadhi did not know, of course.

"Serene of countenance and sweet of voice, the Devi spoke to the gods, saying, 'I am well pleased by your hymn and your worship. Ask whatever you wish, and I will gladly grant it.'

"The gods replied, 'Since you, the glorious Devi, have slain our enemy, this evil Mahishasura, all has been accomplished. For now nothing remains to be done. But if you are to grant a blessing, may we ask that you destroy misfortune whenever it arises. When remembered, may you bring increased wealth, progeny, and success to any mortal who sings your glory. Be ever gracious to gods and humans alike.'

"'So let it be,' the Devi said and vanished from sight."

In his mind's eye Suratha saw the resplendent gods kneeling enraptured before the Mother and receiving her blessing. Recalling the long, sinuous melody of the hymn, the king sensed an eloquence born of true devotion. Now, as he tried to recall the words exactly, he longed to know their deepest meaning, to embrace them in the fullness of his heart and make them his own.

"I don't know where to begin," he said to Medhas almost apologetically. This newfound humility—gratitude might be a better word—was uncharted territory for the king, but deep inside he felt a vague, though not yet understood, sense of trust as he appealed to the guru for guidance.

Medhas, in the fullness of his insight, suggested, "Why not begin at the beginning? Listen again to the first phrase: 'To the Devi, who spreads out this world through her own power.' A lovely image—see how the Mother prepares for her play of creation!"

Suratha thought of his young daughter, Sumitra, when she was about to play—how joyfully she arranged her dolls and other toys on the palace floor before engaging in her games. Perhaps it is the same with the Divine Mother, he thought. She lovingly spreads out this universe, putting everything in its place, and then begins her play.

Medhas continued, "The Divine Mother is the source of all. Everything in our experience flows from her. And everything also flows back—but that's a teaching for another day." The holy man directed this last remark primarily to the merchant.

"You see," he went on, "the extending or spreading out described here means that the Mother projects the whole of creation out of her own being. Besides this idea of emanation, something else that comes to mind is the idea of weaving. We can say poetically that the Mother weaves the fabric of the universe out of her own threads, the three gunas. When woven, thread takes on the form and the qualities of cloth, but in substance that cloth never ceases to be anything other than thread. Do you understand?"

The king deliberated and slowly nodded.

"The thread and the cloth are one and the same substance; only the form is changed," Medhas reiterated. "In the same way, the universe with all its names and forms never ceases to be anything but the divine power out of which it is woven. Everything exists within the Mother and can never be apart from her, because everything is a part *of* her. She is the essence of all that is, whether we recognize it or not.

"Another point," he continued. "When we say that the Devi spreads out this world through her own power, we must remember that she *is* the sole power in the universe, the supreme Shakti. She herself has proclaimed this: 'Through me alone all mortals live who see and breathe and hear what is said, not knowing that they abide in me.'

"Even the gods, who are mightier than any mortal, act only through the power that belongs to the Mother. Indeed, the hymn says that she 'embodies herself as all the powers of the hosts of gods.'

"And next it says that she who is called Ambika—Mother—is worthy of worship by all the gods and humankind. Ambika—what a wonderful name! What relationship is sweeter or more intimate and trusting than that between a mother and her child? Who is more tender or more fiercely protective than a mother? For that reason the gods and humankind alike worship her out of pure love and ask her, trustingly, to grant all good things.

"So great is she that even the greatest among the gods are powerless to describe her might and splendor. How then can we, mere mortals, praise her who is beyond praise? Yet in her infinite tenderness she pays heed to even the smallest voice."

CHAPTER 7

DESTINY AND FREEDOM

"She pays heed to even the smallest voice," Medhas repeated. A palpable silence fell over the room while Suratha and Samadhi reflected on the Devi's unconditional love. The quiet was so engrossing that not even the sound of the cascading rain outside could intrude on either man's thoughts. Medhas sat motionless but for his compassionate eyes, which moved back and forth between the king and the merchant, assessing each one's inner state and seeing what only a guru can see.

After some time had passed, he broke the silence, quoting again from the hymn: "'O Devi, we bow before you who are yourself good fortune in the dwellings of the virtuous and misfortune in the abodes of the wicked.'"

Provocative words, the king thought, coming out of his reverie. So provocative that he felt compelled to challenge them. How quickly his mood had changed! "Does this mean that the Mother, our all-loving protector, is capable of inflicting punishment and misery? If so, how can I trust in her completely, in her whom you just told me to love with all my heart?" The alarm in his eyes all but screamed that something had touched a reservoir of fear.

"There are different ways to understand this, Suratha," the guru explained. "For the worldly, who know little of the matters of the spirit, good and evil appear as two ever-present realities. It is natural for such people to think in terms of reward and punishment. It is natural also for them to think of the Mother, if they think of her at all, as they would their earthly mother, who encourages their good behavior with sweets and spanks them when they misbehave. Such an understanding breeds both love and fear in the mind.

"But for those of deeper understanding, it is a different story. The Divine Mother is far more than even the greatest of persons. Even though she assumes many personal forms, she reveals herself in impersonal ways as well. She is the impersonal intelligence vibrating throughout the cosmos as a conscious, balancing force that insures justice in the end. This principle, ever at work, is called the law of karma."

"I've heard of that," Samadhi interjected. "It means that no good deed goes unrewarded and no evil goes unpunished, or something like that." Clearly the merchant was a man used to thinking in terms of debts and payments.

"I've heard of it too," the king remarked confidently, more sternly adding, "I think it means *fate*."

As if their opinions were weapons held in readiness, the king and the merchant faced each other unblinking, then turned to their teacher. Expectancy hovered in the air, and Medhas could barely conceal his delight—or his gentle amusement at the smallness of their understanding. It would be a joy to stretch their minds.

"The answer to both of you is yes and no," he began, shooting down any sense of certitude in either of the disciples. That was, of course, his aim, because the subject that stretched out before them was not simple at all. To grasp its subtleties they would need to brush aside any preconceptions.

"First," Medhas explained, "let us recognize that there is a principle of cause and effect at work in the world. If I tell you to go stand in the river, what will happen?"

"We'll get wet, of course." The answer was so obvious that the king felt foolish in dignifying it with a reply that any five-year-old could have given.

But Medhas received it with dead seriousness. "Yes, you will get wet. In that sense karma is a simple recognition that certain actions produce certain results. Now is this good or bad, that you have gotten wet? It depends on the accompanying conditions and on your intention. If you are sick with fever, immersion in the river could have severe consequences, but if you intend to bathe, the outcome will be beneficial.

"Next you must understand that this principle at work in the physical world is equally at work in the mental world. Every action, whether in thought, word, or deed, has consequences. There is no getting away from that."

"Are we to understand," the king asked, "that if we do good, good will come to us in return? What Samadhi just said about reward and punishment, with which you seem to agree, isn't borne out by my experience—or by his either!" His voice quavering, the king exclaimed, "Surely it cannot be! Look at our excellent characters and meritorious deeds and then at the calamities that befell us!"

"You prefer to blame your present condition on fate?" Medhas interposed. His face softened in an expression midway between sadness and compassion. "Karma is not a simple matter. It is about *what we do* and also about *what happens to us*, not just here and now but over the course of lifetimes. I repeat, it is no simple matter.

"There are different kinds of karma. One is called *prarabdha*, which means 'commenced.' It refers to events that have already been set in motion as the result of actions in past lives. This kind of karma sets the conditions into which one is born in the present life. The fact that you, Suratha, were born a king is a result of prarabdha karma. This form of karma creates not only the circumstances of your birth but also your inborn character. What are your inner qualities? Your habitual tendencies? Are you compulsive, willful, or drawn to higher aspirations? All such qualities of mind and heart are born of your past thoughts and deeds.

"Like an arrow shot from a bow, prarabdha karma cannot be stopped. Once set in motion, it brings about events that are beyond your control. So even though, as you say, you and Samadhi are men of virtuous character and meritorious deeds, you are each reaping the calamitous harvest of seeds sown in past lives."

At this revelation Suratha and Samadhi contemplated each other dismally, scarcely daring to suspect what evils haunted their respective pasts and would return to plague their futures.

The guru continued, "This teaching should not come as a total surprise! How often when misfortune strikes, do you not lament, 'What did I do to deserve this?' Eh? That simple question, asked without thinking, harbors at least the suspicion that you are suffering the consequences of previous actions. Is that not so?"

The king and the merchant had to agree.

Medhas's face brightened as he introduced a new idea. "Tell me, have you ever thought back later on a particular misfortune and found that it was a blessing in disguise? Often the most painful lessons are the most instructive. Illness may cause us to appreciate health and to take better care of our bodies. Mental agony may cause us to reconsider what is truly important in our lives. Emotional suffering may awaken compassion toward others and make us into better people. And adversity may inspire heroic resolve and reveal strengths we never knew we had."

Again, the king and the merchant had to agree although somewhat reluctantly. All that Medhas said rang true, very true, but at the same time it called for no small effort.

Medhas continued, "Do you remember earlier when our merchant friend here suggested that karma was a matter of reward and punishment? I explained that the result of standing in the river is getting wet, and I asked if that was good or bad. The answer, you recall, is that it all depends. Do you understand this now?"

Considering his point made, the seer went on talking. "Now, Suratha, you said you thought that karma means fate, and indeed prarabdha karma seems to fit that description. It determines what happens to us and sometimes what we do. Events that happen through the agency of other people, the forces of nature, or anything else outside ourselves can be the result of this kind of karma. And so can the way we respond. Through force of habit and ingrained tendencies we often react without thinking. Our very character is formed by our past deeds and the attitudes we have acquired, and in any situation we are more likely than not to call upon an established pattern of behavior and to repeat it, for better or worse. I shall say more about this in a little while.

"But first, what I have explained so far is too simple and only part of the picture. There is another kind of karma called *sanchita*, which means 'gathered up.' Again, imagine an arrow, but this time one that has not been shot. It rests in the quiver. In the same way, sanchita karma is the collection of deep impressions, created in previous lifetimes or in the present life, that lie dormant for now.

"A third kind of karma is called *agami*, which means 'coming up.' It produces results quickly and comes to fruition as a consequence of actions performed in this lifetime, even recently. When you see instantaneous results, know that agami karma is at work.

"Finally, there is a kind of karma known as *kriyamana*, which means 'being done.' This concerns actions done in the present moment. As I explained before, even what we do in the present moment is likely to be influenced by the underlying mental impressions and patterns of behavior already present in the mind due to prarabdha karma. *But we need not be bound by them.* Hear me, and hear me well. What I am about to say is supremely important.

"The present moment—the *eternally* present moment—offers the freedom of choice to follow your existing tendencies or to act in a new and different way. This freedom of choice is a gift of divine grace. If you ignore it, you will act according to your prarabdha karma and continue to be enslaved. If you drive an oxcart down the same road repeatedly, the ruts made by the wheels will get deeper each time. The deeper they become, the harder they will be to avoid or to pull out of. It is the same with the mental ruts that you create in the road of the mind. But if you seize the moment, determined not to repeat the same patterns, little by little you change your character—and your destiny. So you see, Suratha, in one sense it is true that karma is fate—but a fate we ourselves have created. In another sense, to one who is spiritually aware, karma is also the freedom to direct the course of what is to come. Why not avail yourself of that?"

"What you say is inspiring," the king remarked, "but something still troubles me. Is there no escaping what yet lies dormant? Will I still have to suffer my due, however painful it may be, until all those arrows in the quiver have been shot and have hit their mark?"

"In the world of commerce, debts are sometimes forgiven," Samadhi interjected hopefully, still thinking in mercantile terms.

"Even to evildoers—," Medhas began, but at that moment the howling wind tore into the hut, its chill breath extinguishing the oil lamps. A lone flame flickered in the farthest corner, and in the near darkness the three figures, mere silhouettes, sat motionless under the beating of the relentless rain.

"Oh dear," Samadhi said after a while, his dull voice attempting to pierce the gloom.

"Oh dear?" Medhas erupted. "Oh dear? Was everything I have said lost on you? When something unexpected happens in your life, is it your habit to sit passively and lament? When your family cast you out, did you sit in the dust of the road and mutter, 'Oh dear,' before you came slinking into the forest? Show me that you have the sense to seize the moment and act!"

This was the first time Samadhi had been scolded by the holy man, and he wasn't sure what to do. It seemed like a woefully small gesture, but he stirred, stood up, headed toward the far corner, and began relighting the lamps.

"And you," Medhas exclaimed, fluttering his hand impatiently at the king, "make yourself useful. Help him."

Suratha hesitated. As a king he was not used to taking orders or doing menial tasks that could be done by someone else. By now he should have learned his lesson, but once again an inner wave of resistance swept through him, just as Medhas added, "You were so eager to learn the words of Indra's hymn. Have you forgotten this part—'O Devi, we bow before you who are modesty in the hearts of the high-born'?"

Suratha was grateful for the semidarkness, which he thought concealed the flush of humiliation warming his face. He arose, not knowing how fully aware the guru was of his inner state of mind. As he helped the merchant light the lamps, a wave of an entirely different kind arose in him, its motion the opposite of the resentment that had flared up only moments earlier. This one felt like the outgoing tide, draining away his pride. In its indefinable flow, everything suddenly seemed so right.

Soon the lamps' warm glow revealed the reassuring kindness that had returned to the guru's face. Medhas resumed his teaching as if nothing had happened, but he knew that in his two disciples something had shifted.

"Even to evildoers the Mother is most gracious," he said with gentle certitude. "But at the same time, consider how in our ignorance we remain unaware, or at least uncaring, of the evil we do. How could Mahishasura, seeing the Mother's gently smiling face as radiant as the full moon's orb, be moved to strike it?" Medhas was referring to a line of the hymn. "Even in the face of all the beauty and goodness we witness in the world, we are still driven by our human passions to commit terrible, profaning acts.

"Under your benevolent rule, Suratha, the people of your kingdom prospered. Hunger was driven out, and justice and peace prevailed. Yet certain men allowed their minds to be poisoned by greed and the lust for power; they armed themselves and brought calamity upon the land. To satisfy their own desires they wantonly destroyed the common good and left strife in its place. How much destruction and human suffering their violence caused cannot be reckoned. And for what? The satisfaction of a few selfish men. Is it not an affront to all we hold sacred?

"In smaller and more subtle ways, such profaning ignorance reveals itself whenever we engage in unkind thoughts, harsh words, or injurious actions toward anyone or anything in this world. We become like Mahishasura, striking the Mother's smiling face. Often the evil we do is so slight that we are not even aware of it. But even in seemingly insignificant thoughts or deeds we deny the ever-present sacredness all around us and within. That is the fundamental definition of ignorance or evil."

The guru leaned back, drew a deep breath, and looked directly at the king. "As a man who now travels the spiritual path, you must remain ever vigilant of such unknowing, even in its subtlest, most hidden forms. Be always aware of the thoughts of your mind and know that at all times, in all places, you carry the Mother enshrined within your heart."

Medhas paused to allow his words to impress themselves on Suratha's mind. "But to return to the point I began to make about the lingering effects of karma, the Mother is most gracious and benevolent toward all. Whether chastening the wicked or conferring blessings upon the righteous, she is ever intent on the victory of spiritual truth and enlightenment over human ignorance and darkness. Even someone destined to be kept long in torment by the consequences of evil deeds will be purified by the touch of the Mother's weapons, so to speak, and be brought to blessedness. In other words, sincere devotion to her reveals a grace that is unconditional and withheld from no one.

"Suratha, as you learn to recite this hymn that Indra and the hosts of gods sang to the Divine Mother Durga, meditate on its truths. Through her own power of consciousness, the Devi spreads out this world. She herself assumes every form, indwelling as the essence of all; yet untouched by any imperfection, she abides as the supreme reality beyond all manifestation. She embodies herself as the diverse powers of all the gods, yet even the mighty Brahma, Vishnu, and Shiva, foremost of the shining devas, are powerless to describe her might and splendor, which surpass all thought.

"To the virtuous she is gracious, granting all manner of blessings: material bounty, serenity of mind, and the liberating knowledge of the spirit. To the foes of righteousness she is also most gracious, subduing their misconduct and destroying their wickedness so that they also become purified and attain blessedness. Through forms both gentle and terrible she moves through the three worlds, ever showing her limitless compassion and unconditional grace."

Medhas continued, all his attention fixed on the king. "This teaching has been directed to you, Suratha. Reflect daily on the story of Durga and Mahishasura. Its inner meaning will instruct you how to live in the world, dedicated to right understanding and right action. Watch your mind and heart, take heed of every impulse, and allow the Mother to eradicate every imperfection. She herself has said, 'Hear me as I speak the truth to you. I myself proclaim this, which is pleasing to gods and men alike: I make mighty whomever I wish. I make him devout and open his eyes to right understanding. For the god who puts evil to flight,

I draw the bow, that his arrow may strike down the hater of devotion; such is the fervor I stir within that man.'

"In other words, Suratha, through divine grace you will succeed in conquering your lower nature. Surrender to the Mother and you will overcome enslavement to all the passions that Mahishasura and his demon hordes represent."

"How do I surrender?" the king asked, suddenly feeling tired. He felt barely able to absorb more teaching, but he had to know.

"Ah, that is the supreme secret," Medhas beamed, then whispered so only the king could hear. "I have told you this before. It is so simple. Love, simply love, the Mother with all your heart. She will take care of the rest."

The seer leaned forward and pressed his palm firmly to the king's brow with a gesture that signaled both blessing and empowerment. Humbled, the king raised his folded palms in salutation and bowed.

Medhas responded, saying, "Reflect on what I have said. Put these teachings into practice and return here with the merchant when I call for you." Turning toward Samadhi, he added, "For you I shall reveal further truths through the story of how the Mother appeared once more for the destruction of two demon brothers named Shumbha and Nishumbha. I shall relate it exactly as it happened."

The two disciples took their leave of the holy man and disappeared into the rain, one filled to overflowing, the other filled with anticipation of what he was yet to receive.

CHAPTER 8

APARAJITA

Just before dawn Suratha and Samadhi awoke to the roar of a torrential storm that continued hour after hour, bringing with it the dullness of confinement. The king did not mind at all. He had settled into quietude after the previous day's visit with Medhas and remained seated on his cot, alone with his thoughts. Samadhi noticed the change that had come over him. No longer restless or angry or despondent, at least not visibly so, Suratha sat in thoughtful introspection that might almost be taken for contentment.

Samadhi soon understood that his attempts at conversation intruded into a very private realm, and he fell into a quiet of his own that belied his inner restlessness. He tried to think of ways of leaving the king to his solitude, but the unrelenting downpour ruled out strolling around the ashrama or tending the gardens or even leaving the hut. Samadhi thought of Medhas's capacious dwelling and wished he were there in the guru's company, but one did not simply drop in on the holy man as a casual visitor might go to see a friend. In order not to disturb the king, the merchant forced himself to sit quietly, but he only found his own disquiet increasing. With nothing else to do, he lay down hoping for the relief of sleep, but it was only mid morning, and sleep would not come again so soon.

After what seemed liked hours, Krishanu appeared at the doorway, announcing from under his dripping umbrella that the disciples had been missed at the morning meal. "I've brought you some food," he smiled, producing two neatly folded leaf packets. "You're welcome to help in the kitchen," he told the merchant. After a backward glance at the flooded path, he added brightly, "It's not as bad as it looks."

Samadhi ate quickly and set out with Krishanu through the ankle-deep water, thankful for a place to go and something to do.

Hours later Samadhi sloshed his way back along the submerged path, each step tentative in the darkness. He carried with him the king's evening meal and the contentment of a day well spent. At one time or another during the day several of the ashrama's residents had gathered under the roof of the communal dining hall and when not preparing food in the adjoining kitchen, they engaged in sometimes lively conversation. Toward late afternoon, when little remained to be done, they turned their attention to *kirtana*—singing the Divine Mother's praises. Samadhi drank in the resounding elixir of sacred words, pulsing drumbeats, and the bright accents of tiny cymbals and let his own voice blend into the outpouring of devotion. Now, the echoes of those melodies accompanied him along the dark, wet way back to his hut, where a night of contented sleep awaited.

Three more days passed in this way. The rain continued to fall, the king continued to contemplate, and Samadhi, absenting himself from the hut, spent his time with Medhas's other disciples in the dining hall.

On the fourth day, gentle Ushas revealed a cloud-free sky. Stirring every creature from its sleep, she heralded the rising of mighty Surya on the eastern horizon. Soon the sun god would fill heaven and atmosphere and earth with his splendor. For now the rain had ceased, and Surya would look down on the creatures of the world below, all going about their appointed tasks.

His bright rays illuminated the soggy path along which Suratha and Samadhi headed, eager to sit once again at Medhas's feet. Krishanu had told them that the guru would receive them after the morning meal. Suratha, his regal locks now shorn and his golden headband nowhere in evidence, was possessed of a quiet joy. He hardly spoke while his companion chattered enthusiastically about what the holy man had taught so far and about what he still might teach. How different Samadhi appeared from the dejected merchant in tattered clothes whom the king had first laid eyes on. To the king, Samadhi's babble was like the sound of a water jug being submerged in a well. When full, its gurgling would cease, and it would be quiet, just as the king was quiet that morning.

They found Medhas standing outside his hut, surveying the clearing. He motioned for them to sit on a mat in the warm sunlight, away from the still damp shade of the kadamba tree.

"The teaching I begin now is especially for you, Samadhi, but even as you benefited from the story of Durga and Mahishasura, which reflected the king's situation and duty and interests, he also will learn from what I say to you."

And so the seer began.

LONG AGO TWO DEMON BROTHERS, named Shumbha and Nishumbha, grew arrogant with power. Like Mahishasura before them, these fearsome daityas wrested control from Indra. Not only did they cast him out of his heavenly abode; they also seized his sovereignty over the three worlds of heaven, atmosphere, and earth and claimed for themselves his share of the sacrifices so reverently made by unsuspecting mortals.

Next they stripped the other gods of their powers and stole whatever belonged to them. Defeated and driven out, the dispossessed gods remembered the boon that the Great Goddess Durga had granted them: "Whenever you remember me in times of distress, from that very moment I will put an end to all your worst calamities."

And so, the assembled gods approached Himalaya, the mighty lord of mountains, and there praised the Devi, who is called Aparajitā, the invincible one:

Salutation to the Devi, to the great Devi. Salutation always to her who is auspicious. Salutation to her who is the primordial cause, to her who is gracious. With minds intent we bow down to her.

Salutation to her who is terrible. To Gauri, the eternal, shining one; to her who sustains the universe, salutations again and again. Salutation always to her who is moonlight, who has the form of the moon and is blissful.

We bow to her who is auspicious beauty. We make salutations again and again to her who is prosperity and attainment. Salutations again and again to her who is the fortune and misfortune of kings, to Sharvani, the consort of Shiva.

Salutation always to Durga, who takes us through difficulties, who is the creator and indwelling essence of all, who is right knowledge, and who also appears dark as smoke.

We bow down to her who is at once most gentle and most fierce. Salutations to her again and again. Salutation to the support of the world. To the Devi, who is creative action, salutations again and again.

To the Devi, who in all beings is called Vishnumaya, salutation to her, salutation to her, salutation to her again and again.

To the Devi, who in all beings is seen as consciousness, salutation to her, salutation to her, salutation to her again and again.

To the Devi, who abides in all beings in the form of intelligence, . . .

To the Devi, who abides in all beings in the form of sleep, . . .

To the Devi, who abides in all beings in the form of hunger, . . .

To the Devi, who abides in all beings in the form of shadow, . . .

To the Devi, who abides in all beings in the form of power, . . .

To the Devi, who abides in all beings in the form of thirst, . . .

To the Devi, who abides in all beings in the form of forgiveness, . . .

To the Devi, who abides in all beings in the form of order, . . .

To the Devi, who abides in all beings in the form of modesty, . . .

To the Devi, who abides in all beings in the form of peace, . . .

To the Devi, who abides in all beings in the form of faith, . . .

To the Devi, who abides in all beings in the form of loveliness, . . .

To the Devi, who abides in all beings in the form of good fortune, . . .

To the Devi, who abides in all beings in the form of activity, . . .

To the Devi, who abides in all beings in the form of memory, . . .

To the Devi, who abides in all beings in the form of compassion, . . .

To the Devi, who abides in all beings in the form of contentment, . . .

To the Devi, who abides in all beings in the form of mother, . . .

To the Devi, who abides in all beings in the form of error, salutation to her, salutation to her, salutation to her again and again.

To her who presides over the elements and the senses and is ever present in all beings, to the all-pervading Devi, salutations again and again.

To her who pervades this entire world and abides in the form of consciousness, salutation to her, salutation to her, salutation to her again and again.

Praised long ago by the gods for fulfilling their desires and likewise honored daily by the lord of the gods, may Ishvari, the source of all good, create happiness and prosperity for us, and may she destroy our misfortunes.

Tormented by arrogant daityas, we gods now honor her, the supreme power. With bodies bowed down in devotion, at this moment we remember her who destroys all afflictions.[3]

"This hymn to Aparajita celebrates the Divine Mother's presence in the world," Medhas explained. "How fitting that we have this beautiful day to contemplate its meaning." While his right hand gestured gracefully to acknowledge the glory of nature all around, his eyes sparkled with the sheer joy of being alive.

"The gods' first words are, 'Salutations to the Devi.' With this phrase they invoke the Mother in personal form. She promises to rescue from misfortune anyone who calls upon her. Next the gods salute her as the Mahadevi—the great, formless reality of which all forms are her many expressions. Whenever remembered, she is present—and even when not remembered, for she is the ever-present source, sustenance, and underlying reality of all creation. *Her every form offers a possible connection, a way to relate to the infinite Divine*, and that is what the gods celebrate.

"The Mahadevi is auspicious by her very nature. Ever abiding in formless, self-luminous perfection, she is pure consciousness. Through her creative power, which is not different from her infinite, blissful being, she sends forth this world. You see, the Mother is simultaneously unmoving and incessantly in motion."

In his eagerness Samadhi tried to hang on to every word, and Medhas, sensing his struggle to understand, returned to an analogy he had used before.

"When the Mother abides in perfect oneness, she is like an infinite ocean of clear, absolutely still water. When she is active—creating, preserving, and destroying—she is like water in motion. Such water loses its clarity in the swirling currents, bubbles, and froth. Waves rise and fall, and what was formless takes on form. The forms come and go, but water is water whether it remains still or moves. The Absolute and its creative power, Shakti, are one and the same.

"Shakti herself has become all this." Medhas's sweeping gesture punctuated that thought while a thrill of recognition coursed through the merchant's mind. A flash of light that was not physical light, a moment of transfiguration, a new panorama opening out before him, and then a longing such as he had never known before as his heart reached out to grasp the already receding vision of—of something he had no name for.

How much time passed, if any, he could not say, but suddenly he was aware of Medhas's voice asserting, "—and it is she herself who has proclaimed, 'Through heaven and earth I extend. At the summit of creation, I bring forth the heavens. My creative power flows from amid the waters of the infinite ocean. Thence I spread through all the worlds and touch yonder heaven with my vastness. I breathe forth like the wind, setting all the worlds in motion. So great have I become in my splendor, shining far beyond heaven and earth.'"

Samadhi wondered if that was what he had glimpsed, then attempted a smile when the guru looked at him knowingly.

Medhas went on, "Everything emanates from the ever-gracious Mother and is filled with her presence. 'Salutation to her who is terrible,' the gods say. They worship her not only in her serene benevolence but also in the raw power of nature, in her destructive fury—in the howling of a tempest or the crackling roar of a conflagration raging through a dry forest. And they remember that however impetuous or violent she may appear at times, she remains the eternally changeless, self-luminous support of all.

"The gods say, 'Salutation always to her who is moonlight, who has the form of the moon and is blissful.' What does that mean? The Devi who is the moon—that is to say, the source—and the Devi who is moonlight—that is to say, its emanation, this universe—are one and the same. What a poetic image to express the philosophy of nondualism—that there is one reality and nothing exists apart from it."

Next Medhas explained that the Devi appears in many forms, shining through all creation as auspicious beauty with the power to inspire the mind and gladden the heart. She grants prosperity and attainment.

"She is the fortune and misfortune of kings," he said with a meaningful glance toward Suratha. "Just as she presides over growth and fulfillment, she reigns also over decay and death. As Sharvani, Lord Shiva's consort, she appears as the power at the end of a cosmic cycle. The same Devi who sustains life and makes it enjoyable eventually calls it into dissolution.

"But again, the gods say, 'Salutation always to Durga, who takes us through difficulties.' Do you remember when I told you that of all her names Durga is the one dearest to the Mother? Durga, meaning 'difficult of approach,' is an unassailable fortress in whom we find refuge from *durga*, which means 'rough going' or worldly adversity. The hymn makes a play on words to impress this teaching on the mind. Likewise, it continues to say poetically that she is the essence of all, who possesses both the concealing and revealing powers that make worldly existence and spiritual liberation possible. In this play of existence, how easily the Mother is overlooked or forgotten! Yet she is everywhere present, if only we allow ourselves to be aware.

"Now since the day is so beautiful, I suggest that the two of you go for a walk."

Dismissed abruptly but lovingly, Suratha and Samadhi headed uphill on the path to the river, hiking without a word until the guru's hut passed out of view. Then the king, who had been inclined not to speak, came to a standstill and broke the silence. "I remember once, after the rain, walking through the palace garden. It was late afternoon, toward evening. The sky was only beginning to clear, and the scent of the wet earth wafted up through the pure air—cool air that made me aware of the comforting warmth of my clothing. Just then, the inner and the outer existed in perfect balance, and I was supremely happy. I don't know why I'm telling you this. It's just that it has remained fresh in my mind all these years. There are far grander moments to remember—after all I enjoyed the privileges of kingship for a long while. But somehow those memories have faded—lost their luster—but that simple moment in the garden after the rain has lost none of its beauty. I can't tell you how much I treasure it. Does that seem strange?"

Samadhi looked up at his taller companion, at a loss for words. He wondered what Medhas would say. In view of his own recent, inexplicable moods, what the king described did not seem strange at all. "No," he finally managed to reply, "I suspect that these uncommon feelings come to most of us at one time or another. We just don't know how to talk about them—and maybe they're not for talking about anyway, not in an everyday sort of way."

The companions resumed their ascent along the curving path toward the promontory that overlooked the river. About halfway there, Samadhi noticed a narrow trail on the left, descending into the forest. "I wonder where that goes," he remarked.

"Let's find out." Without waiting for the merchant to agree, Suratha plowed into the greenery and set out along the unexplored route. Samadhi followed, close behind at first but soon at a greater distance to avoid the branches rebounding in the king's wake.

After some distance, they stopped to admire the lofty trees that reached skyward from the damp forest floor. They rejoiced over the emerald ferns and sun-splashed shrubbery that sparkled like gold amid the deeper greens. It was then that they became aware of the surrounding sounds. The rustle of leaves filled the air to a gentle fullness that sang against the babbling of the unseen river. The calls of birds and the buzzing of insects added their melodies and harmonies to the music of the forest, and now and then a small creature, skittering in the underbrush, added its percussive accent.

Something he had not thought about for years surfaced in Samadhi's mind. "When I was little," he confided, "my grandmother used to sing a song about the forest goddess, Aranyani. It's been so long, and I don't remember the exact words, but it went something like this: 'Aranyani, lady of the forest, who show yourself not, why do you not come to the village? Are you not afraid out there in the wild? Amid the grasshoppers' and cicadas' calls you move, ever elusive, with the sound of tinkling bells. I praise you, sweet-scented mother of sylvan beings, who till the land not, yet yield stores of food. I feed on your bounty, gentle Aranyani, then take my rest in your shade.'"

"I think she is with us today," the king remarked, moved by the song.

"She is always here, don't you think? It's just that we don't notice."

"Of course, you're right. Isn't that what Medhas told us?"

Moving on, Suratha reflected on how much he had missed, day after day, year after year, just through his own foolishness—or would negligence be a better word? This was no time for blame or regret, though. This was time for joy in the surrounding miracle.

Samadhi must have felt the same. He followed silently, a smile playing on his lips.

CHAPTER 9

The Divine Presence

That afternoon the guru greeted his two disciples again in the clearing outside his hut and with the sun now bright overhead, they resorted to the cool shade of the kadamba tree. There Medhas revealed more fully the wisdom of the great hymn to Aparajita, the invincible Devi.

With his characteristic gesture that signified the universe in its glorious totality, he began, "All this is filled with the divine presence, the joyful vibrancy of the Divine Mother's own awareness—nothing more and certainly nothing less. The mind cannot know her ultimate purity. Still, her light filters through to illumine all states of existence."

Samadhi scanned the clearing, suddenly captivated by the leaves of the tall trees, shimmering in the breeze and dancing with the sunbeams. Beyond them stretched the clear expanse of sky, on and on beyond the imagination. As he looked on, memory of the morning surfaced, memory of his ecstatic glimpse of he knew not what, an instant that had left him changed. How strange, he thought, that after such ineffable joy he still bore the burden of being himself with all his finitude. He longed to expand again into that awareness, whatever it was.

Sensing his mood, Medhas said, "To understand this fully is beyond the power of thought. Of course, that does not mean you should not try," he added quickly. "This universe flows from absolute unity into the miraculous diversity we see all around. As absolute, self-luminous consciousness, the Mother is aware only of her own divine nature—singular, blissful, eternally free. But she, the supreme Oneness, is endowed with creative power. And so the gods praise her, chanting: 'To the Devi, who in all beings is called Vishnumaya, salutation to her, salutation to her, salutation to her again and again.' Vishnumaya is the power of consciousness to sustain the creation.

"This power is threefold—as tamas, concealing; as rajas, projecting; as sattva, revealing. Through *avaranashakti*, the Mother veils her infinitude. Through *vikshepashakti*, she projects out of herself all this wonder of creation. And through *jnanashakti*, she graciously shines the light of knowledge through it, hinting at the bliss of her infinite oneness."

With a sudden burst of insight, Samadhi asked, "Because the Mother's power is threefold, is that why you said 'salutation to her' three times?" He hadn't stopped to reason this out; the idea simply flashed before his mind.

"Precisely! When the gods offer salutation three times, as they do throughout this hymn, they acknowledge the tamasic, rajasic, and sattvic qualities in everything." His face took on that particular intensity that Suratha and Samadhi recognized as the sign of an important revelation to come. "There is also a second way to look at this. Throughout the universe there are three levels of manifestation—the gross plane of physical matter, the subtle plane of mind or thought, and the causal plane of potentiality. In this way, too, the universe is threefold. Do not think of these planes as high, middle, or low levels—or as places at all. They are states of awareness relative to the transcendental unity of consciousness that lies beyond.

When I use words such as *proximity* and *beyond*, I speak in terms of space to express something beyond all idea of space. *Beyond*—a spatial term! There is no way to express it. Speech and mind cannot be freed from the boundaries of time and space. Such is the limiting power of maya.

"Everything evolves from the unity of consciousness to unity in diversity and then to diversity. Try to imagine the supreme Devi as absolute subjectivity, the ultimate 'I'—nothing more. Nothing at all. Then imagine that she wills, 'I am one; let me become many.' In this way she brings forth the creation. For the 'I' to have something to experience, there has to be a 'this,' and so, within the single divine awareness, the sense of an object arises. At first this sense of subject and object—of 'I' and 'this'—remains within the One, like the two halves of a sesame seed. They are joined together and each is the same, yet each is a mirror-image of the other. This is what I mean by 'unity in diversity.' Like the seed, which contains the entire sesame plant in potentiality, this state of consciousness is the seed of the entire cosmos. When the gods sing, 'To the Devi, who abides in all beings in the form of consciousness,' that is what they mean."

The king's attention had wandered, and Samadhi, though intrigued, sat as if stunned, striving but unable to take it all in.

True, the guru thought, this matter was very abstruse and he should not have expected too much of his disciples so early on. "It all seems remote and abstract, does it not?" he proffered. He thought, When one approach fails to work, try another. "This is something profound," he resumed, investing every word with weight. "Wherever there are two, there is always a third."

His revelation did not produce the desired effect, but only more blank incomprehension.

Now Medhas spoke crisply, as if starting all over at the beginning. "You see, the infinite, formless Devi is One without a second." He allowed time for that to sink in. "When one becomes two, there is always a third, which is the *relationship* between the two. The power of consciousness shines in the Mother as 'I,' the knower. It reflects outwardly as 'this,' the object known. There cannot be a knower without something to be known, and there cannot be something to be known without a knower. But there also has to be a connection, and that is the knowing. And so, divine consciousness pulsates continually—creation materializes from the divine will, overflowing from its blissful fullness. Knower, knowing, and known—another example of the threefold nature of everything!"

While the king drummed his fingers on the ground, Samadhi exclaimed. "Of course!" This was exactly what Medhas had hoped for.

"Time and space are also threefold, aren't they?" the merchant said. "I mean, time is either past, present, or future; and space has three dimensions—height, breadth, and depth."

"Of course."

Lest he appear uninterested or less informed than his companion, the king interposed, "And matter also exists in three states. Water, for example, is usually a liquid, like the water flowing in the river or filling a cup. But put it into a cooking pot over a fire and it turns to steam and rises into the air, just as the water drunk by the sun's rays forms the clouds. And when water becomes very cold, it turns solid like a rock. People who have traveled to the mountains tell us this is true."

"You don't have to go that far," Samadhi chimed in. "All you have to do is sit here and wait for a hailstorm."

"And do not forget language," the guru added. "When you say 'I,' that denotes the speaker. 'You' is the one spoken to. 'He, she, or it,' is the person or object spoken about. Three grammatical persons, and another threefold way in which we experience the world."

"And speaking of how we experience the world," the king added, "everything has a beginning, a middle, and an end, doesn't it?" He thought longingly of his lost kingship.

"That is true. And do not forget that we inhabit the three states of waking, dreaming, and dreamless sleep. But beyond the three there is always the fourth—*turiya*—the unmanifest, transcendental consciousness. That reminds me of another name of the Divine Mother—Tripurasundari. What a wonderful name! It means 'she who is before the three' or 'she who is beyond the three.' In other words, the source of all this and also its goal."

Samadhi felt overwhelmed by a teaching that he saw as the fruit of great intelligence. When he voiced that thought, Medhas reiterated, "Emanation flows from absolute consciousness to the Mother's intermediate consciousness pregnant with this universe, to the individual consciousness of you and Suratha and everyone else. About this last one the gods sing, 'To the Devi, who abides in all beings in the form of intelligence.'

They mean *buddhi*, the highest form of consciousness within the human being. It discerns, reasons, determines, understands, and wills. Think of this intelligence shining out from all eyes—yours, mine, his." Excitedly the guru pointed to the king. "*That* is buddhi! That is a hint of the divine essence we all carry within. But how many of us recognize it?

"I shall tell you something practical, yet which is not given to everyone to hear. Because buddhi is the highest mental faculty, it is the part of us that is closest to divine awareness. Through it we approach the supreme Self that lies within. So is it taught that 'the Self, hidden in all beings, does not readily shine forth but is seen by the seers of subtle things with the buddhi focused.' Medhas punctuated the quotation with a long silence so that its meaning would impress itself on his disciples' minds.

After what he considered a suitable wait, Samadhi asked what was meant by focusing the buddhi.

"To focus the buddhi is to make a disciplined mental effort."

"What sort of effort?"

"Ah! The effort to turn the light of consciousness upon itself! You do not understand yet, because your understanding is veiled. Your awareness is constantly absorbed in bondage to actions and the residual impressions they leave on the mind. Your mind is ensnared in the chain of cause and effect of your external life. Because you associate yourself with this web of maya, you have fallen prey to the mental impurity that deludes even the wise. You must practice constantly to peer into the true nature of yourself and all things."

"How is that?" Samadhi asked, not even sure of what he was asking.

"In the embodied state we are physical, mental, and spiritual beings; but it is the mental part, the buddhi, that can lead us beyond this ordinary existence. That is why we must focus our efforts there."

Still not satisfied, Samadhi asked if enlightenment, then, was purely a matter of reason or self-effort. If so, what role was there for the Divine Mother, or any god or goddess?

Of course, the holy man had an answer. "First, you must remember that reason is only one of the buddhi's several functions. I do not see how reason alone—which follows a course from premise to conclusion and is a mental chain of cause and effect—can break the binding chain of cause and effect that we call *samsara*, or embodied existence. Of course, reason can clarify—to a point—and plays a role in spiritual practice.

"Then again, the matter of self-effort is an age-old question. What frees us? Self—effort or grace?"

That is what Samadhi wanted to know. He stared with pleading eyes at the guru.

"Perhaps even self-effort is the result of divine grace," Medhas suggested. "After all, does this hymn not praise the Mother as dwelling within all beings as the very faculty of awareness by which we can strive to attain her? To me that means that grace and self-effort are intimately linked. The philosophers will debate this endlessly, you know. Let them. But you, Samadhi—see where your practice leads and give no thought to the rest. What does all this speculation accomplish? Your own realization is proof enough." Medhas smiled so sweetly that Samadhi momentarily felt engulfed in peace.

Suratha, now heedful of the conversation, grew curious, and asked, "If human beings are all endowed with this divine intelligence, why did their thoughts, speech, and actions not always reflect it?"

"But they do!" Medhas laughed heartily. The outburst, so unexpected, unsettled the king. The holy man went on, "An excellent question. You must remember that Shakti expresses herself through the three gunas. Awareness in the form of buddhi takes on those three qualities and every combination of them. Tamasic buddhi, for example, is human intelligence used for evil purposes, such as the plotting of a crime. Rajasic buddhi would be the intellect applied to the arts and sciences and constructive endeavors. Sattvic buddhi strives toward the higher spiritual knowledge. In every case the light of consciousness is present, dimly or more brightly, for awareness is the very nature of buddhi, but it appears veiled by the gunas and takes on many forms of expression. What matters is how we use that intelligence."

Samadhi inquired, "A while ago you said that waking, dreaming, and dreamless sleep are states of consciousness. When I'm asleep, I don't know *what's* going on around me. How can I be conscious?"

While the king struggled to suppress a laugh, Medhas turned to Samadhi and countered, "What do *you* think sleep is?"

"A state of rest when the body and mind are quiet?" Samadhi's rising inflection signaled uncertainty.

"A good starting point, but let us go deeper. In dreamless sleep you are not aware of the outer world, the body, the mind, or the ego. But dreamless sleep is not unconscious, for every state is a form of consciousness. In deep sleep, physical and mental activities cease, but consciousness remains, though devoid of content. That is why on awakening you have the awareness either that you knew nothing or, at most, that you slept well. And so we say that the Devi, who abides in all beings in the form of consciousness, abides in all beings in the form of sleep. Additionally, if you like, you may take this state of sleep as a metaphor for the spiritually unawakened state in which all creatures of this world exist, be they plant, beast, or human being.

"Now I have a question for you. The Devi abides in all beings in the form of hunger. What does it mean to be hungry?" the guru asked.

Samadhi described feeling empty in the stomach and wanting to eat.

"And when your hunger is satisfied after a good meal, how do you feel then?"

"Full."

Medhas waited to see if his disciple would pursue this line of thought, but Samadhi seemed disinclined to travel beyond his momentary, imagined satisfaction.

And so the guru explained, "The divine reality, the Absolute, is said also to be full. Out of this fullness everything emerges, and in it everything has its being. Yet we feel hungry. As physical hunger signals the lack of food in the stomach, spiritual hunger indicates another kind of lack—the incompleteness of being cut off from the divine plenitude. In the embodied state we are separated from our true fullness, our infinite being, by the limiting power of maya.

"To sustain life in the physical body, every creature must eat, and so through hunger the Mother keeps her play of creation going. At the same time," Medhas observed with eyes sparkling, "this hunger of the spirit is a reminder of the loving Devi who beckons to us from her blissful abode beyond the world of appearances. Is there any way in which she does not show her grace? Even this hunger is a sign of the Mother's love!"

"But why would she keep it hidden?" Samadhi was growing persistent in his questioning, and Medhas was delighted.

"Do you remember what the gods sing next? 'To the Devi, who abides in all beings in the form of shadow.' You can look at this idea of shadow in two ways, maybe more. But for now, two will suffice. Or maybe one of you wants to explain." Seeing the disciples' reluctance, Medhas laughed.

How joyful he is, Samadhi thought, but neither he nor the king spoke.

"Very well. A shadow results when light is blocked, so it is a product of tamas, is it not? It comes about when Mahamaya's veiling power blocks the light of pure consciousness. By 'shadow' the gods mean the material universe—the ultimately formless Devi appearing as form. She is at once the source of light and that which casts the shadow—as well as the shadow itself! You see, nothing is apart from the Mother."

As if reading the merchant's mind, Medhas veered to a new line of thought. "If you were thinking of tamas as something negative, consider this: We are enjoying a beautiful afternoon with the sun shining brightly. We appreciate it all the more from the shade of this tree. Out there," he said, pointing to the sun-drenched clearing, "we might wither in the heat. The shade or darkness, which you call tamasic, is in this case beneficial, offering us refuge or protection. And the brilliant sunlight, which sustains all life, has its harsh, destructive side. The world is a complex place indeed!

"Next the gods sing, 'To the Devi, who abides in all beings in the form of power.' That power, Shakti, is the Mother's very essence. It is one of her primary names, in fact," Medhas explained, "and it carries the idea of ability, energy, force, and strength—and of possibility.

"I told you that at the moment before creation the Mother's power becomes concentrated in a single, dimensionless point, which is the womb of all possibility. Whatever exists—all that we know and do not know and that which we cannot even dream of—is possible because of the Mother's creative imagination, her power of consciousness. Consider all the ways in which Shakti reveals herself as this universe. Through her alone the sun rises and sets, the moon waxes and wanes, the stars travel on their courses. Mother is the sum total of all the energy in the universe."

Samadhi protested, "But if she dwells in all beings as power, how can we be so small, and the events of our lives—my life for example—so overwhelming? I'm reminded constantly of how weak and powerless I am."

Medhas flashed a compassionate smile. "Behind everything lies the power of divine consciousness—Shakti. The energy of your heartbeat—Shakti; the heat in your belly that digests your food—Shakti; every movement you make—Shakti; every word and thought—Shakti. Granted, you live in a world where everything is relative, and so you feel weak or powerless whenever a stronger expression of Shakti than your own comes along. Look at the king here. Once he was the most powerful man in the realm. The greatest generals bowed before him and did his bidding. Yet of what use was his mighty army against a howling tempest or a raging forest fire? Again, though he possessed enormous power over other people, how much power did he possess over himself? When he arrived here in the forest, suffering the agonies of loss and betrayal, he knew no peace simply because he had no power over his own mind."

Suratha absorbed these remarks without protest, while Medhas continued, "And can I not say the same of you, my dear merchant? Do you not still long for the wife and sons who cast you out? Do not the memories of your lost wealth still stab like daggers at your heart?"

"That's just my point."

"It does not have to be that way! The Mother abides in all beings—you included—in the form of power. Use that strength to overcome the illusion of smallness that keeps you in misery. You may not have the power to set the stars in the heavens or to make the sun rise and set, and anyway, those are all external things. You, Samadhi, have the possibility to realize your own divine nature, and there is no greater power than that! When you know the Self, what else can ever exert power over you?"

That was more than Samadhi had bargained for. Medhas approached vehemence in his exhortation, and his disciple sensed a challenge being thrown out—a challenge like he had never faced before and one he was reluctant to accept. He felt relieved when Medhas, barely pausing, recited the next verse.

"'To the Devi, who abides in all beings in the form of thirst.'"

"What is the difference between hunger and thirst?" Samadhi queried eagerly, glad to change the subject. "Aren't they both about filling the stomach?"

"Poetic convention, perhaps," Medhas mused. "But, truly, the Mother created the senses outgoing in order to enjoy her creation. She sees through every pair of eyes, hears through every pair of ears, tastes through every mouth, and so on. She dwells in every creature as the thirst for life, to enjoy all the pleasures of body and mind. This thirst can be colored by any of the gunas. Tamasic thirst, for example, could be sexual desire. Here the mind is most completely identified with the body, the densest dimension of one's being, through which the light of the spirit least penetrates. When physical lust overcomes the mind, one's total awareness becomes engrossed in the confines of the flesh and isolated in the pursuit of fleeting pleasure. Of course, in love-making, the body becomes, more nobly, a vehicle for expressing affection between two lovers. Certainly there is sacredness in that intimacy. And of course," Medhas added with a twinkle in his eye, "without sex, where would babies come from?

"When this thirst for life is colored by rajas, then one desires excitement. Maybe dancing or lavish feasting or driving a chariot at breakneck speed just for the thrill of it." Medhas glanced knowingly at the king, who wondered if he had any secrets left. "But when this kind of exhilaration seizes the mind, where is tranquility?"

"Forgotten?" the merchant queried.

"So right you are! And so I tell you, there is a superior kind of thirst—the attraction to inspiring, uplifting things. When you go to a temple or sit to meditate with the same sense of thirst you once held for worldly pleasures, then this thirst is said to be sattvic. It leads toward the quiet joy of the divine presence. The Devi dwells in all beings in the form of every kind of thirst, of course, but be aware of where true satisfaction and lasting peace abide."

Suratha cleared his throat. "Samadhi and I have felt this thirst for life, and we've enjoyed it in its worldly forms. Then it all came to a crashing end for both of us before we had any inkling of the higher thirst. So here we are now, caught in between and not yet free of the darkness that torments us."

Medhas looked radiant. "Of all the verses in this wonderful hymn, this is one of the most precious: 'To the Devi, who abides in all beings in the form of forgiveness.' Both of you believe you have been sorely wronged. Sovereignty, riches, respect, family—all gone! I do not dispute that, nor the wrongdoing of those who dispossessed and betrayed you. What suffering they have caused! But you must not discount the role of karma, either. Remember, every human life is caught up in the web of cause and effect. Why should yours be any different?

"Now consider this: To live with resentment is to nourish continually the mental impression of the wrong done to you. It grows only stronger, and the sustained ill will that results grows ever heavier and binds ever tighter."

Suratha and Samadhi exchanged sympathetic glances. Then the king spoke for both of them. "What you say is true, but what is the way out? Are we merely to turn our backs on injustice and pretend it doesn't matter? Or are we to remain indifferent to our feelings and think we've attained dispassion?"

"Suratha, as a king and warrior you cannot turn your back on injustice. Your moral duty is to uphold the dharma, but in acting you must recognize the difference between justice and revenge. And I say this to both of you whatever feelings arise: You must be honest with yourselves. You must not suppress your feelings, and you must not fool yourselves into mistaking indifference for detachment. Now, what is the opposite of resentment?"

"Forgiveness. That's what we're talking about, isn't it?" the king replied.

"And what is forgiveness?" Medhas challenged. A pleasant word, he thought to himself, one dipped in honey. But he wanted his disciples to penetrate the facile sweetness and sentimentality.

"Saying that whatever was done is pardoned?" The king sounded as if he were still at the royal court.

"No!" Medhas exploded, and the disciples winced. He breathed in deeply, gathering his thoughts, then proceeded calmly. "It is not enough to say, 'I forgive you, you are pardoned.' If you truly feel that, by all means say it, but do not stop there. Listen well: *forgiveness is severing the bonds of attachment to your own hurt feelings.* That is the first step and the last, and without understanding that, nothing that happens in between counts for anything. It is all empty words and falseness. When you let go of your own hurt, you feel your heart expand beyond yourself, and that expansion frees you from the prison of your own resentment.

"Forgiveness heals in three ways. If others have wronged you, your forgiveness of them releases you from the burden of resentment, anger, or hatred that *you* carry. If you have harmed others, their forgiveness ennobles you by its goodness and frees you from your burden of guilt. And if you have harmed yourself by failing to recognize your own worth, by failing to act in your own best interests, or simply by harboring negative attitudes, the forgiveness of self is a great healer. In every way, forgiveness releases you from the past and opens your life to renewal. Let go! By holding on to the small and particular, how can your arms be free to embrace the fullness?"

"That's easier said than done," the king objected, sure he was speaking for the merchant as well. Maybe he risked the guru's ire, but it would be worth it, because the matter at hand directly touched on the calamities that had brought them to the forest retreat. Medhas's reaction was not what Suratha feared. Instead, the guru beamed.

"Of course! Who ever said that spiritual life is easy? You have to make the effort, and keep on making the effort even when it seems futile. Never be discouraged. I assure you that you will not be disappointed. What I am telling you works, and that alone is what matters.

"One other point: the word that the gods use for forgiveness also means 'patience' or 'forbearance.'"

Those terms prompted another insightful flash, which Samadhi tried to put into words. "I understand now that to forgive is to let go of something painful in the past. Can I think of patience as letting go of something *before* it happens? I mean—whenever I anticipate something, I create an expectation. I set myself up to be pleased or displeased, disappointed or angered. I've prepared myself beforehand to be affected by something that hasn't even happened yet, and I've bound myself to reacting in a certain way."

"Yes, yes," Medhas interrupted. "You have discovered something important. So many people, even intelligent ones, go about expecting things to be a certain way and only that way. They expect other people to hold opinions that agree with their own. And then, look at what happens. Perfectly rational people, or so we think, speak and act rashly, as if they have been offended. Over what? How does it serve them to be critical and judging? What is impatience, but unkindness? But forbearance frees one from the tyranny of expectation. However you look at this question of forgiveness, it all comes back to letting go, freedom, and an expansion of spirit."

Turning the conversation in a new direction, Medhas prompted the disciples to look around. They would observe an order in the world, for the Devi abides in all beings in the form of order. Each object and creature has its own form of existence, he explained, determined by its birth or manner of creation. "Plant a mango seed and up comes a mango tree, not a tamarind. A woman gives birth to a human baby, not to a monkey or an elephant. We do not live in a random universe."

The seer explained that everything takes on its own form of existence through a series of underlying cosmic principles, or *tattvas*. Philosophers describe these in minute detail, but the basic fact is that every principle flows out from the pure unity of divine consciousness as a modification of that consciousness itself. The stages of cosmic evolution proceed in a natural order from initial unity to all the differentiations of intellect, ego, mind, the organs of perception and action, all the way outward to the five physical elements of space, air, fire, water, and earth.

"You see, the very existence of all this," Medhas explained, "implies consciousness as its guiding force. All life, be it plant, animal, or human, is sentient, and to be sentient means to be endowed with consciousness. Take even a seemingly lifeless stone. There are many different kinds of stones with diverse color, shape, hardness, and texture, yet each has a characteristic structure. Are we to deny that these are devoid of a creative principle? Of course not! There is order in the universe from the very largest things to those too small to be seen. Everywhere in nature there is pattern, order—consciousness. Know that to be the Divine Mother's creative intelligence. This sense of order works in two ways. Through evolution it brings into being all the diversity that makes this universe so endlessly alluring. Then this sense of order allows everything to exist and function interdependently and harmoniously. So, you see, diversity and coherence go hand in hand. Philosophers rightly say that the order inherent in the universe necessarily partakes of and reflects the Mother's own divine nature.

"That nature is most clearly revealed in the person who exhibits qualities such as intelligence, patience, forgiveness, serenity, and compassion. Some of these we have talked about already. The gods also say that the Devi abides in all beings in the form of modesty." Medhas shot a penetrating glance at the king. "You are beginning to know what that means, I think."

"I remember that Indra and the other gods praised the Devi as 'modesty in the hearts of the high-born,' and, yes, through my own experience I'm beginning to understand."

"And you, Samadhi," Medhas queried. "what is your experience of modesty?"

The merchant blushed and bit his lip. "When I was rich and somewhat powerful, I'd sometimes feel proud. My fine clothing marked me as superior to people who were poorly dressed. At least that's how I saw it. Maybe I came across as arrogant, and I'm sorry now. I'm no better than anyone else, and there are others, such as you, who are far better than I could ever hope to be."

Medhas was not pleased at Samadhi's sincere but misguided attempt at humility, and the merchant, unnerved, wondered what he had said wrong. If there is such a thing as an emphatic gaze, Samadhi found himself at the receiving end of one, not where he wanted to be. After a prolonged silence Medhas said, "You must understand that modesty is not self-abasement. True humility lies not in thinking yourself beneath anyone else, but rather in recognizing the divine essence in everyone. One who is truly humble makes the other person feel important, but never at the cost of denying his own worth. Self-denigration only denies the divinity in oneself and so dishonors the

Mother. Rather, know that true humility lies in setting aside the ego-sense and acknowledging holiness in and through all beings. With this comes a sweetness of character that others will be drawn to respect." Medhas smiled at the paradox—that true humility, and not arrogant self-assertion, commands respect.

"Humility is a way to peace, and as the gods proclaim, the Devi abides in all beings in the form of peace. But peace, *shanti*, is one of those pleasant words we like to throw about until it is almost meaningless. What does it really mean?" Again Medhas intended to provoke his students and succeeded. Samadhi struggled to think through the vagueness of what he thought of as peace.

Suratha, the warrior and sovereign, stated, "Peace is the absence of war, people living together in harmony and cooperation rather than in open conflict."

That definition fits the outer world, Medhas thought, but he wanted to take his disciples deeper. "Do you see any war raging about you now?" he challenged, referring to the tranquility of the forest.

"No."

"And are you experiencing peace?"

"Not entirely."

"Ah!" Medhas exclaimed.

"May I say something?" the merchant interposed. "The king is just thinking of the outer world and not the inner world of the mind. There, neither one of us can say we've found peace, not even here in these peaceful surroundings."

"Precisely!" Medhas uttered his favorite word of approval. "Now the opposite of shanti is *ashanti*—restlessness, anxiety."

It was beginning to make sense. For Samadhi and the king the idea of peace was moving from a hazy abstraction to something intensely personal.

Medhas went on: "Inner disturbance takes many forms, from mild discontent to violent turmoil. We have seen such states of mind in the story of Mahishasura. The story of Shumbha and Nishumbha that I intend to tell you will make all that even clearer. But that is a matter for the days to come. For now, simply think of peace as the absence of any kind of dissatisfaction."

Maybe it was the mention of anxiety that prompted Samadhi to confess. Whatever the reason, what he said poured out in uncharacteristically high-flown language. "All that you've taught is appealing and rings true, yet from time to time the chill grip of doubt seizes me and leaves me despairing. Then the pain crashes down on me again in unbidden waves that threaten to sweep me away. I'm overcome with uncertainty, even though I want to believe that what you say is true."

Medhas exploded. "Don't talk to me of belief! Do you think you can keep your fear at bay through self-deception? Is fooling yourself the way to overcome ignorance? I could tell you what to do with that kind of belief, but it wouldn't be polite."

Managing to suppress his own amusement, the holy man observed Samadhi's obvious perplexity with some relish. The king sat by, dumbfounded. Uneasy moments passed until Medhas said quietly, "The Devi abides in all beings in the form of faith. Do you know what that means? Do you think, Samadhi, that by merely saying 'I believe, I believe,' all your distress will vanish? Do you think that I would teach you blind acceptance of something you could not prove to yourself? Faith is trust in your own experience—not believing what someone else tells you. Only through your own experience will you gain the unwavering sense of strength that is true faith."

The conversation had unfolded in unexpected ways, with unimagined new insights, until late in the afternoon. Now the setting sun flooded the western sky with vibrant pink, purple, and orange, merging into cool violet in the east.

"Magical, isn't it?" Medhas remarked. "I shall have more to say about this later. Now go, take your evening meal, and return here tonight."

ॐ ऐं ॐ

CHAPTER 10

CELEBRATION

That evening, outside Medhas's hut, the moon hung huge and luminous, a yellowish white orb crossed by interlaced wisps of black and silver cloud, suspended low in the sky's expanse of deepening blue. As if by design, nature's enchantment heralded the guru's opening words.

"To the Devi, who abides in all beings in the form of loveliness." The holy man appeared radiant, savoring the moment. He pointed to the moon with a graceful gesture that verged on benediction. "Look! The Mother abides in all this in the form of beauty. The joyful wonder you feel at this sight, the expansion of your heart, is a response to the Mother's self-revelation. Everywhere in nature's luminous visage she shows herself."

Overflowing with joy, he continued, "Think of the red hibiscus flower in the perfection of full bloom. Or any other flower for that matter. When we worship, we offer these flowers to the gods and goddesses. But when you see these same flowers blooming in nature, are they not the Mother's own joyful worship of herself? Think of the dark blue butterfly borne on the gentle breeze. Or of the green parrot with red eyes in the depths of the verdant forest. Or of the thundercloud that floats on high, its dark billows shading into brilliant white. Think of the sunlight sparkling on the river's current like countless diamonds. Or of the night sky glittering with stars beyond number. All this is the Mother reveling in her own glory.

"We experience beauty not only in the constantly changing face of nature but in countless other ways as well. There is no greater artist than the Mother, of course, but consider the beauty in objects that women and men create—silken textiles interwoven with gold, magnificent pottery vessels, exquisite paintings. Is this artistry not also a sign of inspiration? Is the Mother's beauty not revealed in those human works as well? Think of the poetry and the music that speak to our nobler selves and celebrate the breadth and depth of our human feelings. Do they not also reflect something greater than our smallness? From what do such wonders arise? Even in our mundane actions we see beauty in human kindness. In every act of generosity and compassion, in every caring word and benevolent thought, there is beauty and its power to transform.

"How often we speak of 'truth,' 'goodness,' and 'beauty,' all in the same breath. Do you think this is merely by accident? How do they differ from one another? Where any one of them is present, holiness abides. In all the ways I have just described, the Devi reveals herself and inspires us. Beauty is the Mother's way of reminding us of her presence."

Medhas looked at his disciples. They appeared like living sculptures in the play of moonlight and shadow—two more of the Mother's works of art, he thought, admiring the rugged strength of the king's well-formed features and the bright innocence of the gentler merchant's inquiring face. Patiently he waited for either man to speak.

"We are fortunate," the king remarked at last.

"Yes, and the gods agree. They say, 'To the Devi, who abides in all beings in the form of good fortune.' She is the source of all good. She offers material bounty, such as gold, cattle, and horses. Through the abundance of crops she provides food to sustain us. Health, satisfaction, increase, and happiness are all her gifts. Yes, Suratha, we are indeed blessed."

Recalling Indra's earlier hymn, the king recited a verse that was now engraved in his memory: "O Devi, we bow before you who are yourself good fortune in the dwellings of the virtuous and misfortune in the abodes of the wicked." He wanted the seer to comment.

"We have already discussed that verse at length in relation to karma and the idea of reward and punishment," the guru noted. "Still, I shall say something about the connection between virtue and good fortune, which is the import of your question. The Devi inhabits all beings as good fortune, or *lakshmi*. We can think of her personified as Lakshmi, the benevolent goddess who rests upon a lotus and dispenses her blessings. The wise, hoping for favor, seek to please her through self-purification and virtuous conduct. They entreat Lakshmi to banish their ill luck and their enslavement to maya in both the outer affairs of the world and the inner movings of the mind and heart. Do you see how personal this becomes?

"When you think of good fortune, know that the outward signs of blessing are indeed the Mother's gift, but remember also that greater abundance still lies in the inner felicity she grants by dispelling ignorance and illusion. Yes, you may enjoy prosperity, but think of what greater treasure awaits where there is neither anger nor spite, where neither greed nor impurity of thought intrudes! Therefore, be grateful to the Devi Lakshmi and as a sign of your gratitude, worship her in all you do that she may ever remain radiant in the dwelling place of your heart."

"A beautiful teaching," Suratha murmured. "Thank you."

"But that's easier said than done," the merchant protested.

It was not the first time Medhas had heard this objection, and he put little store in it.

"You can start out with resolve," Samadhi defended himself, "but five minutes later it's gone, as if it never crossed your mind at all. Life sweeps you up in the momentum of all sorts of everyday matters, large and small, important and trifling. Immediately they divert your attention and before you know it, that higher resolve is forgotten, and another day is gone."

Medhas smiled, understanding fully his disciple's complaint. "Very well, let us talk about this world that the Mother has so graciously spread out before us. All this—we call it *vishva*, the universe—is in constant motion and that is why we also call it *jagat*, 'that which moves.' No one can deny that in this world things are always changing. Day follows night, night follows day, the moon waxes and wanes, the seasons come and go, the rivers flow ever onward in their courses. The tide erodes the shoreline, and the wind wears down the mighty mountain peaks. Humankind journeys through infancy, childhood, adolescence, adulthood, and old age. And against this backdrop we journey through the doings and happenings of each day, while nothing ever stays the same. The world is teeming with *vritti*—activity! And it is the Devi that abides in all beings in the form of activity. That is what you must remember."

Samadhi prompted the guru. "In other words, we have to keep in mind that the Mother is the animating force behind all this, right?"

"Of course." Medhas acknowledged the obvious, then added, "Perhaps this will help you to remember. This busy world is called jagat, and the Devi is called Jagadamba, 'the mother of the world.' A beautiful name and one to treasure. But back to you. I would like to know what else you have to say."

Samadhi's lack of reply answered more loudly than words. He knew Medhas was prodding him, and he wanted to be forthcoming with some insightful comment, any insightful comment, but regrettably thoughts and words failed him.

And once again, as so many times before, Medhas elucidated. "Behind the physical motion of the material world we have the constant, inner activity of the mind. This mental activity is the movement of consciousness within each one of us—in you, in Suratha, in me. What lies beyond that? Do you ever stop to wonder? Hear me well: your individual awareness flows from the supreme, divine consciousness, and this too has motion. The movement of divine awareness is the vibrant joy in and through and beyond all the fabric of this universe, this realm of beauty. From this joy we are born, by this joy we live, and into this joy we return. Its vibrancy is the inherent bliss of the Mother's own self-awareness, which some philosophers call *spanda*. It is mirrored dimly—ever so dimly—in the activity of our own minds, in the thought waves that arise."

"Thought waves?" Samadhi asked.

"Yes, and wherever there are waves, there is a medium in which they arise. Can you have the ocean's waves without water? Now I ask you, in what do these thought waves arise? They have to arise out of something."

"Of course," Samadhi murmured with a glimmer of understanding.

"They arise out of the undifferentiated ocean of pure consciousness, the substratum of all awareness," Medhas continued. "These thought waves, or vrittis, take on many different forms. Some flow out through the doors of the senses and back again to the perceiving mind, the *manas*, in order to bring knowledge of the outer world. From the perceiving mind the waves flow back to the buddhi, the intellect, which we have spoken of before. And along the way they pass through *ahamkara*, the ego sense, where they acquire all the colors of personality." Medhas chuckled at that last thought.

"Practically speaking," he went on in all earnestness, "this mental activity, which seems so enlightening because it gives us knowledge of the world, actually keeps us in delusion. Think of your own restlessness and discontent and misery, or even the exhilarating sense of displacement that pleasure can bring. Do all these not have one thing in common—an unsettling sense of distraction? But this same mental activity that enslaves can be harnessed and turned back toward the supreme knowledge. When the activity of the mind is controlled, when the thought waves are restrained, then there is only indescribable peace."

"At the risk of repeating myself," Samadhi interjected, "that's easier said than done."

"This time I countenance your remark and am glad that you wonder how to achieve this. I shall tell you. First, you must recognize that some vrittis increase ignorance and bondage, and other vrittis foster knowledge and freedom. Whenever a negative wave arises in the mind, such as anger or despair, you can neutralize it by raising an equal and opposite thought, such as love or joy. In this way, you must consciously replace a 'bad' thought with a 'good' one. Assuredly it takes time and practice, so you must not become discouraged even though you seem to fail.

"When you have gained some control over the mind, then you will be ready for the next phase, which is to still even the 'good' thought waves. Only when you have succeeded in completely stilling the mind's activity will you experience the clear, contentless consciousness, the infinite awareness beyond all form. Only then will you know true and lasting peace.

"But I am getting way ahead of myself," Medhas declared briskly, "and for now there are other things to talk about, such as how the Devi abides in all beings in the form of memory. You see, along with the faculties of perception, ego sense, and intellect, memory also forms part of the inner organ we call the mind. And so, once again we are dealing with thought waves. Like all other forms of mental activity, memory is nothing more than a modification of consciousness, but it differs from all the others in one way: Memory is not an immediate experience. Rather, it is the revival of an impression already present in the mind.

"Memory is indispensable for ordinary knowledge. It provides the continuity needed to sustain the world of our experience, because all knowledge of the world is relational. When you see an object, confront a situation, feel an emotion, or consider an idea, you compare it with something you already know. That is how the mind works. Without the storehouse of memory, the mind would be devoid of all content and there would be nothing to relate the immediate experience to, nothing to give it any meaning whatsoever. But because we embrace all we know and hold it in memory, that memory becomes the bridge of continuity that spans our countless experiences and, indeed, makes our experience of the world possible.

"This is a technical matter, of course, but if you remember nothing else about memory, take to heart what I tell you now. This whole hymn to Aparajita is an ecstatic celebration of the Divine Mother's presence in the world. It exhorts us to see holiness everywhere, because the Mother herself abides everywhere, in everything. We need only *remember*. And as a sign of her boundless grace, she herself dwells in each of us in the form of memory."

Samadhi fell into a deep, inner quiet. Fully attentive to Medhas's discourse all along, he had managed to grasp intellectually much of what was said, but it was the seer's final thought that touched his heart.

Sensing his mood, Medhas leaned over and whispered, "The Mother abides in all beings in the form of compassion."

Tears welled up in Samadhi's eyes. Already moved, the merchant felt his heart open wide. He recalled his loved ones, driven to despicable acts by the power of greed, and any bitterness he might have harbored before—bitterness blended so troublingly with his feelings of affection—began melting away. Now, feeling compassion for his wife and sons, he wept at the thought of those unfortunate souls, poisoned by an avarice that could surely bring them no joy.

Nor was the message lost on King Suratha, who sat quietly in the silvery moonlight, contemplating all that had gone wrong with his kingdom. He deplored his usurpers' evildoing and the injustice that no doubt brought misery upon the land, but now, more than anything else, he regretted the suffering of the people. And for the first time he genuinely regretted abandoning his lost kingdom. How could a beautiful word like *compassion* arouse such strongly conflicted feelings in him? The king, though a warrior, wanted to cry.

"Compassion," Medhas explained, "is an opening of the heart, a reaching out that allows us to understand the suffering of others. Compassion takes us beyond our own petty concerns and tears down the walls of self-centeredness. But again, it is not enough merely to feel pity toward someone else; you must *do* something to help. True compassion is any action that diminishes the suffering of others. Your dharma, good king, is to be committed to such action.

"You saw how the Devi came to rescue Brahma from Madhu and Kaitabha's mindless attack. You saw how she came to rescue the gods after Mahishasura had wrested power from them and how she promised the gods and mortals alike that whenever they remembered her in times of distress, she would put an end to their calamities. There are many stories of the Mother's unfailing kindness toward those in need. As her children, should we do any less toward one another? The Devi is present within each of us in the form of compassion; when we reveal this in our own actions, our very lives become a blessing to others."

"That's what I would like," the king sighed.

Medhas drew a deep breath and let it out slowly. Regarding his disciples in the moonlight, he appeared the very picture of contentment. Did the king and the merchant comprehend his mood? To test their understanding, he intoned, "'To the Devi, who abides in all beings in the form of contentment.'" And then he asked what they thought contentment was.

Samadhi answered first. "It's the satisfaction that comes when our needs are met, and when we get what we want."

Before he could elaborate and before Medhas could respond, Suratha interrupted, "Earlier the gods praised the Devi as abiding in all beings in the form of hunger, which you said meant a fundamental lack. Then they praised her as thirst, which you said meant a thirst for life—a desire to experience this world. If she is lack and desire, how can she be contentment? Isn't this all a bit contradictory?"

Medhas did not see it that way. "Suratha," he said, attempting to clarify, "you are approaching this in terms of 'either this or that.' Either the Devi reveals herself as hunger and thirst or as contentment. Why only one or the other? Why do you limit her? Can she not show herself in any way she pleases? It is time for you to broaden your thinking.

"What I said before is true. What I say now is also true. The Mother is everything. Her maya creates the lack and limitation on which our individuality depends. It creates the thirst for life that follows upon that condition of individuality. But then the Mother reveals herself also as the fulfillment of every longing and as the satisfaction that follows."

Medhas turned to the merchant. "What you said about contentment being the satisfaction of fulfilled desires is true, but that is only the beginning. I believe you were speaking about worldly and material desires. Know that such contentment is fleeting indeed—here for a moment and then gone. There is no lasting satisfaction in the finite. In the infinite alone is there true and lasting satisfaction. Contentment in its highest sense is a fullness that arises only with the cessation of desire. Ask yourself: is it better to fulfill a thousand desires or to conquer one? When you know the answer, you will know true contentment.

"Are the two of you beginning to understand that it is the Mother herself who has become all this—she who abides in all beings in the form of mother?"

Samadhi blinked, wondering how the principle of motherhood could possibly dwell within him, a man, or in any man for that matter. Momentarily he had the horrifying vision of himself pregnant. He glanced sideways at the king, hoping to gauge his reaction, but Suratha's impassive face revealed nothing other than self-contained masculinity. Next the merchant tried furtively to scan Medhas's face for a clue, but the guru met his glance head on and laughed.

"Are you confused or embarrassed?" he asked.

"Both," Samadhi admitted nervously.

Medhas laughed again, heartily. "I shall explain. It is easy to understand how the Mother can abide as mother in female forms. It is the female that gives birth, nurtures, and displays maternal affection. In giving birth it is the female alone who wraps spirit in matter, so to speak. Doing so, all mothers of living creatures emulate the universal Divine Mother, who gives birth to all this.

"Put aside your masculine prejudices for a moment," he went on, addressing both disciples. "Because male children also come from the Mother, they are ultimately not different from her. We men too partake of her nature, because we have our being in her. And what is her nature? Divinity. The Devi abides in all beings, male and female alike, as the indwelling, divine Self. This we have heard from the knowers of truth. And I tell you this: The Devi's indwelling presence reminds us that we are never alone. At all times, wherever we go, we carry the Mother enshrined in our heart."

Abruptly Medhas recited, "'To the Devi, who abides in all beings in the form of error, salutation to her, salutation to her, salutation to her again and again.'"

If Samadhi had blinked at the previous verse, this one jolted both him and the king as if they had been slapped in the face. Error? Whatever could that mean? True, they had already heard the word when Medhas first recited the hymn in its entirety, but then one verse had followed rapidly upon another with precious little time to contemplate the meaning of any, as they were doing now. The disciples made no attempt to hide their bewilderment at this shocking turn in a largely ecstatic litany.

Not for the first time Medhas sighed to himself, thinking that by now they should know better. Still, he spoke patiently. "Do you remember

Vishnumaya, who obscures her self-luminous infinitude in order to project the world as we know it? Well, here we come full circle. We experience this sometimes dark, sometimes dazzling world of multiplicity only because our individualized awareness is limited and imperfect. We do not know the shining wholeness directly. For that simple reason we are subject to error."

"Just what do you mean by error?" the king inquired.

"A mistake?" the merchant chimed in.

"Yes, a mistake, but what kind of mistake? The root meaning of *error* is 'to wander.' Error is nothing more than a wandering away from the truth, in this case a misreading of reality that takes the finite parts for the infinite whole. Error is mistaking the fragmented, imperfect appearance for the reality and becoming caught up in it. In terms of the individual, error is misidentifying the true Self with the body, mind, and personality, and thus wandering away from the truth of one's being and into the captivation—or should I say captivity?—of this world with its ever-repeating cycle of birth, death, and rebirth and all the attendant woes.

"So you see, error is what makes the world go round!" Medhas concluded jauntily. There was no consternation in the serene detachment of his worldview, where joy alone reigned. "And so I ask you," he said, "how do we experience the universe just described? As an up-and-down course through happiness and sorrow or through a clearer understanding? It is the power of the Devi's own consciousness that pervades the elements of creation and the senses that perceive them. This single consciousness expresses itself and experiences itself in an endless multiplicity of ways. Who but the Mother herself is the knower, the knowing, and the known? And so I urge you to cultivate the awareness that *the world is saturated in divinity*."

The conversation had lasted late into the night, and now the moon shone higher, smaller, and brighter in the inky blue sky. As Medhas repeated the hymn's closing verses—the gods' plea for deliverance from the torment of dispossession—the words reminded the disciples that much more still lay ahead.

ॐ शांति ॐ

CHAPTER 11

THE MERCHANT'S TALE

Suratha and Samadhi followed Krishanu along the trail into the deep forest, mystified by the earthenware jar that rested in his hands. The jar was globular with a narrow neck, and something inside it rattled as they walked along.

Krishanu had announced the outing after the morning meal. "Today we're going hunting," he said but would disclose no more. When questioned, he responded only with an amused smile and an enigmatic, "You'll see."

After leaving the compound and walking for quite some time along a poorly defined path, the three men came to a sunlit glade where Krishanu halted, looked about, and listened—for something. "This will do," he grinned, setting the jar down in the middle of the small clearing and motioning for his companions to follow him into the concealing vegetation.

When they had crouched down out of view, Samadhi whispered, "What are we doing here?" Whatever it was, it was nothing he had ever done before.

Just then a troupe of monkeys appeared in the trees above, and one of them, spying the jar, swung down and dropped to the ground.

"There's your answer," Krishanu whispered. "We're going to catch a monkey."

"But why?" Samadhi inquired.

"You'll see."

The monkey looked around, then cautiously approached the jar. He circled it twice, then pushed it tentatively. The spherical object rocked back and forth and made a rattling noise. The monkey pushed again, this time harder, and the jar rattled louder. He looked at it quizzically, then sniffed at the narrow neck. Next the three observers saw the monkey thrust his hand and forearm into the opening. It was a close fit.

"Now watch," Krishanu instructed. "He knows there are treats inside—nuts and other things that monkeys like to eat—but when he grasps a fistful, he can't pull his hand back out. The opening is too small."

"Then what happens?" Samadhi asked.

Really, Samadhi, the king thought, you haven't figured it out?

"Stay here and watch," Krishanu said, standing up and stepping out into the open.

The monkey looked toward the sound, a startled expression crossing his tiny face. He tried to flee, but the cumbersome jar dragging along behind him impeded his escape. Krishanu approached, bent over, and gingerly picked up the jar and its screaming, furry appendage.

"Careful he doesn't bite you," Suratha cautioned, stepping out from the underbrush.

"I already learned that lesson—the hard way," the young man laughed, all the while attentive to his tiny captive, who was by now chattering furiously. When Samadhi joined them in the clearing, Krishanu set the jar and monkey down. This time the animal made no attempt to escape. Instead his attention fixed on extracting a handful of delicacies from the jar. While the three men sat in a semicircle, watching, now and then the monkey gave his observers a perplexed look, as if he wanted them to share in his frustration.

This went on for quite some time.

At last Krishanu stood up and said, "Let's go."

"What about him? We're not going to leave him here like that!" Samadhi exclaimed.

"After a while he'll get bored and let go. Then he'll figure it out. If he turns the jar upside down, the contents will spill out." Krishanu regarded Samadhi thoughtfully, then said, "There's a lesson here. He'll get what he wants. He'll have his freedom and the treats as well. *But not until he lets go.*" Starting back toward the ashrama, the young man added casually, "Sri Medhas wanted you to see this."

On the way back through the dense forest, the three men failed to notice an unnatural darkness that came on without warning. By the time the gate of the enclosure came into view, huge raindrops began spattering down, slowly at first.

"We'd better run," Krishanu directed with a note of urgency. He dashed toward the gate, and his two companions followed close behind—into the compound, up the main path, to the left along the path to the dining hall. By now nocturnal darkness enveloped the day, and the blackened, pregnant heavens rumbled, on the verge of release. The drops descended faster and faster and just as the breathless trio reached the shelter of the dining hall, water cascaded from the sky, no longer in drops but in solid sheets.

"That was close!" Krishanu gasped. "This time of year the rain can take you by surprise."

"Welcome!" a jovial voice rang out. "Are you planning to stay awhile?" The three men turned and saw slender Hiranya emerging from the kitchen.

"You got here just in time," a deeper voice added. The burly Lambana stood close behind, a vegetable cleaver in hand. Two younger disciples, Dhataki and Vashya, appeared smiling in his wake.

Within minutes lamps were lit to ward off the gloom, and trays of sweets, fruits, and beverages were laid out on the reed matting. While the rain continued unabated, the seven men sat down together. It was an impromptu gathering, to be sure, and a convivial one, but before long the conversation took a purposeful turn and focused on the merchant.

"You've been here for a while now," Hiranya began, "but you've told us very little about yourself."

Samadhi recalled the day the two of them had spent working together in the vegetable garden and how friendly and reassuring

Hiranya's manner had been. His curiosity now seemed born of genuine solicitude and was in no way offputting to the reticent merchant.

"Yes, how did you come here? And where do you come from?" Dhataki chimed in. It was the first time the fair-skinned, curly-haired questioner had actually spoken to the merchant, but Dhataki's sincere interest put Samadhi at ease, even in this company of near strangers. During his months of wandering with no one to listen to him, the merchant had been forced to keep his grief and all his other thoughts to himself. Even here at the ashrama he found it hard to break through the wall that his bitter exile had built around him. True, he had disclosed fragments of his past to the king, but only fragments. Now he had an audience and now seemed like the time to tell his tale of woe. Shy before their eagerness, he cleared his throat nervously and began.

"I come from a town far to the north. For the past year or so I've been wandering here and there and after crossing seven rivers, I came to this forest. As you know, I am, or was, a merchant. My family was well-to-do, because my father and his father and his father before him built up a thriving trade in textiles—fine woolens imported by ship from lands far to the west, silks brought overland from the east, and the finest cotton produced close to home.

"Anyway, when I was young, my father arranged for me to marry the daughter of a bead merchant in a neighboring town. Her name was Mohani. Her father dealt in high-quality beads made of carnelian, lapis lazuli, and shell. The idea was that his trade and ours would go hand in hand, and both families would benefit.

"At first everything went well. Mohani was a devoted wife, and within three years she gave me two sons. We named them Jalada and Kushala. The business prospered, and we grew richer and richer. That's when the trouble started. Something happened to Mohani—I can't say exactly what, except that she seemed never to be satisfied with anything. It started in small ways. She'd come to the shop and pick out the finest cloth and the best jewelry for herself. If I said no, she'd demand it. She said she took pleasure in being the best dressed among all her women friends, and who was I to deny her that? If it had gone no further, I suppose I could have lived with it. But next our house wasn't good enough, or grand enough, I should say. First it was the inner court, where we entertained our guests. She wanted it paved in marble. It was a big expense, as you can guess, but to keep her happy I saw that it was done. After that, the rest of the house didn't seem grand enough to match the inner court, and Mohani whined and wheedled until the other rooms were made finer and some new ones added.

"To pay for all this I had to earn more. I began to work longer and longer hours in order to expand my trade. I looked for new markets and additional sources of supply. It worked. The business grew and flourished, but I spent less and less time at home with my family. My sons grew distant—and luxury loving like their mother.

"Then an opportunity came along—the kind of opportunity that merchants dream of—but it meant that I'd have to be away for a long while. I had my doubts about going, because by then we already had more wealth than we needed, and I couldn't see that the way we lived was making us happy. But Mohani insisted. Six months later, when I returned home, I was like a traveler coming to an unfamiliar place. There were all new furnishings throughout the house—lavish furnishings. Some of the woodwork was even gilded! Can you imagine the extravagance? There was no need for this huge, glittering palace of a house! My parents had died some years before, when the boys were still small. Shortly afterward Mohani drove out my brother and his new bride. She insisted there wasn't room for a second woman in the household, and I foolishly gave in. Now, in my absence she had dismissed the entire staff of servants and hired new ones. I recognized no one. I was a stranger in my own home. An unwanted stranger, it turned out. Instead of the homecoming I'd looked forward to—"

Here Krishanu broke in. "Pardon me for asking, Samadhi, but when so much was already so very wrong, you still anticipated a joyous homecoming?"

"Every man has his dreams, I guess. Or maybe needs them. I needed the illusion of a loving family and a place where I belonged. Anyway, it gets worse. Jalada and Kushala, my own sons, treated me coldly at first. Then they were openly disrespectful. While I was away, they and Mohani had conspired to take control of my wealth. It was very clever how they did it, and underhanded, of course. I won't bore you with the details. The outcome was that I was thrown out on the street with nothing but the clothes on my back and a small amount of gold I had with me. Thrown out of my own house by servants whose names I didn't even know, while my wife and sons stood by watching!"

By now Samadhi's voice quavered, and he struggled to hold back his tears.

"If this is too painful for you, we can talk about something else," Dhataki suggested.

"No, I want to go on, now that I've started. Please, just give me a minute." Samadhi rose and walked to the edge of the room and looked out. There, silhouetted by the storm, his shoulders sloping, he seemed once again the broken figure the king had encountered only days before.

A gloomy silence, imparted by his sorry tale, fell over his audience—an almost silence, accompanied only by the relentless drumming of the rain. It penetrated every heart, and each listener solemnly imagined himself in the merchant's place.

From where he stood gazing, Samadhi contemplated the gray majesty of the waterlogged sky, its vastness, and his own smallness.

Then, returning to his seat, he said, "I'm sorry, I didn't mean to drag you down into my misery."

"It's all right." Krishanu said. His usual, affable charm had evaporated, revealing a depth of concern. "Please continue whenever you feel ready."

Samadhi stared at a nearby oil lamp. Its flame, like liquid gold, cast a circle of warm light on the reed matting that covered the floor, displaying its woven pattern in bold relief. The merchant glided his fingertips lightly over the matting and found its orderliness reassuring, unlike the amorphous, wet grayness outside at his back.

"There I was, out on the street, not knowing what to do or where to go. At first I was too stunned to think—I just couldn't believe it was happening—and that was better than what followed: the rage and disappointment and hurt and self-doubt. I should have known better. I should have seen what was coming all those years, but in my foolishness I didn't want to know.

"I headed toward the house where my brother and his wife lived. They went to stay with her family when Mohani made them leave our home. We hadn't had much contact since then. I was away a lot of the time, and feelings were, well, strained. When I got there my brother refused to see me at first, and when he heard what had happened, he refused to take me in. He said I hadn't come to his defense when Mohani drove him and his bride out, so what did he owe me? Our father had set him up in business before the marriage, and he was doing all right.

"For the second time that night I was turned away. And now I had nowhere to go at all. I thought of taking a room at an inn, but even at the cheapest place, the gold I had with me wouldn't last for long.

"And so began my months of wandering and hardship. The awful reality began to set in that I had been torn from my comfortable life. Until then I had enjoyed power—economic power at least," Samadhi laughed ironically. "With my wealth, I could do pretty well what I wanted. I lacked nothing in material comfort. Now for the first time I had to wonder where I was going to sleep, how long the little gold I had with me would ward off hunger. Those were my first two concerns, but as the days wore on, more and more problems came up.

"I had to learn how to survive. I didn't know exactly how, and matters that were once so small that I hardly gave them any thought loomed large. I learned some hard lessons. On the second and third days, I ate at roadside inns along the way. 'The way,'" he laughed bitterly. "The way to what? I couldn't tell you. By the fourth day, after spending three nights in the fields, I was starting to look disreputable, but I was too unhappy to think about how I looked. All I could think about was this awful thing that had happened to me. Toward mid afternoon I came to a town and found an inn. When I walked in, the innkeeper took one look at me and ordered me out. 'Filthy beggar' was what he called me. 'Get out, you filthy beggar! We don't want you here.'

"At that moment I realized that I'd have to keep up appearances. My stomach ached, but I found a street vendor and was able to buy some food. It wasn't good, but at least it would keep me alive.

"I left that town as soon as I could, and since it was built along a river, I followed the bank until I came to a secluded spot. There I sat down and tried to think. There was little current at the bank, and something shiny in the shallow water caught my attention. A clam shell. At first I gave it no thought, but then I figured that I could sharpen it against a rock and use it as a razor. I could keep up some appearance of respectability, and maybe then I wouldn't be shunned like the outcast I was.

"I'd lost so much—almost everything—but I still had my wits. I worked for a long while sharpening that clam shell against a stone, and finally I had a suitable blade. I shaved, bathed in the river, washed my clothes, and spread them to dry in the late afternoon sun. Then I tied the razor and whetstone into a corner of my cloth. I'd need them again, because my beard would keep on growing, of course.

"I wandered for days on end, following this road and that, not knowing where I was or where I was going. It was strange. I had been so well positioned in life before. I knew my town and all the roads leading in and out of it. I knew the trade routes to neighboring and distant places. I had traveled them all in style. And now here I was on foot, headed in a different direction where nothing was familiar. I wanted my life to be as it had been before. Before, I always knew where I was going, where my life was headed.

"Can you imagine how powerless I felt now? Stuck in the middle of nowhere, able to go only as fast and as far as one step after another could take me? I'd see something in the distance, a hill or the edge of a forest, and make that my goal for the day. But I knew that it was a goal to nowhere. And the next day I'd set off to another pointless goal.

"One day I came to a large city. It was a rich city with wide, paved streets lined with shops and a bustling marketplace in an open square. The place was a feast of sights and sounds and colors. I drank in its life and felt alive just being there. On one street, just off the main square, vendors prepared and sold all kinds of foods. I ate well that day. I still had some gold, which I spent with the greatest care. Then I explored the city, up one street and down the next, until I came to a shop where luxurious fabrics were on display. I thought of asking the proprietor if he'd let me work for him. Certainly I had the knowledge and experience, but I was too sick at heart to make the effort to ask. Even if he said yes, what good would it do? Was it worth it to start all over again?

I was just so tired. And what if he said no? Was I strong enough to bear another rejection?

"And so, I turned away and continued along the street, watching the life around me. No one spoke to me, and I spoke to no one, but still I took some comfort in being there among all those people. Then, as evening approached, the shops began to close. The market folded up, and I was left there alone. I looked at the shuttered store fronts, now closed off and dark, and thought of the people who had gone home to their own lives. I imagined their houses glowing with lamplight, and families together, eating and talking about the day's events, while I faced the lifeless city streets and the empty square. I had never before felt so alone. I had to get out of there. I turned and left that city, weeping.

"Some weeks later, I passed through a village where the people were poor. The countryside in this region was arid, and I suspected the villagers had little means of supporting themselves. I saw no reason to stop there but went on along the road that ran through a huddle of miserable dwellings. When I reached the outskirts on the far side, some children playing in the field caught sight of me, a stranger, and pelted me with rocks. For the rest of the day I tried to put as much distance as I could between myself and that mean place.

"That night, after a tiring day of hurrying along in the heat and dryness, I lay down in a field and fell into a deep sleep. Sometime in the middle of the night I was awakened by a sharp blow to the top of my head—a kick, probably—and then I blacked out before I could see my attackers. When I woke up hours later, the sun was high in the sky. A pool of blood had formed under my head—my hair was sticky with it—and flies buzzed around me.

"I staggered to my feet and then noticed my gold was gone. No, it can't be, I thought. I closed my eyes, thinking that when I opened them again, the gold would be there, where it belonged. It wasn't, of course, and I had to accept what had happened. At least I'm alive, I thought. They could have killed me. They had cut off the corner of my cloth where the clam shell and stone were tied, thinking it held something valuable, and those two articles, worthless to the thieves but precious to me, lay on the ground. I picked them up and thought, I suppose I could end it all here and now. The shell razor rested in my palm, and it wouldn't have taken much to slide it across my wrists and finish what the thieves had started. I thought about this seriously, but, you know, even in this darkest hour I felt a clinging to life. At least I'm alive—that had been my first thought on coming to, and now that phrase repeated itself in my mind. I said it out loud over and over and finally shouted it, defiantly, to the empty field and the cloudless sky.

"Then I tied the razor and whetstone in my cloth again. By now, you can imagine, my clothing was tattered, and even though I kept it as clean as possible, I couldn't pass for anything but a mendicant or some poor madman. Sometimes that's almost how I felt. I had lost everything else, why not my mind? But that day, at least I was alive.

"I found a small stream nearby—almost dry—but I dug into the gravelly riverbed with a broken branch and uncovered a flow of water that allowed me to wash off the blood. I needed to wash off the impurity of the assault and be free of it. There wasn't enough water to immerse myself, of course, but I scooped up handful after handful of the bubbling spring and poured it over my body until I felt the defilement leave.

"By now I'd learned enough about survival that I could go on, even without my gold. I learned to beg. Some days I succeeded; other days I went hungry. Overall, there were enough kind people to keep me from starving to death, although by now, when I saw my reflection, it was shocking to see how gaunt I had become.

"Now and then I'd pass a group of religious mendicants on the road. They always looked well fed, especially compared to me. One day I got the idea of passing myself off as one of them. As the next village came into view, I headed into a thicket not far from the road and left my clothing there—all but my loincloth—and went into the village. At the first house a woman came to the door, looked me up and down, and told me to wait. Moments later she reappeared with a leaf plate, folded over and stuffed with food. As she handed it to me, the look in her eyes was one of pure goodness. I accepted her gift and thanked her for her kindness, but as I walked back to where my clothes were hidden, a deep sense of shame set in. The more I thought about it, the worse it got. I thought of the purity in her eyes and knew I had betrayed the trust of that woman by pretending to be something I was not. Remorse thrust into me like a dagger. Betrayal was something I knew all about, and now I had betrayed that good woman's trust.

"I found my clothes, dressed, and sat down to eat. At first I didn't want to touch the food. I didn't deserve it. I got it by lying about who I was. That woman's loving, trusting look—I couldn't get it out of my mind. And suddenly I understood. Her gift to me wasn't this food at all, but that look. I cried, and I ate as if that food were sacred, as if it would purify me. And it did: I vowed never again to be untruthful. Whatever might happen, I would hold fast to the truth.

"There were many other incidents, of course. Altogether I wandered for about a year until coming here. And that's my story. Please don't judge me too harshly."

"No one is here to judge," Krishanu said. "Every life is a drama, or sometimes a comedy. Some lives are filled with suffering, some with enjoyment, most with a mixture of the two. You've known both, to be sure. And you still aren't sure what this is all about, are you?" He smiled ever so sweetly. "Don't despair, Samadhi. Sri Medhas has the answers."

CHAPTER 12

THE DEVI AND THE MESSENGERS

Samadhi spent a fitful night drifting in and out of sleep that came only unwillingly and refused to stay for long. Fragmented recollections of the past swirled about in the whirlpool of his mind, threatening to engulf him while he lay awake in the darkness.

Toward morning he became aware of raindrops falling on the thatch overhead, at first slowly, then with insistent regularity. Across the hut the steady rise and fall of Suratha's breath signaled the king's untroubled sleep. Samadhi envied his companion and lamented his own lack of peace. Turning over yet another time in the hope that bodily comfort would beckon slumber, he began to reflect on the strangeness of his life.

In a state somewhere between sleep and wakefulness he mused, Whoever could have thought that I, a merchant, would one day share a rude hut with the mightiest of kings? That through a reversal of fortune either of us would fall into such sorry circumstances? I, a merchant; and he, a king! Samadhi's heart swelled with pride at the thought of his improbable adventure. How would his family and friends react? His family! Samadhi's mood instantly deflated. In his worst fears he could not have imagined the loss of their love or respect, let alone their betrayal. A wave of impotent despair jolted him awake, and he thought, It wasn't supposed to be this way!

Just as suddenly another wave arose in his mind—he wasn't sure quite how, or from where—but its words rang loudly in the quiet: *It isn't supposed to be* any *way*.

Sensing wisdom in this, Samadhi reflected that his present misery came from the sense of expectation. He expected that his trade would prosper, that his wife and children would be loving and loyal, that he would have a good life and a comfortable old age. He expected what he had been taught to expect. Yet the present betrayed his dreams from the past, and if he entertained any further dreams now, might the future not betray them also?

This flash of insight shattered Samadhi's former, unquestioning ideas of how the world should be. They were wrenched out from under him in an instant of release, an instant that did not even allow his insight to be put into words. He understood that it is a matter of seeing things not as we think they should be, but as they appear in and of themselves. To see in that matter-of-fact way is to attain some degree of freedom. Samadhi's joy lasted less than a moment, an immeasurable fraction of time. Still, something in him had shifted like an earthquake and had refashioned his worldview into a strange, yet strangely familiar, new landscape.

He thought about anticipation. To look ahead to pleasant events was to risk setting himself up for disappointment. He winced at the recollection of many times when joy eluded him, all because he had expected too much or something other than what he got. By the same token, he considered, to anticipate the unpleasant was to feed his fear and in his mind to go through something awful many times over before it actually happened. More often than not the actuality turned out to be less awful than the anticipation. How needlessly he brought misery on himself!

But before long Samadhi began to wonder if his revelation had any real substance, or if his disturbed sleep had merely played an odd trick on his mind. How weary he felt—too weary to try to make sense of it all.

His gathering clouds of doubt mimicked the rain clouds overhead and when the fair goddess Ushas arrived, she only managed to light the world in somber gray. The rain was still falling in full, wet force when, at the appointed hour, Samadhi and the king hurried to the guru's hut. There Medhas awaited them with another story.

ONE DAY CHANDA AND MUNDA, two servants of the daitya brothers Shumbha and Nishumbha, espied a young woman of surpassing beauty, who sat casting her radiance upon the Himalayas. They hastened to their masters' glittering palace and breathlessly told Shumbha of this unknown woman, saying, "Never has such beauty been seen before! She is effulgent like the moon shining at the edge of a cloud. Surely you, great lord of asuras, must learn who she is and take possession of her.

"Master, since all the wealth of the gods and all the riches of the three worlds now grace your palace, since all the powers of the gods are now yours and your brother's as well, surely you must seize this jewel among women for your very own!"

Flattered by their praise and pleasantly aroused by their lustful insinuations, Shumbha gave heed to his obsequious servants. Without delay he summoned the great asura Sugriva and instructed, "Go to that woman whom Chanda and Munda beheld. Go as my messenger to that resplendent, craggy place where she dwells and speak such fine words on my behalf that she will come to me."

Sugriva went to the fair maiden and spoke honeyed words in unctuous tones, saying, "In these three worlds Shumbha is supreme. I have come as the emissary of the lord of daityas, whose command is never resisted. Even the gods submit to his will, each one surrendering his share of the mortals' sacrifices. All treasures belong to my great lord, who takes pleasure in the finest things. Thus he bids that you give him your hand in marriage, and if not to him then to his younger brother, the valiant Nishumbha. In so doing you will obtain pleasure, riches, and dominion beyond compare!"

The Devi—for that is who the young woman was—smiled inscrutably and replied, "You have spoken the truth. Shumbha and Nishumbha indeed rule the three worlds. But how can I go back on my word, on a vow I made long ago? I swore that he alone who conquers me in battle will become my husband. He alone who equals my strength will be worthy of my hand. Let the glorious Shumbha or the valiant Nishumbha approach me now and, having conquered me, take me in marriage."

Though the Devi spoke gently, her words displeased Sugriva, and his honeyed tones turned menacing. "You are arrogant to speak so in my presence. Who in the three worlds surpasses Shumbha and Nishumbha? And who dares to defy them? Not even Indra and the hosts of celestial gods can stand against them in battle. How then can you, a mere woman alone? Come willingly to Shumbha and Nishumbha's presence and suffer not the indignity of being dragged there by your hair."

The Devi Ambika replied softly, "I made a vow long ago. What else can I do? Go back to your glorious chief and repeat exactly what I have said. And let him do what is fitting."

"Sugriva was lying, wasn't he?" Samadhi queried.

"Let us just say he was making every attempt to appear not to deceive," Medhas replied, "and the Devi saw right through his ruse. Did neither of you catch the ironic tone of their exchange?" he chuckled.

"When the story begins, Shumbha is sitting in his palace amid the glittering hoard of treasure stolen from the gods. He should be well satisfied but, as the saying goes, all the wealth in the world is not enough to satisfy one greedy man. When the two fawning servants arrive with news of the beautiful young woman, they appeal to their master's vanity and insatiable greed. Shumbha, now inflamed with lust, resolves to claim the lovely maiden as his own, just as the worldly-minded want to possess all that they find attractive and desirable. To that end he sends the smooth-talking Sugriva to entice the Devi with a marriage proposal. Of course the messenger fails to mention that his master is a hideous demon and boasts only of his dazzling wealth and power."

"That's what I meant when I said he was lying," Samadhi interjected.

"Sugriva fully intends to mislead, and the all-knowing Devi knows it. She agrees that what he says about Shumbha possessing all wealth and power is true, but she knows the full truth and is merely playing along with the messenger. Do you not see the irony here? It is really quite amusing," the guru laughed.

Then he said seriously, "Think back on your life, Samadhi, as a boy and a youth and a merchant and the head of your family. Do you not recognize in Sugriva's behavior any instances when you were less than completely honest? How many times, under the cover of so-called truth, have you attempted to deceive even in small, seemingly harmless ways?"

The regret in Samadhi's dark eyes revealed that he was more like Sugriva than he wanted to admit. Maybe the quality of the goods he sold was not always as fine as he made it out to be, and maybe—but only now and then, of course—he availed himself of a little unentitled profit. If his behavior was not completely honest, it was not completely dishonest either. As merchants go, he could feel far better about himself than most. But now he regretted that his honest, good—hearted reputation was not quite as untarnished as people thought. The taint of even minor infractions and small character flaws loomed large in Samadhi's growing awareness and brought no small discomfort.

"Truthfulness is the highest virtue and the greatest spiritual discipline—the indispensable one, in fact," Medhas declared. "Where truth is absent, all other virtues are compromised. Hear me well: Always practice truthfulness in thought, word, and deed. *Make your heart and your lips one*. And remember that to succeed requires constant vigilance."

He continued, "The Devi counters Sugriva's deceitful proposal with the vow she made and the need to abide by it without exception. Her steadfastness stands opposed to Sugriva's mendacity. It is likely that you have heard the worldly-minded say, 'Vows were made to be broken.' But you see, Samadhi, in spiritual life there is no room for compromise.

Even in conflict the Devi holds to her vow and refuses to submit to Sugriva's threat of force and humiliation."

The merchant grew reflective, and his thoughts traveled back to the kind village woman who had given him the resolve for truthfulness. He remembered his vow, kept unbroken ever since, and wondered if he should disclose it to the holy man. He wondered if Medhas, in some way, already knew. Then a somewhat different question arose.

"If I want to see the depth of this story," Samadhi began slowly, "I should understand the Devi and the asuras as different states of my own mind, shouldn't I? If I see the Devi Ambika as the best in me, then it follows that Shumbha and the other demons are my weaknesses and failings. Is that right?"

"Go on," Medhas urged.

"Then Chanda and Munda would stand for my vanity, greed, or lust. Sugriva would be the temptation that pulls me toward worldly enjoyment."

He trailed off momentarily, allowing Medhas to comment, "A better word would be *beguilement*—a pleasurable misleading—"

"Because what Sugriva promises is not exactly what he delivers!" Samadhi finished the guru's sentence excitedly, showing a deepening insight that he phrased, nevertheless, in terms of his mercantile past.

Typical, thought the king, who interjected wryly, "Sometimes you get more than you bargained for. *I* think Sugriva personifies hypocrisy—saying one thing but meaning another. Believe me, as a ruler who had to deal with ministers, advisors, and ambassadors, this is something I know all about."

"You are both correct," Medhas said. "And therein lies the beauty of a story such as this. Depending on one's own experience and temperament, the story will reveal different meanings to whoever hears it. Now to return to what Samadhi was saying, the messenger's attempts to beguile mirror the delusion of the mind when faced with the allure of possessions, power, and prestige. Such a mind tries to convince the nobler awareness within to turn away from the higher ideals. We call that temptation.

"We shall go one step further and look at this philosophically. Sugriva's attempt to deceive the Devi stands for the imperfect way that our senses and mind perceive the world. As I have said before, nothing in this world is as it seems to be. On the other hand, the Devi represents purity and truth—the perfection of wholeness. The mind's fragmented awareness of the finite world is fraught with deceptive promises of enjoyment and lasting satisfaction. Like Sugriva's honeyed words, those promises ultimately ring hollow."

Silence ensued until Samadhi asked, "What happened next?" Medhas continued his story.

SUGRIVA RETURNED TO SHUMBHA and indignantly related everything in detail, whereupon the king of the daityas flew into a rage and summoned his general, Dhumralochana. With face contorted, the mighty Shumbha said, "I, who am not to be refused, command you to hasten with your army and bring that trollop here by force, kicking and screaming if need be. If anyone should foolishly rise up to save her—be he a man, a god, or a celestial being—kill him on the spot!"

And so Dhumralochana, with forces sixty thousand strong, set out for the snowy mountain where the radiant Devi dwelt. Arriving there, he thundered, "Come to the presence of Shumbha and Nishumbha! And if her highness will not come gladly, she will come in dishonor, dragged by her hair."

From her lofty seat the Devi replied, "O Dhumralochana, how mighty you are, and mightier still with your demon army! If you take me by force, what can I do?"

Hearing her words but failing to consider them, Dhumralochana charged up the mountainside but was quickly reduced to ashes by the power of the Devi's contemptuous outcry. Then his great army attacked, and the Devi's magnificent lion leaped with outstretched claws upon the demon horde. Asuras tumbled down the mountainside, their entrails trailing behind them, tracing bloody patterns on the pure white snow. Some, without heads, arms, or legs, followed not far behind, drained of their life's blood, until none were left to follow. Thus perished Dhumralochana and his demon forces.

Learning of the rout, Shumbha shook with rage in his glittering palace and grimly planned his next move.

Again Medhas reminded his disciples to identify the Mother's successive victories over the demons with their own efforts to purify themselves of every imperfection and misconceived notion.

"First," he explained, "a story such as this turns a mirror on your own feelings, thoughts, and behavior. Then you are drawn in deeper to observe the mind and its workings. How deep can you go? You will be drawn in deeper still," he said enigmatically, "but for now, what do you think about Dhumralochana?"

The merchant replied, "If lying and cajoling don't get us what we want, why not try force? That's a common tactic, isn't it?" Samadhi generally phrased his observations to Medhas as questions, partly out of respect but more out of uncertainty. How could he be sure that his understanding would match the guru's, or even that it was correct?

"That is true," Medhas replied, "but it is only part of a larger picture, which this story illustrates. Shumbha allowed his thoughts to dwell on the Devi's beauty, and desire to possess her took hold of his mind. When the first attempt failed, notice how in his agitation the 'jewel among women' became 'that trollop.' In sending out the thuggish Dhumralochana, Shumbha resorted to brute force, even if it meant that the Devi might be brought to him disheveled and battered. You see, when we set our minds to something and our intention is frustrated, that desire becomes an end in itself. How it affects others—even the object of desire—no longer concerns us. What was at first so alluring became the cause of Shumbha's misery, and his only desire then was for the triumph of his own will at any cost.

"We find a broad principle at work here. Dwelling on the objects of the senses, one becomes attached. From attachment springs desire; from desire, anger; from anger, confusion; from confusion, the loss of judgment; and when the lessons of experience are lost, one goes to ruin."

Samadhi's face went dark while he recalled the times when he reacted, or overreacted, to frustrating circumstances. How easily things could spiral out of control!

Medhas went on, "Dhumralochana—that name means 'the smoky—eyed one,' someone whose vision or understanding is obscured by ignorance. Like his master, Dhumralochana acted out of anger, and from anger arose confusion. Not understanding who the Devi was, he addressed her sarcastically out of his own excessive arrogance as 'her highness' and threatened her with force. She replied, 'If you take me by force, what can I do?' That sounded innocent enough but, as you see, Dhumralochana was not exactly the brightest flame on the lamp. When he mindlessly rushed at her, his poor judgment led to unintended, and for him most unfortunate, consequences."

"Really unfortunate," Samadhi echoed.

"You may have noticed that Dhumralochana is much like those stupid oafs, Madhu and Kaitabha. Those who understand only brute force often fall victim to it themselves. Violence begets violence. Does that not sum up how Dhumralochana met his end?

"Meanwhile," Medhas added, "Shumbha's continuing frustration rose to a fever pitch. Listen while I tell you what happened next."

CHAPTER 13

Kali and the Mothers

Suratha and Samadhi sat like two small boys before a storyteller, wide-eyed at the drama of Shumbha's rising passion. Their eagerness delighted Medhas, and he continued his tale.

SHUMBHA STORMED THROUGH his glittering palace, consumed by rage that the fairest among women had dared to refuse his command. His lower lip quivering, his cheeks fiery with chagrin, he raged oblivious past coffers overflowing with sparkling gems, past Brahma's swan-yoked chariot, past all the treasures plundered from the gods. The daitya king's footfalls thundered along the polished floors. At length his frenzied screams brought his two loyal servants scurrying to kneel at his feet. Knowing their master all too well, they wavered somewhere between expectation and dread.

"Chanda! Munda! Go with immense forces and bring that vile woman back at once! But should you lack the nerve to do this deed, let all the asuras slay her lion and strike her down in battle. Then bind her, seize her by the hair, and drag her here to my presence!"

With epic fanfare Chanda and Munda and the fourfold army set out. Trumpets blared and drums throbbed while elephants, charioteers, cavalry, and foot soldiers streamed forth, an implacable river with the multicolored banners of countless legions flapping in the wind like waves.

At the foot of the mountain where the resplendent Devi dwelt, the army of foul and fearsome asuras brandished weapons beyond number, all glinting in the sunlight, while portentous clouds spread like flaming blemishes across the sky. High above, on the peak of the snowclad mountain, the Devi smiled down gently while the asuras, at first hesitant but then with growing purpose, began to ascend the slope with swords drawn and weapons poised in readiness.

Without warning Ambika cried out wrathfully, and her radiant face turned as black as ink. From her scowling brow emerged the Great Goddess Kali, frightening and awesome to behold, clad in a tiger's skin and bearing a skull-topped staff. Armed with sword and noose, Kali descended slowly down the mountainside, the silence broken only by the rattling garland of skulls around her neck and every snow-crunching step. From her gaping mouth her lolling tongue dripped a trail of blood along her path. Her emaciated black flesh scarcely concealed her bones, and her sunken eyes glowed red. The horrifying figure drew ever closer, then stopped. Deathlike quiet reigned until Kali, tilting back her head, filled the four quarters of the sky with a roar such as the asuras had never heard.

Swiftly she fell upon them and single-handedly flung the enemy hosts into her mouth. Elephants and drivers, horses and charioteers, cavalry and foot soldiers—all these she ground between her gnashing teeth. Others she crushed beneath her feet or slammed against her breast. Battering the rest with her skull-topped staff, she ravaged the demon foes.

Chanda rushed at the glowering Kali and unleashed a shower of arrows as relentless as the monsoon rain. Munda hurled discuses by the thousands, which vanished into her mouth as so many solar orbs into the denseness of a cloud. Kali laughed in fury, her fangs gleaming in the ghastly light. Chanda and Munda looked on transfixed while the black goddess mounted the lion, swept down on them with brandished sword, and severed their heads.

Panicked, the remaining asuras fled in all directions while Kali triumphantly dangled the heads of Chanda and Munda and approached the Devi Ambika. Mingling raucous laughter with courtly manner, she proclaimed, "I present to you two offerings in the sacrifice of battle. You yourself shall slay Shumbha and Nishumbha."

The auspicious Devi replied, "Because you, O Kali, have delivered Chanda and Munda to me, henceforth you will be known in the world as Chamunda."

The king furrowed his brow, and Medhas, sensing the reason, reminded him, "The Devi appears in many forms. We have spoken of this before. Like Malati, who is wife to you, mother to your children, daughter to her parents, queen to multitudes—who fulfills all manner of functions—the Devi reveals herself in various ways. There is no end to the ways in which she reveals herself. And for now she is both the auspicious Ambika and the terrible Kali."

"Tell us about Kali," Samadhi pleaded with awe. To the guru he looked like a small child sitting there. Was he not, after all, a child of the Mother?

"Kali appears here in a particularly frightening form to embody the Devi's wrath. The Devi, in her lovely form as Ambika, projected the horrific Kali from her own scowling brow."

"Wasn't the description of her coming down the mountainside enough to give you chills?" Suratha asked with relish.

Samadhi nodded, childlike.

The guru went on, "This form of Kali bears the imagery of death and destruction: the emaciated flesh hanging loose upon the bones, the skull-topped staff, the all-devouring mouth. Kali is the relentless power of time, which in the end swallows up everything.

"But there is more to Kali than this. Her flesh is black, her tongue is red, her teeth are gleaming white. Black, red, and white represent the three gunas—tamas, rajas, and sattva. Kali embodies all the energy of the universe. She is Shakti personified. Hers is the power to create, sustain, and destroy. She is indeed supreme."

"But she's so frightening," Samadhi whimpered.

"She is the Mother," Medhas countered. "You must go beyond your fear and come to her in love."

This is all too strange for me, Samadhi thought but dared not say it. Instead he averted his eyes. Looking up again, he saw Medhas regarding him intently. He felt utterly transparent, as if his body were as clear as water. The guru seemed to be peering into his very soul. Is there nothing, the merchant wondered, I can't hide from him? But Medhas's face was all solicitude and reassurance, and any discomfort on Samadhi's part quickly melted away.

"What you love, you cannot fear," Medhas continued. "And Kali takes us beyond all fear. She has many forms. This wrathful form is called Chamunda. When she appears on the battlefield with bloody mouth and glowing eyes, she is the night of death who laughs derisively and binds men and horses and elephants in her terrible snare. When she haunts the cremation ground, she is Shmashanakali, the embodiment of destructive power who reduces all created things to ash. Is this a terrible thing? No, because in fact Shmashanakali presides over the dissolution of matter back into spirit. When she is pleased, she is the benevolent Bhadrakali. As Shyama, she is worshiped in household shrines as the tender dispeller of fear and the granter of boons. She is also called Bhavabhayaharini, 'she who removes the fear of worldly existence.'

"What a beautiful name!" Suratha and Samadhi exclaimed almost simultaneously.

Medhas certainly had his disciples' interest and knowing there was much more he wanted to impart, he forged ahead. "You may find the descriptions of Kali unsettling at first, but know that behind every detail of her appearance lies a sublime truth. Usually we think of Kali in a more benevolent form than Chamunda. For example, the auspicious Dakshinakali. Her untamed hair hints at unrestrained power and boundless freedom. Some say it represents the veil of illusion, woven from the strands of space and time. Her three eyes represent omniscience, for she sees past, present, and future. Nothing is unknown to the all-knowing Mother. The garland of skulls around her neck is not a symbol of death, as you might think, but of creative power. How can that be? you wonder. Each of the fifty skulls stands for a sound of the alphabet, and from these sounds, these vibrating energies, the Mother brings forth the entire universe. So this garland of skulls is, in fact, the alphabet of creation! Kali's full breasts show how she nurtures us. The girdle of severed arms around her waist betokens her power to sever the bonds of karma—to free us from the accumulated deeds that keep us in bondage. Her nakedness represents freedom from illusion, and her blacker-than-black skin, like the endless blackness of the night sky, tells us that she is infinite."

Medhas explained that Kali's paradoxical mixture of maternal tenderness and destructive terror appears polarized on right and left. "She often appears with four hands," he said. "Her lower right hand extends itself in the offering of a boon, as if to say, 'Ask of me what you will.' How many of us know what to ask for? Wealth, power, fame?" He shook his head. "Health, happiness, peace of mind? Perhaps. The welfare of others? All right. Pure love and surrender at her holy feet? Much better!

"One of Kali's greatest boons is fearlessness, which she signals with her upper right hand, the palm held outward. 'Be not afraid!' this gesture proclaims.

"Now, how to dispel fear? Consider the Mother's upper left hand, which wields the bloodied sword of knowledge. This is a strong image. It represents the power of discernment—the ability to separate what is transitory and fleeting from what is real and abiding. This power cuts through appearances and reveals things as they really are. Use this sword to cut away the mental clutter; focus your attention solely on that which leads toward the liberating knowledge of the all-pervading oneness.

"In her lower left hand the Mother dangles the freshly severed head of a demon. This represents the limiting sense of ignorance that she slays. Taken together, Kali's four hands say, 'Take refuge in me, let go of your fear, let me slay your illusion of smallness and separation, and you will merge into my infinite bliss.'"

Medhas tilted his head slightly back. With half-closed eyes and a smile breaking on his barely parted lips, he took on a beatific glow and whispered softly, "How beautiful the Mother is! Her dazzling darkness—I try to tell you, but I fall tongue-tied, mute, as words melt into amazement."

Dumbfounded, Suratha and Samadhi regarded the guru, then each other. Neither knew what to say or dared to break the mood, to intrude into something very sacred, which both recognized but neither could fully comprehend. And so they sat, wordless, until the seer's ecstasy passed. Then Medhas resumed his tale.

AT THE NEWS OF ANOTHER FAILED MISSION, Shumbha, now bereft of all reason, ordered the marshaling of the remaining demon clans. Three hundred thirty clans he called up and still others, until all had arrived: the violent, the plundering, the benighted, the corrupt, the villainous—asuras who embodied every sort of evil the three worlds had ever witnessed.

And so it happened that Shumbha, the despotic lord of demons, went forth attended by the most formidable of forces to wage war against the resplendent Devi, her noble lion, and the terrifying Kali. Seeing the demon hordes approach, Kali emitted from her gaping mouth a howl that heralded a sight to behold. From the bodies of the onlooking gods—Brahma, Shiva, Skanda, Vishnu, and Indra—sprang forth their *shaktis*, their embodied powers.

Whatever the god's form was, whatever his weapons, adornments, and mount, those too his shakti displayed. From Brahma came forth Brahmani, prayer beads and water pot in hand, driving a swan-yoked chariot. Astride a great bull rode Maheshvari, Shiva's trident-bearing shakti, great serpents entwining her arms and the crescent moon adorning her brow. From the war god Skanda's youthful body, Kaumari rode forth on her peacock mount, dazzling, with spear in hand. Vaishnavi, on Garuda, the eagle mount, flew out from Vishnu's resplendent figure, displaying the splendors of conch, discus, mace, and sword. Flower-garlanded Varahi, the shakti of Vishnu's boarlike form, trotted forth with tusks gleaming. Fierce Narasimhi roared forth from Vishnu's man-lion form, with the toss of her mane scattering the constellations on high. And the regal Aindri, thousand-eyed with thunderbolt in hand, rode out from Indra's shining form, swaying majestically on her elephant mount.

When these seven shaktis had assembled before the Devi Chandika, Shiva stepped to the center and declared, "Let the asuras quickly be slain for my satisfaction."

What effrontery! Shiva, a mere onlooker to the Devi's battles, now issuing commands! Thereupon the earth rumbled and from the Devi Chandika's own body came forth another form, savage in her fury and howling like a hundred jackals. This, the Devi's own unvanquished shakti, said to the moon-crowned Shiva of dark, matted locks, "Go, my lord, as my messenger to Shumbha and Nishumbha and say to them that Indra must regain sovereignty over the three worlds, that the gods must again receive the sacrificial oblations that are their due, and that the asuras must return to their lightless abode in the netherworld And tell them also that if through the conceit of strength they are still desirous for battle, they are to come and let my jackals be satiated with their flesh!"

So was the great god Shiva commanded by the Devi's own shakti, and so is she known as Shivaduti, because she sent Shiva as her messenger.

On hearing the Devi's ultimatum from Shiva's lips, the asuras, filled with indignation, strode to where the Devi stood and rained torrents of arrows, spears, and lances upon her. Playfully she split asunder their hurtling weapons in mid-flight with great arrows shot from her own resounding bow. While Kali roamed the battleground, destroying asuras as she had before, the lovely Brahmani moved serenely through the fray and

> sapped the demons of strength by the holy water she sprinkled gently from her water pot. In like manner each shakti moved through the battle with her own array of weapons and assailed the enemy hosts. Demons, torn asunder, discharged torrents of blood upon the earth, and while Shivaduti devoured them in between fits of violent laughter, those asuras who could still escape took flight.

Not for the first time did one of Medhas's tales leave Suratha and Samadhi speechless.

"Do you want to know more about the shaktis?" the seer inquired to break the silence. "They are called the Seven Little Mothers. Though they are mostly fierce, they are also fiercely protective. You should understand them not only as the gods' powers, but as the diverse expressions of the Divine Mother, the one Shakti to whom, after all, the gods owe their powers. As I said a little while ago, the Mother reveals herself in many ways. There is no end to the forms she can assume.

"Now, having multiplied her forces to face the onslaught of Shumbha's demon throngs, she has appeared as Brahmani, Maheshvari, and all the others."

"What, exactly, does this have to do with me?" Samadhi queried. "I know you are telling this for a reason, but you'll have to explain so I can understand."

"Do you not see? The Seven Little Mothers are not only the diverse expressions of the one Shakti; more importantly, they are the diverse powers of your own awareness."

The merchant closed his eyes and tried to imagine the strange figures rampaging about inside his head. Really, they were too much for him to deal with but soon his frustration was relieved by Medhas's patient guidance.

"Were you ever on the verge of doing something you knew to be wrong and then sensed an inner voice restraining your action—call it conscience or perhaps your own innate decency? Do you know what I am talking about?"

"Yes," Samadhi replied, and the king also nodded his assent.

"Good!" the guru exclaimed. "Know that to be Brahmani's doing. That nobler impulse, that appeal to your higher sensibility, is symbolized by the sprinkling of her holy water, which leaves her enemies—your disgraceful urges—sapped of strength. In Brahmani, who is purity itself, the sattva guna prevails. Her water pot is the emblem of the ascetic, and the drops of holy water carry the power of self-restraint, the strength to forego that which you know to be wrong or contrary to your higher values. The swans that draw her chariot—do you know what they symbolize?"

Suratha and Samadhi did not.

"The swan has the ability to separate milk from water with its beak, in other words, to discern what is true and abiding from what is impermanent. So, like Kali's curving sword, the swan is a symbol of discernment. One who becomes discerning turns away from the lesser, fleeting pleasures and delights instead in contemplating the Divine. That contemplation is symbolized by the prayer beads that Brahmani holds.

"I'd hardly call Brahmani fierce," Samadhi objected. "Doesn't she seem out of place with the other Little Mothers, who seem so bloodthirsty?"

"They run the gamut from raw and brutal to auspicious, but you must remember that, in the end, whatever they do is beneficial."

Medhas continued, "Maheshvari is the shakti of Shiva when he appears as the great Maheshvara, the lord of ascetics and the destroyer of ignorance. Her mount is a white bull, who symbolizes the dharma. Her trident holds the powers of creation, preservation, and destruction. The lovely crescent moon that glows softly on her brow reminds us of passing time, which we measure by the lunar waxing and waning. The serpents entwined around her arms as adornments signify fertility, regeneration, the eternal cycle of time, and finally immortality.

"Do you not see?" Medhas uttered excitedly. "Each of these Little Mothers is one facet of a single, sparkling gem!"

Samadhi's face shone with joy at his teacher's revelation. These alien, mythical figures were beginning to make sense. Now he was eager to know what bearing Maheshvari had upon the conduct of his own life, and Medhas gladly explained.

"The ultimate goal of existence is to reunite with the divine oneness that is the source of everything. That state of blissful union is called *yoga*. Maheshvara—Shiva—is the lord of yoga, and Maheshvari is the power by which this state of enlightenment is achieved.

"Listen well: Yoga is the cessation of the thought waves in the mind. To arrive at that state is to take a journey within. The Mother, in the form of Maheshvari, rides a bull—Nandi." Medhas giggled, visualizing the unlikely image of traveling inward on a white bull. Regaining his composure, he went on, "This journey becomes an entire way of life, and because it leads to the innermost Self, it necessarily begins somewhere else—on the outside. So, the beginning steps are the ethical precepts, which have to do with living in relation to the exterior world. This is dharma; this is what Nandi stands for. His four legs are truth, purity, compassion, and generosity. When you follow these principles, you do not deceive anyone, you do not disrespect your own self-worth, you do not cause injury to others, and you do not take anything that does not belong to you or any more than you need.

"Once you have cast off the outer faults, you next cultivate positive inner qualities—right attitudes, contentment, self-discipline, attention to sacred matters, and devotion to your chosen form of the Divine. These are the two preliminary steps on the path of yoga. You will learn about the remaining six later on. For now, you need only know that Maheshvari is the shakti that will carry you along."

"What about Kaumari?" the king asked. As a warrior, he felt that this goddess would have special relevance for him.

"Shiva's son Skanda, or Kumara, is a beautiful youth and also the god of war. Kaumari, his shakti, is the power to challenge ignorance. She offers an opportunity for spiritual growth. Her peacock mount represents the glory of the manifest universe, but you must remember that such glory has the power to enthrall. So with Kaumari there is the celebration of divine beauty but also the danger of delusion."

"Then in Kaumari, there is a sense of conflict?" Suratha asked.

"Yes, I suppose you could say that. She *is* the goddess of war, after all, and what is war if not conflict? But of course I am speaking of the inner conflict that subdues the lower urges and draws us toward the nobler aspects of existence."

Next Medhas spoke of the three shaktis associated with Vishnu—Vaishnavi, Varahi, and Narasimhi. "Vaishnavi," he explained, "is the power inherent in Vishnu's supreme form. Like him she rides on the fabulous bird, Garuda, and holds the symbols of universal power. Her conch destroys ignorance, because its auspicious sound awakens us to divine awareness. Her discus is the inexorably turning wheel of time, which in the end devours all created things. Her mace destroys unrighteousness, and her sword is the power of right knowledge that severs the apparent from the real. In other words, your own consciousness holds the potential for spiritual awakening, for transcending the limitations of name and form, for being in harmony with the all-pervading divinity, and for recognizing its constant presence.

"Vishnu has ten *avataras*, or earthly incarnations, who follow a pattern of evolution from lower to higher life forms. Varahi is the shakti of the third incarnation, the boarlike Varaha. How boldly and bluntly Varahi confronts the asuras! She stops them in their tracks with blows from her snout and pierces them with her tusks. She is the power of restraint, which reveals itself as the ability to stop unwanted thoughts and impulses.

"The ferocious Narasimhi, half woman and half lioness, is the shakti of Vishnu's man-lion form, Narasimha. Once there was a righteous youth, Prahlada, whose devotion to Vishnu angered his demonic father, the God-hating Hiranyakashipu. The father had the boy tortured, and when Prahlada prayed for deliverance, Vishnu appeared in the form of Narasimha and disemboweled the demon king. Narasimhi, his shakti, is that fierce power that arises to defend in the face of great evil."

The guru appended an afterthought. "Consider also the image of the heavenly constellations being scattered by the toss of her mane. How poetic! It means that human consciousness is not limited to the confines of the body and immediate surroundings but can soar through the power of imagination to the realm of the stars!" Medhas fell silent to let his words make their effect.

Then resuming, he said, "Aindri is the power of Indra, king of the gods. Like him, she rides with regal bearing upon an elephant. She is the inherent nobility within everyone. And like Indra, she has a thousand eyes, for hers is the power of omniscience. Her weapon, the thunderbolt, signifies specifically the power of illumination."

Thoughts raced through Samadhi's head. What an overwhelming display the Seven Little Mothers presented. What an awesome array of powers resided within his own consciousness, there within his own reach, if only he knew how to use them.

Wanting to know more, he asked, "Can you explain the part about Shiva and Shivaduti? What was *that* all about?"

Medhas laughed. "Ah! The original teller of this story was having some fun. You see, the devotees of Shiva raise him to the level of supreme godhood and consider Shakti, the Divine Mother, as slightly subordinate. We Shaktas, who are devoted to the Mother, are likely to do the reverse and say that Shakti, the divine power, is supreme. Our story was told by a Shakta, who wanted to make the point that the Mother is supreme." He laughed again, this time as though enjoying a private joke. Then he let his disciples in on it. "After the Mother summoned this whole shining array of her powers, Shiva, who had thus far been a bystander, said quite unexpectedly, 'Let the asuras quickly be slain for my satisfaction.'"

"Just who does he think he is?" King Suratha blurted out. His vehemence betrayed that he was still sensitive to the violation of authority.

Medhas knowingly concurred, "Exactly. The Devi's reaction must have been just that. She decided to teach him a lesson and so revealed her own shakti, the fiercest and strongest of all, who then commanded the mighty Shiva himself to act as her messenger—a humbling role."

The point was not lost on the king, but the pain of Samadhi's not fully comprehending face called to Medhas for more explanation.

"Shiva and Shakti are the two poles of one reality—Shiva the quiescent, unchanging ground of existence, Shakti the dynamic power that expresses herself through the creation. You might call them the Absolute and the relative. Though they appear different, they are one and the same, for the ultimate truth is one and only one. It is neither male, nor female, nor neuter. It is pure consciousness as well as the energy of consciousness. Between them there is no difference. It is that ineffable reality we Shaktas worship as Mother in her supreme formlessness—and the Shaivas worship as Shiva." Medhas laughed again. "The rest is only sectarian partiality, like a child saying, 'My father is stronger than yours,' or some such nonsense. The Divine is one."

His point made, the holy man concluded, "Imagine these battle stories as your own internal conflicts. You have overcome many faults, conquered many inner demons. Still, the war is not over, and other battles remain to be fought. Tomorrow I shall tell you about the most formidable demon yet."

CHAPTER 14

SEEDS OF BLOOD

"Well, are you ready for the next part of the story?" Medhas asked the following morning when the king and the merchant entered his hut. The question was a mere formality, because he had already quickened his listeners' interest with the promise of a demon more imposing than any they had yet encountered. Within moments, the holy man resumed his narrative, right where he had left off the day before.

> EVEN AS THE DAITYAS FLED from the enraged Little Mothers, the mighty Raktabija strode onto the battlefield, a demon among demons. He stepped forth proudly, possessed of a power unlike any the onlooking gods had ever seen, unlike any they could have imagined. Wherever a drop of his blood fell to the earth, there a demon of equal might and measure would rise up.
>
> Swinging his heavy club with irresistible verve, the ruddy daitya advanced toward the regal Aindri, and she, from atop her elephant mount, released her shining thunderbolt. It struck with a resounding crack, and from Raktabija's stricken flesh

a crimson flow streamed to the ground, giving birth to warriors of identical form and force. For as many drops of blood that touched the earth, so many demons of equal size and strength arose, an army of Raktabijas that fell fiercely upon the Mothers.

Aindri's thunderbolt flashed a second time and found its mark on Raktabija's brow. Vaishnavi's discus and Kaumari's spear and Varahi's sword and Maheshvari's trident likewise wreaked their damage on every part of Raktabija's body, and out of the blood from this single demon's wounds, myriad asuras multiplied and pervaded all the world.

Utter terror seized the gods.

The Devi Chandika burst into laughter at their despair and summoned the fearsome Kali, saying, "Chamunda, open wide your mouth! Drink in the spattering blood and consume the great asuras born therefrom! Roam the battlefield and devour this demon's spawn."

Then Chandika herself impaled the mighty Raktabija on her lance and slammed him to the ground. Stunned, he staggered to his feet and fought back valiantly, frenetically, while from his battered body the glistening crimson of his demon blood oozed all about. Kali, emaciated and ravenous, rushed to lap it up and ground between her gnashing teeth the great demons that sprang from the bloody flow until the formidable Raktabija, now drained of blood, toppled lifeless to the ground. When he and all the demons born from him lay dead, the gods rejoiced.

Samadhi marveled at the contrast between this grisly tale and its narrator's demeanor of pure kindness. Not for the first time was he perplexed by the holy man. He wondered how many more times his comfortable ideas of how the world ought to be would be turned upside down. Things simply did not add up. Add up? There he was again, thinking like a merchant, only this time he noticed his mind's ingrained tendency to follow familiar, habitual routes. Maybe the ability to observe his own thoughts was a step in the right direction. Whatever was happening, Samadhi felt both encouraged and unsettled.

The guru, increasingly responsive to his disciple's unspoken questions, inquired, "Is something disturbing you?"

At Samadhi's nod Medhas continued, "The story of Raktabija can be understood in more than one way. Listen, and I think your questions will be answered.

"Raktabija's name means 'he whose seed is blood.' On one level the glistening red drops stand for the overwhelming allure of desire. Like a seed, every desire that falls on the fertile soil of the mind grows to maturity and then new seeds for the next planting burst forth. Every desire produces the seeds of many more, and we are never satisfied."

"Are all desires to be avoided, then?" Samadhi wanted to know. "For example, I desire to learn everything you can teach me. Is there anything wrong with that?"

Medhas smiled almost indulgently. At one moment Samadhi displayed all the signs of a shrewd tradesman; in the next, the innocence of a child. It was this curious mixture of acuity and naiveté that accounted for the disciple's unpredictable charm and the holy man's affectionate patience. "You see, Samadhi, we must recognize that not all desire is wrong. Like everything else, desire comes in many colors, depending on the mixture of the gunas. What color stands out in the story of Raktabija?" It was the kind of question one would ask a child, as much as it was a portal to deeper understanding.

"Red, of course, with all that blood spurting and spattering and gushing and oozing," Samadhi replied, compelled to let out his critical opinion of the revolting imagery, an opinion that Medhas chose to ignore.

"Yes, and red is the color of rajas—activity, restlessness, and passion. That is Raktabija's nature. He does not represent the sattvic desire to experience the joy of learning or to know the divine fullness of creation as you are beginning to do. The desire he stands for is Shumbha's aggressive, wrong-headed grasping. Such desire never remains satisfied for long. The more you feed a fire, the fiercer and hotter it blazes. So too with the flames of desire. The more you gratify them, the more they proliferate. As our story puts it, the world is soon filled with Raktabijas. And then, can there be peace? Far from it! The clamor of battle only intensifies."

"The gods were overwhelmed and filled with terror."

"Indeed they were. In other words, all sense of peace and virtue was lost. That is what happens to a mind inflamed with desire.

"Next, Chamunda Kali avidly laps up the flow of Raktabija's blood, which swarms with demons taking shape. Do you understand?"

Samadhi struggled to visualize the gruesome scene, then gave a typically questioning answer. "Desire is conquered most easily when nipped in the bud?"

"Precisely!" Medhas exclaimed. "Before it gets out of hand. Never forget that for all the horror of the imagery, Kali's destructive power is for you a protective, beneficent force. But not for Raktabija!" The guru laughed delightedly as if this were all great fun, even though to Samadhi it seemed a very serious matter.

"Now I shall tell you the hidden meaning of this tale, which takes us deeper into the mind. You must think of everything in terms of consciousness. As I told you yesterday, the state of yoga is achieved through the control of the thought waves in the mind. Raktabija represents the nearly unstoppable power of thought."

Samadhi tried to understand.

"Can you stop the wild wind?" Medhas asked.

"No, of course not."

"The mind is almost as hard to control. If you have ever tried to sit quietly, completely still, you know exactly what I mean. No matter how hard you try to calm the mind or hold it to a single thought, it wanders or jumps from here to there, always in motion. Incessantly one thought gives rise to another, like the endless Raktabijas born from the demon's own blood. These are the vrittis, the thought waves of the mind. They continually spring up from the normal, unruly state of human consciousness, wherein mental energy is scattered and unfocused, always dividing itself.

"You asked before if all desires are wrong. Let us apply that same question to the thought waves. The answer is the same. There are vrittis colored by every possible combination of the gunas—harmful thoughts, restless thoughts, virtuous thoughts—thoughts of every possible quality and relative value. First you must replace the undesirable ones with beneficial ones, as I have taught you, but in the end, mental activity is mental activity, and if you are to achieve true peace, the restlessness must be stilled. Raktabija must be conquered."

"How do I do that?" Samadhi asked, propelled by a wave of enthusiasm.

"Who conquers?" the guru countered. "Not you, but Chamunda Kali! She is the Divine Mother's power of concentrated awareness that subdues the thought waves on the stormy sea of samsara and carries us across to a calmer, purer state. In calming the incessant waves, the undisciplined thoughts, Chamunda severs the knot of ignorance, cuts through the illusion of duality, and reveals the pure underlying consciousness, the infinite unity of the Absolute."

It all sounded very good but way beyond anything Samadhi felt within his reach. Still, he hesitated to draw the conversation down from such exalted heights and back to his own mundane mental life, which he now saw as increasingly valueless, if not downright sordid.

"Is something still disturbing you?" The guru's question drew Samadhi out of his troubled reverie, and he groped for an honest reply.

"Your teaching is beautiful, so why does it makes me feel so much worse? Really unworthy. Raktabija's swinging club—that's my mind, in a constant whirl. That's bad enough in itself, but more and more I'm haunted by thoughts of my own faults. During the year I wandered and then into my first days here, I was overwhelmed with agony over my loss and betrayal. Thanks to your teaching, those feelings began to fade, but suddenly I'm plagued by memories, regrets, failures. Whatever these things are, they make me suffer as much as before—all over again—and maybe even worse." Choking back a sob, the merchant confessed, "I feel so awful about myself."

"You must not," Medhas said comfortingly but firmly. He had little patience for self-pity or self-deprecation, but he recognized both the sincerity of Samadhi's confession and the fragility of his present state. He also recognized spiritual progress when he saw it.

"What is happening to you is natural," he reassured. "You see, you have managed to withdraw somewhat from the concerns of the outer world and have laid them to rest. Your conflicts with others may be over, but now you see revealed the conflicts raging within yourself. The battleground has shifted to the inner world of the mind, where subtler thoughts or tendencies long buried are rising to the surface. What you once shrugged off as no more than inconsequential thoughts or feelings now looms large in your mind and causes you inordinate grief. Am I right?"

Heartened by the guru's understanding, but still a little wary, Samadhi bit his lip and nodded.

Medhas sensed the merchant's reluctance to bare his soul, especially in front of the king, and proceeded to speak in generalities. "Let us examine some of these mental disturbances that are, after all, obstacles to spiritual progress. We have already spoken at length about desire—just now in connection with Raktabija and earlier in connection with Mahishasura. Desire is a longing for gratification. Why do you suppose that longing is there?" Here Medhas paused.

"We want what we don't have?" Samadhi guessed. It was a superficial answer, not well thought out, but it held a grain of truth that Medhas seized upon.

"We desire because we feel that something is lacking. We feel deficient or incomplete, limited or separated, and we look for ways to fix that. We think that by acquiring this or that or by having a pleasant experience of some sort we will be fulfilled." Turning to the king, Medhas continued, "When we fail to satisfy a desire, we often become angry. Suratha, do you recall saying that your young son's tantrums at not having his way reminded you of Mahishasura's rage? And Samadhi, do you not see how Shumbha's unfulfilled desire to possess the Devi has brought him to his present sorry state? Instead of possessing her, he is possessed by his anger and has lost all reason.

"Now what happens when a desire is satisfied?" Medhas hoped to provoke some discussion.

"I'd like to think that one becomes happy and contented," Suratha declared. Then recalling the lessons he had already learned from the seer, the king wished he had not spoken so soon and added, "But I suspect it's not as simple as that."

"What do you say, Samadhi?" Medhas asked. "What happens when a desire is satisfied?"

In all his years of selling things, the merchant had seen that scenario played out countless times. "People who get what they want are usually satisfied for a while, but soon they're back to buy something more."

"Precisely! And that is called greed. The pleasure of fulfilling one desire makes them want to repeat the experience again and again. One desire begets another and soon the world is swarming with Raktabijas! You see, greed is the sure sign that desire is insatiable."

Samadhi felt a glow of satisfaction at the superiority of his response over the king's, but not for long.

"Pride," Medhas cautioned, "is a false sense of superiority that aims to convince us that we are better than anyone else. In its own twisted way it is actually an unspoken admission of our own shortcomings."

Now Samadhi had something more to feel bad about.

"Pride takes different forms—personal pride, such as I have just described, or pride in your own cleverness or accomplishments." Samadhi's mood grew more unsettled.

"There is also the pride of one's good looks; this is called vanity. And the pride of family, ancestry, or lineage. If your father was a great man, does that necessarily make you great? If your grandfather excelled in virtue, do you? Do you see the fallacy of such pride? Just as empty is the pride of caste or rank or station or birthplace, yet how often our attitudes and behavior are governed by such artificial distinctions!

"Know that we are all children of the Divine Mother. Her essence drives our very life breath and courses through our veins! Knowing that, how can anyone feel superior to anyone else?

"Through pride we delude ourselves into feeling good about who we are, what we do, and what we possess—until someone else comes along whom we see as happier, richer, more powerful, or more attractive. Then we fall prey to jealousy. Why should another's good fortune, well-being, or happiness poison our minds? Because we resent in another something we think should be ours. Again, we are reminded of our own sense of lack.

"Yet another form of pride is known as self-righteousness. This is the pride of good conduct, masquerading as virtue but only concealing the hollowness within.

"My brother's wife is like that," Samadhi interrupted. "Always so pious—and always finding fault with others. No wonder my Mohani didn't want her under our roof. In the few months she lived with us, I can't remember when she wasn't stirred up over something. She never gave anyone a moment's peace, thanks to her constantly taking offense. It was as if everything disgusted her. Of what use is her self-righteousness? For people like her I have nothing but contempt."

"And so another Raktabija is born!" Medhas exclaimed.

At first the remark was lost on Samadhi, but when he realized the depth and breadth of his admission, he cringed and awaited a well-deserved rebuke.

Instead, Medhas said, "Do you see how all these disturbances—desire, anger, greed, pride, and jealousy—are connected? How one gives rise to another in an endless chain? No, more like a web, where each point is linked to several others. Such is the complexity of the mind and of the thoughts that enmesh us. In the course of our high-minded conversation Samadhi has let slip that he harbors hatred!"

Neither the merchant nor the king could have anticipated that their conversation with the guru would have come to this uneasy pass. Suratha sat immobile, dreading where it might lead to next, while Samadhi struggled to hide his discomfort. How could he have been so foolish?

"Samadhi," the guru said earnestly, "even though you have advanced somewhat along the spiritual path, you still retain traces of former tendencies, and even such traces must be erased. Where shall we begin?"

Samadhi lowered his eyes and whispered, "Shame."

With the conversation now focused on the source of the merchant's distress, Medhas explained, "Shame is a formidable obstacle to spiritual progress. It is, in fact, the reverse side of pride. Whereas pride is a lie designed to conceal your imperfections, shame forces you to dwell on those flaws, or on past mistakes, in the very act of trying to keep them hidden. As long as you do, you will remain in bondage. Inwardly, if you continually tell yourself, 'I am no good,' you will begin to believe that, and from then on it is downhill all the way."

Having come this far, Samadhi saw little reason to keep up his defenses any longer. "Sometimes I feel so guilty," he sighed, then spoke with increasing eloquence. "Not about any major offense—I don't think I've ever done anything really bad. But I regret certain past deeds that now seem selfish or thoughtless, maybe even harmful to others. I've said some things in the past that I wish I could take back—even some well-meant things that didn't come out the way I meant them. I may have offended someone, not meaning to, but the memories of even an unintended unkindness spring up unbidden. Like clouds drifting before the sun and darkening the day, those feelings of guilt and shame cast a chill shadow over me. How can I be free of them?"

Not unexpectedly, Medhas had some advice. "Whatever you may have done in the past, let it go. Every saint has a past, and every wrongdoer has a future. Shame? There is nothing you can hide from the all-knowing Divine Mother. Why do you even try? Do you think she loves you any less for your mistakes? Once a great sage called us children of immortal bliss. You are the Mother's child. Remember that and cast off all sense of unworthiness!"

Samadhi's confession reminded the king of his own failure to fulfill his duty. Instead of defending the kingdom from anarchy and moral decay, he had taken the coward's way out and fled. Rather than wallow in self-blame, he resolved now—somehow—to set things right.

"One more thing I must tell you, Samadhi," Medhas added. "Your concern shows a dawning of love. That is a sure sign of spiritual progress. Agonizing over minor infractions is not the behavior of the worldly-minded, and while it pains you just now, it means that inner purification is taking place. Do not despair, but be thankful. Clearly it is a sign of grace."

Nothing in this world is as it seems to be, Samadhi thought, applying Medhas's familiar teaching in a whole new way.

The guru continued, "Shame is the opposite of pride. What would you say is the opposite of desire?"

The merchant knew to expect something insightful.

"Fear is the negative form of desire," Medhas declared simply, but his words carried enormous weight. "A desire is something you want to happen. A fear is something you want not to happen. Either one is a form that takes shape in your awareness, a thought wave, and as you attract what you desire, you also attract what you fear, because of where your attention is."

That revelation unsettled the disciples. How many times might they have brought misfortune upon themselves inadvertently, purely out of ignorance of this simple truth?

"Now you know," Medhas remarked dryly, "and you need not make that mistake again. Like everything else we have spoken of today, it is a matter of controlling the thought waves."

"But how?" the king asked, the memory of his ignominious flight from his capital city still fresh in his mind. "How can I suppress my fear?"

"It is not a question of suppressing anything. How can you be free of something you have forced into the recesses of your mind? Do you not continue to carry it with you?" Medhas waited a moment, then revealed, "It is *knowledge* that dispels fear. Fear is a powerful adversary, and it engenders a host of other enemies, such as suspicion, distrust, hatred, secretiveness, and shame—all causes of misery and bondage. Do you understand how these demons join hands, as it were, and cavort about in the mind, just as the nascent demons swarmed in the ruddy flow of Raktabija's blood? Fear feeds on ignorance, thrives on it. But knowledge—right understanding—reveals the falsehood of everything that causes you to be afraid. The Divine Mother is that fear-dispelling knowledge. When you begin to see things as they are and not as they merely appear to be, so much in life loses its fearfulness.

"Also, fear gives rise to hatred, the most violent and divisive of all mental modes. See how contrary, how antithetical, hatred is to the goal of blissful oneness with the Divine! The path to the Mother is love, but hatred leads one away.

"So," Medhas continued, drawing a deep breath, "the battle with Raktabija tells how this web of thought works. Now go and reflect on what I have explained. Sit quietly, both of you, and observe the mind. Focus on the clarity of its awareness. Thoughts will arise. Watch their flow, let them go, and when you find that your attention has strayed along with them, bring it back again to the pure awareness and try to hold it there. It will be difficult at first, but little by little you will succeed. Even as the replicated Raktabijas were devoured by Chamunda Kali, who is the power of concentrated awareness, your unruly thought waves will be absorbed into the single thought of the Mother. Practice this, and return here in three days."

CHAPTER 15

MISTAKEN IDENTITY

For the next three days, reflecting on the holy man's teachings, Samadhi found rare contentment. But on the morning of the fourth day, in this haven of peace, he awoke to a disquieting sadness that caught him off guard. No, not so much sadness as a despairing, sickening regret that all this would pass. He had weathered the adversity of worldly life and the loss of family and fortune, and he was beginning to find a new sense of calm that he was loath to lose. But suddenly he felt a desperate clinging to that which would most certainly slip away. He mourned the eventual passing of his body, mind, and personality and felt in his heart the chill grip of a terror never faced before—the terror of annihilation. Is this creation nothing more than a cruel, cosmic joke? he wondered. Is Medhas's fine teaching just a wishful fantasy?

Try as he might, Samadhi could not shake off his paralyzing doubt.

"So, you have had a presentiment of your own mortality," Medhas observed when the merchant took his place beside the king at the guru's feet. "Worldly attachment does not go away all at once, and doubts may plague you now and again. But you must understand that every created thing is evanescent, fleeting.

"Can you grasp the passing breeze or a lovely reflection on the water? Can you stop the sunset at the peak of its beauty? Life is meant to be savored moment by moment—there can be no doubt of that—but when you try to hold on to the ungraspable, only suffering can result. Now imagine that you awoke today not to this panicked realization of your own impermanence but to a glorious dawn brimming with the promise of the new day.

"Do you know how our ancestors welcomed the dawn? Gathered outdoors in the darkness and looking toward the eastern horizon, they would chant a prayer like this: 'We have stepped over the boundary of night's darkness; now Dawn's rays uncover the mighty gloom, and her bright, far-shining glance stirs each living creature to motion, each one to its own pursuit. Bright Ushas, bounteous giver, we awaken to welcome you. Graciously shine your light on us! Hear our songs of praise and answer them with gifts of abundant happiness, O you who illumine this radiant realm!'"

"Beautiful," Samadhi whispered.

"But there is more. Listen. 'Reborn each day, in timeless beauty clothed, the first of endless dawns to come, fair Ushas wastes away the life of mortals. Like a skilled hunter hacking away at his prey, each radiant dawn diminishes the days of our lives. At her rising she urges forth the living but wakens not the dead from their slumber. Gone are they who beheld her radiant light in days before us. Now we, the living, welcome her brightness. How long before those who follow us will greet the future dawns?'"

Under the poignant weight of those words, Samadhi crumpled back into dejection, his haunted expression moving the holy man to pity.

"You must understand, Samadhi, that you are not alone in what you feel. Our ancestors spoke eloquently about this very matter—first, ecstatic optimism at the joy of living and then the aching reminder of their own mortality."

Medhas drew a thoughtful breath, then asked abruptly, "What is it about diamonds and gold that makes them so desirable to the worldly-minded? Is it the sparkle, the luster, the rarity, the cost? Maybe all of those, but do you know why people truly value gold? Because it does not tarnish or rust away. You—a merchant—have you not heard it said that diamonds are forever? You see, these things are valued for their seeming imperishability. Even in material objects we seek that imperishability, even though what is material, by its very nature, eventually perishes. In short, we seek lasting satisfaction and peace in all the wrong places."

While Medhas spoke to Samadhi, the king allowed his thoughts to wander. His own concerns were very different from his companion's. He turned over and over again the memories of abandoning his kingdom when he should have stayed and fought. Could he do something now to undo that mistake? At length a lull in the conversation allowed him to interject, "Revered sir, I wish to hear more about what Shumbha and Nishumbha did after Raktabija was killed."

"And so you shall," Medhas responded. Then he advised the merchant, "As you listen to what I tell the king, remember that this story is more than a tale of military conquest. For you, the battle is an interior one, the battleground is your field of consciousness, and the Devi's swift arrows and other weapons are the powers of consciousness that will speed you on to spiritual victory. Everything in the story is symbolic of something deeper. Hear me well."

> WHEN RAKTABIJA LAY DEAD, Shumbha and Nishumbha's fury knew no bounds. Surrounded by their grim forces, the demon brothers advanced to slay the Devi Chandika. Like two thunderclouds, they rained down torrents of arrows on her, which she gracefully repelled with arrows of her own.
>
> In a flash Nishumbha attacked the Devi's mount, the mighty lion of dharma, and swiftly Chandika unleashed her power. Nishumbha's shining shield, emblazoned with eight moons, gave little protection against her onslaught, and soon the asura lay senseless on the ground. When Shumbha saw his brother fall—his younger brother who was dearer to him than life itself—he sped forward in his magnificent chariot. Enraged beyond measure by the pure-toned fanfares of the Devi's conch, by Kali's menacing taunts, and by Shivaduti's peals of laugh-

ter, which pervaded the space between heaven, earth, and the netherworld, the daitya chief lost all reason and flung himself at the Devi. Wounded by her counterblow, he fainted and fell to the ground.

Meanwhile Nishumbha staggered to his feet. Sprouting ten thousand arms, he flung as many discuses at the glorious Durga, but she who destroys adversity cut through them effortlessly with her arrows. He lunged at her with lance in hand, only to be pierced through the heart by her swiftly hurled spear. Then from his gaping heart wound stepped forth an identical figure, who commanded her to stop. But the Devi merely laughed and effortlessly lopped off his head with her gleaming sword. Thus did the mighty Nishumbha meet his end.

"You asked me to listen to this story as if it were told in symbols," Samadhi reminded the sage. "I'm not sure how much I understand. I still don't know just what Nishumbha stands for except that he's horrible and powerful."

"It is easier to understand Nishumbha when you know Shumbha," Medhas explained. "You have learned that the two brothers are almost inseparable, that Nishumbha is the younger brother, dearer to Shumbha than life itself. Did you notice that when Nishumbha is knocked unconscious, Shumbha comes forward, and when Shumbha falls into a faint, Nishumbha rises up again? They are like two partners dancing."

A grotesque dance, the merchant noted to himself.

"Do you remember when Sugriva delivered the marriage proposal to the Devi? He said that his master, Shumbha, bade that she give him her hand in marriage, and if not to him then to his younger brother, the valiant Nishumbha."

"At the time I thought that was strange." Samadhi blushed. "But I didn't want to ask."

"Well, now I shall tell you." Medhas cast him an expansive smile. "Shumbha is the ego, and Nishumbha is the sense of attachment, the tag-along sibling that follows him everywhere.

"Earlier, when I told you and the king about Mahishasura, I said that 'my-ness,' or attachment, is rooted in 'I-ness,' or ego. The ego is the false sense of individual selfhood that depends on the limitations of mind, senses, and body for its very existence. The ego is not the true Self, which is infinite. The ego is only what we call ahamkara, literally the 'I-maker.'

"Along with the sense of its own individuality and separateness, this I-making principle has the power to claim things as its own: thoughts, feelings, the physical body, external objects. This power of appropriation is called *mamatva*, or 'my-ness,' and that is what Nishumbha represents. More than that, this sense of attachment is, we might say, the glue that holds our identity together."

Samadhi gave his characteristic, endearing blink that signaled both surprise at the revelation and an attempt to understand it fully.

"We consciously attach our sense of self to things that are not the Self," the guru explained. "We identify with our bodily characteristics and think, I am a man, I am a woman, I am tall, I am short, I am fat, I am thin, I am fair, I am dark. We rejoice when we think we are young and lament when we think we are old. You see, wherever there is attachment, there is also fear of loss.

"To look at this from a different angle, wherever there is attachment, there is also aversion. So, we define ourselves in both positive and negative terms, by our likes and our dislikes. And then we spend our time either running after what gives pleasure or avoiding what brings misery.

"What is more," Medhas continued, "we use our life's experiences—what we do and what happens to us—constantly to shape and reshape our identity. We define ourselves by the people in our lives and our relationships to them: father, mother, son, daughter, husband, wife, friend, and so on. How numerous are the roles we play throughout the vast web of family and social ties, and how differently we feel about ourselves according to which role we are playing. Our sense of self is colored by our positions and occupations and activities and by countless other factors that combine in ways that make each one of us unique. But this sense of self is constantly shifting, always in flux. How can we depend on it for any measure of peace or security? It is like trying to grasp that reflection in the water."

Samadhi brightened. "What you say reminds me of a man in my town. Every time he came to my shop and bought a new garment, he paraded down the street afterward like a swaggering fool just to show off. How he entertained the townspeople without even knowing it! You should have seen him—and them, snickering behind his back!" The merchant burst out laughing at the memory of pomposity personified. "And then there was this pauper who was known for his humility. He was kind and gentle—until he came into some wealth. It changed him overnight. After that you could hardly imagine how arrogant he was. 'Who does he think he is?' people used to say."

Medhas cast an admonitory glance aimed at Samadhi's own lack of charity embedded in those memories. "These instances that you have seen for yourself illustrate my point. Is the sense of self so fragile that a slight change of circumstance causes us to refashion who we think we are?"

It was a provocative idea, and the holy man gave the disciples some moments to ponder its implications.

Resuming, he explained, "Every factor that we identify with is called an *upadhi*, a defining attribute. But consider: a defining attribute is also a *limiting* one. We go through life acquiring upadhis, thinking they will make our identity bigger and better, but in reality we are merely adding to our limitations. Attachments to fame, influence, wealth, and possessions only make the burden of personal identity heavier. The more we are reined in by our defining attributes, the more we think and act as we are expected to, the more we lose sight of the larger sense of self. When we allow our happiness and misery to be dictated by conditions and objects outside of our true nature and foreign to it, we lose our autonomy. Is that not how both of you feel—that your lives are out of control?"

The king nodded solemnly, wishing himself back on his bejeweled throne, where he could uphold the proper order of things.

Samadhi felt differently. Returning to his family and former life held no attraction, although he was no less unsettled than the king. In truth, his disquiet came from a deeper level of his being. Like Suratha, he felt his life had spun out of control, but in his case the world's former pleasures now seemed empty and no longer beckoned him. Beyond his own despairing confusion, Samadhi felt there was nothing left to hold on to.

Through the dreary mist of this reverie he heard Medhas say, "There is another dimension to this word *upadhi*. It means a substitute, anything that may be taken for something else, an appearance mistaken for reality. Do you not see? In the end our defining attributes are no more than worthless tokens of our separation from the Infinite.

"But look how we cling to them!" the guru quickly added. "When the Divine Mother resolves to slay Nishumbha, the struggle is ferocious. The asura, gloriously arrayed in all the fine trappings of his achievements, represents attachment to fame, influence, wealth, possessions, and the identity they confer. His shield, emblazoned with eight moons, is a sign of his personhood and his own self-importance. When, in all his splendor, he is knocked down to the lowly ground, he rises up again in horrified desperation and sprouts ten thousand arms with ten thousand hands, each grasping a discus. Those discuses are the countless pieces of his individual selfhood."

"But why does he release them?" the merchant asked.

"Think, Samadhi. At this point the discuses he hurls at the Devi become his own defensive thoughts—thoughts that the Devi can't touch him because he is mighty, brave, wealthy beyond measure, important, glorious. He is thinking, Look at who I am! You can't do this to me!"

Samadhi ventured another question. "Don't Nishumbha's ten thousand hands also show just how desperate we are not to let go?" He faltered, then added, "But once he's released his discuses—all those ideas of who and what he thinks he is—the Devi takes him off guard, doesn't she?"

"Just as she took you off guard this morning," Medhas smiled, "when you awoke from deep sleep. But before Nishumbha, now defenseless, can gather up the pieces of his identity once more, the Mother pierces him through the heart with her spear—a symbol for the penetrating power of insight."

"That's not what happened to me, is it?"

"Not quite, Samadhi. The Mother gave you a momentary flash of insight, and your understanding will develop in due course as she wills. In the stories I tell, the events are more concentrated than in ordinary life, because there are points to be made. The point here is this: sometimes spiritual awakening dawns only after the experience of great pain, a severe wounding of the heart."

"That's why the Devi pierced Nishumbha through the heart!" Samadhi exclaimed.

"Yes. Both you and the king can think of your own suffering over worldly losses and the blow to your sense of self as a similar kind of wounding. Beyond that, you each suffer the pain of attachment in your own way.

"Suratha, you know that you have lost your kingdom, yet you still cherish some possessiveness toward it. At the same time, your understanding has gone beyond mere attachment. What bothers you more is your moral failure through ignorance and fear to have fulfilled your duty. Your primary concern is no longer to enjoy the royal prerogatives that once delighted you, but to rule according to the dharma. That, in your mind, remains unresolved."

Dropping the matter, Medhas abruptly turned to the merchant's state of mind. "In your case, Samadhi, your sense of loss no longer relates to external affairs of fortune and family but is penetrating ever deeper into your being. With growing dispassion toward the outer things, your awareness is focused on interior and very personal attachments. Your current distress is understandably more intense. Now listen.

"Nishumbha loses more than his outer trappings; all his upadhis are gone. Early this morning you were given a momentary glimpse of that state. You can sympathize, at least in small measure, with the awfulness of his distress. After the Devi spears him, his essence—the very principle of attachment—appears from out of his heart's gaping wound in the form of an identical demon. In other words, even when everything else is gone, the principle of attachment lingers on, still as reluctant as ever to let go. He cries for the Devi to stop, but this time he stands exposed and defenseless before her gleaming sword."

Even though Nishumbha had never been portrayed in flattering terms, Samadhi suddenly pitied the hapless demon. "Shouldn't the all-compassionate Devi be merciful?" he asked.

"And have him do it all over again? This power of attachment is very persistent, and in spiritual practice halfway measures simply will not do. And so the Mother raises her gleaming sword of knowledge and beheads him!" Medhas's voice rang with triumph, then grew gentle. "This metaphor of beheading means that through the grace of divine knowledge, the Devi puts an end to all the false ideas that have kept us so long in bondage."

"If that's the case," Samadhi asked, "shouldn't that be the end of the story?"

"It would be, except for one thing. Shumbha."

CHAPTER 16

Recognition

The portentous utterance of Shumbha's name echoed in Samadhi's mind, and aftershocks persisted into the next morning.

Stepping out of the hut where the king still lay sleeping, the merchant beheld a band of coral sky flaming across the eastern horizon. Above its ominous glow, clouds billowed up in blackening heaps. By the time the king awoke and joined Samadhi outside, the rising sun shone persimmon red through the thickening atmosphere.

In the eerie light, the two disciples hastily prepared for the day and, after the morning meal, set out for the guru's dwelling. They left none too soon, for already the trees thrashed overhead in the howling wind. Even the mightiest of them shuddered and creaked. Then as suddenly as it had come up, the wind subsided into unnatural calm—a sure sign that the dark clouds were about to burst. The companions exchanged knowing glances, then bolted along the gloomy forest path. In just moments day had turned to night. Overhead, the lightning sizzled and the thunder boomed, and while massive raindrops pelted the lush foliage, flowers rained from the trees, releasing their sweet perfume. The two men plunged on and on through a barrage of falling water, gasping lungfuls of now liquid air, until they dashed breathless and dripping into the holy man's hut.

It took them a moment or two to realize that within the dark interior utter quiet reigned. Medhas, in contemplation, showed no awareness of the raging storm or indeed of the outer world. His eyes were closed, and his lips hinted at a smile. What was he experiencing? Could it be anything like their own growing attraction to the divine presence that occasionally overflowed their hearts, however fleetingly? Was it like that, only multiplied a thousandfold? All that their small understanding could recognize was that they were in the presence of holiness.

After a while the seer emerged from his ecstasy. His face glowing, he invited the two disciples to sit. Each of them wondered what he would say.

"The rain is both beneficent and destructive," he observed casually as if nothing out of the ordinary had taken place. But his next sentence dispelled any such impression. "In the same way, everything that is created is subject to the tension of duality. As long as our awareness is engaged in this play of existence, we remain subject to both its beneficent power and its potential to cause grief. Where is the peace in waiting for the dark clouds to release their sweet moisture to the earth so that the green plants will bring forth food? And when the heavens stream too abundantly and the raging flood devastates the products of our endeavor, where is the peace in waiting for the rain to stop? There can be no abiding peace in this realm of duality and limitation. In the Infinite alone is there true peace."

Suratha and Samadhi knew that the seer's words flowed from experience although his was an experience as yet inconceivable to either of them. Inconceivable but undeniable, they had to admit, for even more than his words, Medhas's demeanor proclaimed the truth of what he said. The disciples sat enfolded in the fullness of the moment, until Medhas suddenly and quite unexpectedly resumed his narrative from the day before.

SHUMBHA REGARDED NISHUMBHA'S body lying lifeless on the ground. Flooded by grief and raging with fury over the fate of the brother who was dearer to him than life itself, the daitya chief approached the Devi and screamed, "O Durga, do not show your pride to me, for though you are flushed with victory, you have fought depending on the strength of others!"

The Devi replied quietly, "I am alone here in the world. Who else is there besides me? Look! All these—Kali, Shivaduti, the Seven Little Mothers—are but projections of my own power. Behold them now, entering back into me."

No sooner had she spoken than the goddesses, led by Brahmani, merged back into the Devi's body, and the Mother alone remained. Her head held high, she addressed Shumbha once more, saying, "I have withdrawn my many forms and stand alone in the glory of my power. Now, I warn you, be resolute in combat!"

While the gods looked on, the Devi and Shumbha engaged in fighting more horrific than any they had yet seen. The Devi showered her terrifying, wondrous weapons on the daitya chief. He sought at all cost to defend himself, but his every weapon, no matter how mighty, proved no match for hers, not even his sword, emblazoned with a hundred moons, or his shield that shone as brightly as the sun. Finally, with every weapon broken, the enraged demon chief seized the Devi and leaped high into the sky. There in midair the two struggled hand to hand until the astonished onlookers saw the Devi take hold of Shumbha, swing him around, and fling him to the earth.

He landed with a heavy thud, sprang up, and ran forward with upraised fist to assault the Devi yet again. Without warning she thrust her spear through his chest and threw him, the lord of all demonic creatures, to the ground. Mountains and oceans, indeed all the earth, shuddered in the cataclysm of Shumbha's departing life breath. When he lay in the stillness of death, the flaming clouds dispersed, the sky cleared, and the sun shone once more in glory. Again the rivers flowed gently along their courses, the winds blew sweetly, and the sacred fires glowed peacefully. On high the celestial musicians sang, and the hosts of gods were overjoyed. The sounds born of the four directions faded away, and the universe rested in bliss.

As beautifully as he had expressed it, Medhas knew that his tale had fallen short of its intended effect. "We are talking of the ultimate realization," he said. "Mere words cannot convey the glory of the Divine. Know that this story—any story—is inadequate to express the experience of enlightenment, the truth of your own being."

This last phrase caught Samadhi's attention, and from his look Medhas knew that the merchant was eager to learn more.

"You see, all these tales I have related illustrate the events of your own mind. Of every mind," he added, acknowledging the king. "Practically speaking, the story of Shumbha's destruction is about the death of the ego. Philosophically speaking, it is a story about the One and the many. In fact they are one and the same story, as you shall see. But mere words can go only so far, and until you yourselves experience the truth of all truths, you can have little inkling of it."

The king and the merchant remembered how they had found Medhas immersed in bliss a short while before. Samadhi longed to be like Medhas, for a moment to *be* Medhas, to know what he knew, which was beyond telling. He listened raptly to the holy man's words.

"When Shumbha faces the Devi Durga on the battlefield, he sees her accompanied by Kali, Shivaduti, and the Seven Little Mothers. He perceives these many forms—in other words, the plurality of this creation. He does not know that the Devi is indeed One. In chiding her for depending on the strength of others in the fight, he betrays his ignorance of her oneness. This primary ignorance is called *avidya*—a not knowing, you might say. It is an inability to recognize the unity pervading all existence.

"And how does the Devi respond? She says, 'I am alone here in the world. Who else is there besides me?' In other words, *'I am One without a second.'* She says that the goddesses who fought beside her are but projections of her own power, as are all the forms she inhabits. It is she herself who has become all this!" Once again Medhas waved his hand in the sweeping gesture that by now had become charged with meaning.

While Samadhi sat hanging on every word, the guru explained that Shumbha can never pierce through Mahamaya's veil. Shumbha represents the primal ignorance of individual selfhood. "Ego is an illusion of separation that depends for its very existence on the distinction of 'I' and 'not-I,'" the guru emphasized. "Unlike the fault-ridden Shumbha, the Devi is pure, undivided consciousness. Now consider this carefully: Consciousness is not thought, although thoughts are forms within consciousness. These mental concepts are finite, multiple expressions within the infinite One. Shumbha is one such entity, one such individualized, localized center of consciousness. We all are. But, you must remember, a tiny bubble can never embrace the limitless and undivided ocean."

Samadhi interjected, "You've told us how Shumbha tried time and again and by every possible means to possess the Devi, and how every time he failed."

"Precisely!" Medhas exclaimed.

Samadhi added, "I wonder—how does the ego come into being, anyway?"

As if he had been waiting for this moment, Medhas got up, disappeared into the hut's dark recesses, and returned with an elaborately carved wooden box in hand.

Sitting down, he resumed his discourse as if there had been no interruption. "Ego arises from ignorance of our true nature. That is a fact, pure and simple. But when philosophers attempt to explain it, they muddle the question with many scenarios and a profusion of different vocabularies, although they are all talking about the same thing. In the end, I ask you, can words reveal the truth that is beyond words?"

Medhas opened the box and took out a brightly polished copper disc. Holding it before the merchant's face, he asked, "What do you see?"

"Myself."

"Do you?"

All was quiet while Samadhi thought.

"I see my reflection."

"Do you?"

The merchant thought again, then answered, "I see the reflection of my face."

"And who is this 'I' you speak of?"

This was getting more difficult. Again Samadhi hesitated before saying, "I am the one who sees the reflection." He hoped there would be no more questions and felt relieved when Medhas smiled broadly and resumed speaking.

"The supreme Self, the *atman*, is the witness of all things, the one that sees the reflection. This eternal subject is not different from the Devi's ultimate being—infinite, self-luminous consciousness. Shining in perfect wholeness beyond time and space, name and form, cause and effect, this highest awareness is called *prakasha*.

"Then again, the radiant prakasha views itself reflected in the mirror of its own pure consciousness as *vimarsha*, its own power of reflective awareness. The pure consciousness of the eternal witness—Self turned upon its own reflection produces the Devi's own sense of 'I.'

"I used the mirror to make this point, but it is not entirely accurate, and I shall tell you why. Your physical form, reflected in the mirror, is an object external to the mirror. In the case of prakasha and vimarsha, there can be no object outside the mirror of pure consciousness. Rather, it is the One alone that reflects itself, appears as the reflection, and perceives the reflection. *Everything exists in the Self-existent*. In its vimarsha aspect, consciousness contains the seeds of the universe, which is in reality the Devi's cosmic body.

"When you, Samadhi, think of yourself as body, senses, mind, intellect, or ego, you mistake yourself for all manner of objectified forms. Because you perceive your body, it is an object. So are your senses, your mind, even your sense of ego. All these are objects of perception and not the perceiver. Do you not you see? Your whole sense of self is nothing more than an objectified reflection; in truth you are the eternal witness."

Samadhi looked down at his body, touched his right hand to his left forearm, then raised his hand to his cheek. In the intense silence he barely seemed to breathe. His mouth opened slowly, then froze, wordless. Looking up, he met the guru's gaze eye to eye.

"I think you're saying," Samadhi faltered, "that I'm suffering from a case of mistaken identity?"

"That is exactly what I am saying!" Medhas answered confidently. "As I said, the ego sense arises from ignorance of our true nature. It is no secret how we identify ourselves with external things. You once thought that material possessions and the people in your life gave you a sense of who you are. That is a lesson you learned the painful way when your wife and greedy sons seized your wealth and cast you out. In spite of those losses your sense of selfhood remained, however miserable you felt." Not waiting for a comment, Medhas pressed on. "Further, the story of Nishumbha taught you the futility of identifying with limiting adjuncts, such as body, senses, and mind. You can no longer take it for granted that you are those. They, too, are as external to the Self as your lost wealth.

"Why do you grieve, Samadhi? You are not a mere merchant, cast out by your family! You are neither the body, the senses, nor the mind. When you fall asleep, you lose all awareness of the body, but have you ceased to be? In your dreams you continue to live within the mind, but when you fall into deeper, dreamless sleep, you lose all awareness of the mind, too. Yet you do not cease to be, do you? What happens when you awaken from dreamless sleep?" This time Medhas waited for an answer.

"I feel refreshed and think how well I must have slept."

"And while you were sleeping, were you thinking this?"

"No." Samadhi murmured nervously, hoping there would be no more probing questions he felt unequal to answering. He added, "When I wake up from deep sleep and try to remember it, all I can think is that I knew nothing."

"Ah!" the guru exclaimed. "Body, senses, mind—all gone! Yet, 'I' remains—and the sense of knowing, even if it was knowing nothing!"

"So is enlightenment no more than the peace of deep sleep?" the merchant blurted out, at the same time thinking what a monumental letdown that would be.

"I was not speaking of enlightenment—not yet," Medhas said—a bit crisply, Samadhi thought. "You see, in deep sleep there still remains the final cloud of unknowing. Philosophers call this innermost veil the causal body. The reason that deep sleep is so peaceful is that the causal body is the state of awareness closest to the blissful Self. When you awaken from having experienced this, you naturally feel a sense of well-being.

"But only when the causal body, that final covering of ignorance, is dissolved, only then is the imperishable Self revealed. Atman, Brahman, prakasha—call it what you will—it is beyond all name. It lies beyond the threshold that neither speech nor mind can cross. Where wisdom becomes silence, there alone shines the inexpressible truth.

"There is no need to grieve, Samadhi. Your individual selfhood is only an illusion, bearing the impurity of limitation."

"Why do you say impurity?"

"Because the idea of limitation creates feelings of incompleteness and dissatisfaction, whereupon follow all desires and their attendant woes. Hear me: You are the supreme Self, beyond all sorrow. Your nature is pure being-consciousness-bliss, imperishable and ever free. *You are that*, Samadhi! Know you are that!"

King Suratha, feeling out of touch with what seemed to him too rarefied a discussion, tried to redirect the dialogue. A man of action, he was interested in knowing more about the Devi's conquest of Shumbha in practical terms.

Obligingly Medhas descended from the heights of his discourse and asked the disciples first to recall Shumbha's demonic companions. "What do you think they are, but the ego's projections," he began. He explained that from Shumbha comes Nishumbha. Sensing its own deficiency, the ego projects the sense of appropriation and attachment. Then the toadying servants Chanda and Munda come along and flatter Shumbha with false praise of his dazzling wealth and power, even though those glories are not his at all, but stolen from the gods. Chanda and Munda are the ego's self-aggrandizing tendencies, which perpetuate one falsehood after another. They plant in Shumbha's mind the desire to possess the lovely Ambika's physical form. They stir up his lust and then drive on his crazed desire.

"Look at your own lives," Medhas exhorted. "Do you not see the same principles at work?"

He asked the disciples to think of Sugriva, the ego's capacity for deceit and hypocrisy, and of Dhumralochana, the willingness to resort to brute force.

"When it comes to having your own way, surely these same impulses are not entirely unknown to you, are they?" he queried. "Then there is Raktabija, insatiable desire that befouls the whole world with its presence. On a deeper level still, Raktabija is the mind's unruliness that allows no peace. Tell me you have not lived with such inner demons!"

Samadhi slowly, shyly, signaled an incipient question, which he tried to formulate even while he spoke. "Earlier the Devi told Shumbha that the goddesses who fought alongside her were projections of her own power."

"Yes."

"And now you tell us that the asuras are Shumbha's projections."

"That is so."

"Then am I right to think that in some way the Devi and Shumbha are alike?" Samadhi phrased this with trepidation, as if the possible implications of what he asked might prove deeply troubling.

"Not at all," Medhas corrected. "You are confused. You must remember that *everything* in the universe is the Mother's projection—even Shumbha. And he is only a small wave of finite awareness, whose rippling in the form of his attendant demons symbolizes all manner of human weakness and evil. Those demons, his projections, are nothing more than the further fragmentations of something that is already partial and imperfect—Shumbha himself. In them we recognize our own faults and failings. But in the Devi we recognize our own ultimate perfection."

"How do we reach that perfection?" Samadhi asked, his heart beating faster.

"As I have said many times before, everything emanates from the Mother, who is the ultimate perfection. Now, to reach that is simply a matter of retracing the steps of creation, of making an inner journey back to the source."

"But how?"

The seer beamed, regarding first the merchant, then the king. "Eventually I will instruct each of you in what to do."

"Must we engage in battle, as in these stories?" Samadhi asked. He hoped not, thinking of his own peaceful nature. The idea of a fight was inherently disagreeable.

"Of course there will be struggles," Medhas began softly. "That is the nature of life in the world, but what are these tales of bloody combat with the demons really about? Something very simple. At every moment spiritual practice is a matter of making the right choices and the right effort. In that way the asuras are defeated one by one.

"But for now, let us consider the Devi's final battle with Shumbha."

The king posed a question regarding strategy. "At this point is Shumbha still fighting to possess the Devi or to destroy her, or is she fighting to destroy him?"

"I think it hardly matters," Medhas replied matter-of-factly. "It is no longer a question of either one or the other. It is a matter of going beyond duality. That is why the battle takes place in midair—to symbolize a state above the realm of ordinary, worldly awareness and beyond even the subtler inner experiences. 'To possess the Devi,' as you put it, here means to know the infinite Self. To attain that knowledge, Shumbha himself must be destroyed. Only by his own destruction is his attainment reached. A paradox? You might say so, until you remember that Shumbha represents the primal ignorance of ego. Believing he is a finite being, he cannot possess the infinite Devi any more than ignorance can reveal knowledge. Shumbha himself is the final obstacle to be removed."

"Then why did the battle return to earth at the end?" Suratha asked.

"A good question. Because the ego belongs by its very nature to the realm of duality and must be left there. What is finite can never enter the Infinite and still remain finite. Put another way, the knower of the Self becomes the Self."

Well, the king might enjoy a good fight, but I wouldn't, Samadhi thought, reflecting on his own very different nature. Medhas seemed to read the merchant's mind and said, "The story of the Devi's victory over the asuras, culminating in Shumbha's destruction, is presented in terms of battle, but really, what sort of a battle is it? I shall tell you a secret. The journey to Self-knowledge need not be a struggle. Granted, it requires discipline and constant mindfulness, but it should be joyful, because it allays our worldly suffering and reveals something new every day. *Sadhana*, spiritual practice, is an adventure. A struggle? Ask yourself, In the long run is it easier to remain in a pit crawling with scorpions and venomous snakes or to make the effort to climb out? Take your pick. Now apply that metaphor to your mental universe. Is it easier to practice mindfulness or to remain at the mercy of expectations and uncertainties, desires, attachments, and fears?"

If it were so simple, Samadhi thought, wasn't it strange that all people weren't pursuing such a path? The way Medhas put it, it seemed only common sense that they should.

Again the holy man smiled and continued, "All people are pursuing happiness and satisfaction, but most of them are looking in all the wrong places. Mahamaya, with her deluding power, casts even the wise into the whirlpool of attachment. When you two arrived here, was that not your frame of mind—grieving over your bitter disappointments, your betrayal and loss?

"Later, Samadhi, when you had that awful presentiment of your own mortality, your fear was all-consuming, but do you not see now that it was groundless? Your experience was actually a lesson in nonattachment—a blessing, even though you did not recognize it as such.

"Sometimes enlightenment is spoken of as the death of the ego, and certainly that is what we find in the story of Shumbha's destruction. But in reality, what is this death of the ego? Only the giving up of a lesser identity for a greater one. When one's own inmost Self and the Devi's essential being are recognized as one and the same, all distinction vanishes in the ultimate, nondual knowledge. So I ask you, what is the death of the ego? Only the melting away of a boundary, the dissolving of that final veil of unknowing."

The holy man, regarding Samadhi knowingly, added, "Now and then the Mother marks a bound soul as her own. From then on, it is all her grace."

While the king lingered inside the hut, carefully examining the carved box and the mirror it contained, Samadhi stepped outside and found to his delight that the storm had passed. A cool freshness renewed the air, and the merchant breathed deeply. In a way he had never felt before, everything was exactly as it should be. Nothing in his experience had ever produced a moment of such contentment, of utter perfection. In the golden light of late afternoon, a single bank of clouds floated far above like a celestial city. Samadhi marveled at the sight and then regarded the surrounding sky. Suddenly it, and it alone, claimed his attention. Its clarity and inconceivable vastness seemed to extend forever, far beyond the reach of his imagination.

From behind, he heard the guru say, "A sky such as this is a visible intimation of infinity. Our ancestors who first beheld such a sky took it as a glimpse of the Mother herself. They called her Aditi, the undivided one. Aditi is the oldest name we know her by. It speaks of unity and boundlessness, of endless expanse, and of infinity beyond the sky itself."

Samadhi gazed raptly on.

CHAPTER 17

NARAYANI

Several days passed before Suratha and Samadhi saw the guru again. Medhas, in his wisdom, had asked them to reflect on his teaching thus far. Over the course of many days and sometimes into the evening, his instruction had been intensive while he informed them through his vivid tales of the Devi and engaged them in dialogue, questioning and challenging them to find the answers within themselves. Now it was time for the seeds he had planted to take hold and be nurtured in the quiet of contemplation.

The two disciples, sometimes together and sometimes independently, spent their days recalling everything Medhas had said. To each of them the forest offered a place of solitude, where their days passed quietly.

Now and then they would meet and sit by the river to converse, their words flowing along with the tranquil murmur of the current. To all appearances it was an idyllic existence, yet the matters they spoke of sometimes belied that. True, the despondency they each felt had lifted, thanks to the holy man's wise counsel, and neither man despaired as before over his memories of betrayal and loss. Day by day the turmoil that once had confounded their minds, even amid the tranquility of the forest, faded in the growing light of understanding. Yet during this quiet interlude the king could not shake off a lingering restlessness that time and again impelled him to recount to Samadhi his last hours in the royal palace, when chaos threatened to engulf the capital. In the grip of terror he had wondered whether a member of his trusted inner circle might deliver the thrust of a dagger or bear a poisoned cup. Fearing desperately for his life, Suratha had taken an ignoble way out. He had mounted his horse and fled to the safety of the deep forest. More plainly put, he had run away.

Much later, reflecting on Medhas's teaching and his own inner stirrings, the king understood at last where his duty lay and committed himself to right action where he had failed before. But now he faced a new conflict. Though eager in his resolve, he knew he was not yet ready to leave the forest. Something was still missing.

A part of Samadhi found the king's story exhilarating, especially since the drama heightened with each retelling. Yet another part of him found the story wearying. The king seemed fired up by his noble cause, but what did his resolve mean for the merchant? For Samadhi the world held little attraction, and the thought of reclaiming his former existence, as the king suggested, was too disheartening to contemplate. He and the king spent hours in fruitless discussion of their respective futures, and in the end Samadhi would always sputter, "It's fine that you have a plan, but what am I supposed to do? Go back and be the ideal merchant? Do you think it's my dharma to keep on selling things? I appreciate—I admire—that you have to go back, and yes, in a sense I have to go back, too, but not to my former life. I have to go back to something before all my former lives. I want to return *there*, but I don't have the words to tell you what *there* is."

Because the king and the merchant no longer shared the misery that once united them, they were perplexed by their emerging differences. Just hours before they were to see Medhas again, they stayed awake long into the night, their unresolved conversation bouncing back and forth to the warm flicker of a single oil lamp that sent shadows dancing along the darkened walls of their hut. It was the conversation that wouldn't go away, and the next morning it resurfaced while Suratha and Samadhi trod the forest path on the way to see their guru.

"As I was saying," the king insisted, "I accept that you and I are very different."

Well, that's progress, the merchant thought, although he wisely refrained from saying so.

The king went on, "I need to do my duty in this world and at the same time to live devoted to the Mother, as Medhas says. I'm still not sure what you aspire to, my friend, nor do I always understand what Medhas means when he talks to you. It all sounds so abstract and elusive, even—I'm sorry—unappealing. There's nothing I can grasp, and your attempts to explain don't make things any clearer. I don't doubt that he speaks the truth—we both know from experience that he's a holy man—but what he tells me and what he's telling you aren't the same at all. At least, that's how I see it."

"I think you're right," his companion agreed. "You and I have entirely different temperaments. As you always say, you're a man of action. I'd rather think things out than act on my feelings. That's been my nature all along, more or less, and certainly more since coming here. We've both lived in the world, but now, let me tell you, I'm tired of the world. No, not just tired, but weary. I've had enough. What do I do, when all that I used to enjoy and cherish has lost its flavor? None of it matters any more. Don't take me for a pessimist, because it's not a sad state to be in, not really. The inner experiences you've heard me talk about have changed everything, maybe in ways you can't understand. There's much that I don't understand yet either, but believe me, I'm not the same person who came to this place any more than you are."

Suratha nodded his assent while Samadhi added, "Whatever we need to know, I expect our guru will reveal it when the time is right."

Coming to the clearing, the two men found Medhas seated outside his hut, enjoying the morning's freshness. He greeted them with an expansive smile and motioned for them to sit down. In the welcoming serenity of his presence, they expected he would ask about the intervening days, but with no such formality he simply resumed his tale from before.

AFTER THE DEVI HAD SLAIN SHUMBHA, the chief of the daityas; there was great rejoicing. The resplendent Agni led Indra and the other gods into the Devi's presence, and after bowing in reverence, they regarded her adoringly and raised their voices in praise:

O Devi, who remove the sufferings of those who take refuge in you, be gracious. Be gracious, mother of the entire world. Be gracious, ruler of all. Protect the universe, O Devi, who are the ruler of the moving and the unmoving.

You alone are the sustaining power of the world, for you abide in the form of the earth. By you, who exist in the form of water, all this universe prospers, O Devi of unsurpassable strength.

Of boundless might, you are Vishnu's power, the source of all, the supreme maya. Deluded, O Devi, is all this universe. In this world you alone, when pleased, are the cause of liberation.

All forms of knowledge are your aspects, O Devi, as are all women in the world. By you alone, the Mother, is this world filled. What praise can be sung to you who are beyond praise?

O Devi, who have become all things, who bestow enjoyment and liberation—when you are praised, what words, however excellent, can extol you?

Salutation be to you, Devi Narayani, who abide as intelligence in the hearts of all beings, granting heavenly reward and final liberation.

Salutation be to you, Narayani, who bring change as the moments of ever-passing time, who are the power at the cessation of the universe.

Salutation be to you, Narayani, who are the good of all good, the auspicious one; to you who accomplish every intent; to you, the refuge, the all-knowing, shining Gauri!

Salutation be to you, Narayani, who are the power of creation, sustenance, and destruction; who are eternal; who are the source and embodiment of the threefold energy.

Salutation be to you, Narayani, who are intent on rescuing the distressed and afflicted that take refuge in you; to you, O Devi, who remove the suffering of all.

Salutation be to you, Narayani, who assume the form of Brahmani, riding in a swan-yoked chariot, O Devi, and sprinkling sanctified water.

Salutation be to you, Narayani, who have the form of Maheshvari, bearing trident, moon, and serpent and riding a mighty bull.

Salutation be to you, Narayani, who have the form of Kaumari, the faultless one attended by peacock and cock and bearing a great spear.

Salutation be to you, Narayani, who have the form of Vaishnavi, holding the supreme weapons of conch, discus, mace, and bow. Be gracious!

Salutation be to you, Narayani, auspicious one, who have Vishnu's boarlike form, grasping a great, formidable discus and uplifting the earth with your tusks.

Salutation be to you, Narayani, who in the ferocious form of the man-lion are intent on killing the daityas and protecting the three worlds.

Salutation be to you, Narayani, who are adorned with diadem, great thunderbolt and thousand-eyed radiance; to you, O Aindri, who took the demon Vritra's life-breath!

Salutation be to you, Narayani, who in the form of Shivaduti, of frightful visage and piercing shrieks, slew the mighty demon army.

Salutation be to you, Narayani, whose mouth bares its terrifying teeth and whose neck is adorned with a garland of skulls; to you, O Chamunda, destroyer of Munda!

Salutation be to you, Narayani, who are good fortune, modesty, great knowledge, faith, prosperity, satisfaction to the ancestral spirits, constancy, the great night, and the great illusion.

Salutation be to you, Narayani, most excellent Sarasvati, who are intelligence and well-being, the divine consort and the dark one, ever constant. Be gracious, O you who are supreme!

O Devi, who exist in the form of all, who are the ruler of all, possessing all power, protect us from fears. O Devi Durga, salutation be to you!

May this gentle face of yours, adorned with three eyes, protect us in every way. O Katyayani, salutation be to you!

May your terrible, flaming trident, exceedingly sharp and destroying all asuras, protect us from dread. O Bhadrakali, salutation be to you!

May your bell that destroys the daityas' life force and fills the world with its ringing protect us from all evils, O Devi, even as a mother protects her children.

May your sword, smeared with the mire of asuras' blood and fat and blazing as the sun's rays, be for our welfare. O Chandika, we bow to you!

When pleased you destroy all afflictions, but when displeased you thwart all aspirations. No calamity befalls those who have taken refuge in you, and they who resort to you become a refuge to others.

O Devi, multiplying your own form into many, you have wrought destruction on the mighty asuras who hate righteousness. O Ambika, who else can accomplish that?

Who other than you abides in all forms of learning, in the sacred texts that are lights of understanding, in the primordial wisdom of the Vedas? Yet who else confounds this universe in the darkest abyss of attachment?

Where malevolent beings and venomous serpents lurk, where enemies and thieves abound, where forest conflagrations rage, there and even in midocean you stand and protect the universe.

O ruler of the universe, you protect the universe. You are the essence of all things, and you support all that is. All kings must praise you, O revered one, and those who bow to you in devotion become the refuge of all.

Be gracious, O Devi. Even as you have destroyed the asuras, protect us always from the fear of enemies. May you subdue the evils of all the worlds and great disasters born of ominous portents.

To those who bow down to you, be gracious, O Devi, who remove the afflictions of all and who are worthy of praise by the dwellers of the three worlds. Confer your boons upon the worlds.[4]

His recitation ended, Medhas said, "This hymn to Narayani sums up what I have taught you thus far about the Divine Mother, her universe, and yourselves. Because it is all-embracing, you will do well to commit its verses to memory and meditate on their meaning. Doing so will give you insight into the many matters you still ponder."

Before Samadhi could bring up the conversation that he and the king had been having repeatedly about their differences, the king said, "I'd like to ask about the name Narayani. What does it mean?"

Medhas smiled as a lover would smile recalling his beloved. "Narayani is the supreme Devi, the universal consciousness that inhabits all forms. She is the divine presence that permeates human beings, animals, and plants, indeed whatever lives. Beyond that she pervades all that is moving and unmoving—the flowing rivers, the sighing forests, the outstretched plains, the solid mountains, and above this earth the drifting clouds, the sky, and the vast heavens. Shining ever vibrant through the sun and moon and distant stars, Narayani pervades everything as consciousness." Medhas stopped, only for an instant, then added, "That is one meaning of the name."

The remark hinted that there was more to come, and when the disciples looked on expectantly, the holy man continued. "The first part of the name, *nara*, means 'man' or 'human being.' The rest, *ayani*, means a going or a progression toward something. It signifies a path as well as a goal. So, Narayani is the one who leads all humanity to the ultimate goal, which is her own infinite being.

"I shall tell you more." Medhas repeated a verse from the hymn. "'All kings must praise you, O revered one, and those who bow to you in devotion become the refuge of all.'" His voice trailed off dramatically, then rose anew. "Tell me, Suratha, do you not see your duty?"

Like a bolt of lightning the question momentarily illuminated Suratha's mind. Earlier, when Medhas had first recited the hymn, the full import of this verse slipped by the king. How had he failed to recognize that it spoke directly to his life? The message, now as clear as could be, thundered through his mind in the profound quiet of true understanding. Silent thunder? An absurd description, yet there was no denying the reality of what impressed itself upon the king in that moment: he was to devote himself body, mind, and soul to the Divine Mother. In turn he would become a conduit through which her grace and compassion would flow to others. That was the purpose of his kingship—not personal ambition, not even righteous action, although that was indispensable, but service born of selfless love.

In the clarity of the moment, Suratha wondered how many other such moments had been lost on him through his past lack of mindfulness. He understood now that holiness was an ever-present reality to which he need only be attuned. It should have been so simple all along, but it had eluded him by its very simplicity. Now, unexpectedly and unforgettably, the Mother had revealed her power.

Watching, Samadhi recognized in the king's glowing stillness and in the guru's intense regard of him that something had happened. The silence thickened. Then, much to the merchant's surprise, Medhas steered the discourse in a whole new direction.

"Human life has four aims that give it meaning. So say the wise. We call these the *purusharthas*. They are dharma, *artha*, *kama*, and *moksha*. You know what dharma is—the fulfillment of moral duty. I place it first to guarantee that righteousness will be the guiding principle for all else that follows. Artha is economic activity, such as the pursuit of a livelihood and the acquisition of material comforts. Up to a point, that is a necessary part of human existence. Next, kama means the fulfillment of desires, and again if dharma comes first, then the desires that follow will be legitimate and non-harmful, spiritually speaking. These first three aims form a class by themselves and relate to life in the world. The fourth aim, moksha, is liberation from this world."

Samadhi's face brightened. "This has to do with what Suratha and I have been discussing these past days—the question of our differences. We recognize that your teaching isn't the same for both of us, and we need to know why."

"I am glad that you have found your way to this question," Medhas responded, not at all surprised. "Listen while I explain. King Suratha is a man of great virtue and growing devotion, yet his concerns remain of this world. His life is governed by the pursuits of dharma, artha, and kama. There is nothing wrong with that. You, Samadhi, have put those behind you, and in your growing dispassion your single remaining goal is moksha, liberation. You seek the supreme freedom, and nothing less will satisfy your yearning heart."

While the guru articulated the contrasting natures of the two disciples, each listened solemnly. Too solemnly, Medhas began to think, and so he cheerfully interjected another verse from the hymn to Narayani: "'O Devi, who have become all things, who bestow enjoyment and liberation—when you are praised, what words, however excellent, can extol you?'"

Their expressions remained unchanged.

"Do you not see?" he exclaimed. "She who has become all this, shining far and wide, she is Bhuktimuktipradayini—'she who bestows worldly enjoyment and liberation.' How wonderful this is!"

The disciples' gazes implored Medhas to elucidate what was so apparent to him but still lost on them.

"You see, Suratha," he began, "to you whose dharma for now is to remain in the world, the Mother grants *bhukti*, or worldly enjoyment. Because you are devoted to her, she will be ever gracious. She makes known her benevolence, saying: 'I bear the nectar of immortality. I support the creator of living beings, the protector of the universe, and the gracious lord of prosperity. I bestow wealth on those who prepare the sacrifices and offer the oblations with an attentive mind.'

"Do you know what it means to sacrifice with an attentive mind? It means to make your life holy through constant awareness of the divine presence, in unwavering devotion. In that state every action becomes an act of worship and connects you to the resplendent Mother, who supports the entire created order. Consequently you exult in the dazzling splendor of her creation.

"But that is not the whole story," Medhas cautioned, his face darkening. "Bhukti entails more than just enjoyment; it encompasses the whole range of human experience and carries an implicit warning for those who are wise enough to see. Here I have to bring in some philosophy. There are conditions woven into the fabric of the universe, some impurities in the creation. Just as you cannot make an ornament of pure gold, the Mother's creative consciousness must have some impurity—that is to say, limitation—in order to embody itself in form. Impurity is only limitation within the limitless.

"The Devi is infinite and absolute, beyond all qualities. Her creative power is the power of limitation, and it works in five different ways to negate her five perfections."

"Wait a minute!" Samadhi burst in, so fired up by his impending question that he failed to notice his rudeness. "How can she who is absolute and without qualities have five of anything? That makes no sense at all!"

Unfazed, the guru continued, "A very logical observation, and you are right to object. Of course the Absolute has no qualities. But we can think of the Absolute only from the standpoint of our own limitations. Do you follow?"

"I think so."

"We are limited in five basic ways; the supreme reality is unlimited in those same five ways. The Absolute is all-powerful, all-knowing, complete in itself, eternal, and omnipresent. Her creative power, her maya, is said to have five 'cloaks' that veil her five perfections when projecting this world and making our human existence possible.

"First, the Mother is all-powerful; we humans are not. Nothing is impossible for her, and she is free to do whatever she wants. Her action is pure, spontaneous, and unbound; it is called *kriya*. In contrast, our human action is binding; it is called karma.

"Second, the Mother is all-knowing—she is infinite consciousness. But her maya limits our ability to know. We humans do not know our own infinite nature, thinking instead that we are the body, the mind, the personality. All our knowledge of ourselves and the world is limited—incomplete, fragmentary, unreliable, and misleading.

"Third, the Mother is perfect fullness or self-satisfaction. But her maya hides that fullness from us. Instead, we experience division. We carry out our lives thinking of 'self' and 'other.' Not knowing our own wholeness, we seek satisfaction and fulfillment outside ourselves, always striving to fill the imagined void with enjoyments and possessions that in the end are never enough. You see, there is no joy in the finite; only in the Infinite is there true and abiding joy. And what is the Infinite? The One, beyond all division. When the impurity of division dissolves, one knows a feeling of oneness with all creation; this is universal love.

"Fourth, the Mother is eternal. We are not, because we are limited by maya's veil of time, which shrouds the boundless eternality of our true being and reduces it to the finitude of past, present, and future, in which we perceive ourselves as mortal beings that grow old and perish.

"And fifth, the Mother is present everywhere. We are not. We are enshrouded in maya's cloak of space. And more than that, we are restricted by the natural law of how things happen in a certain order. For example, in our life's journey we go from infancy to childhood to adolescence to adulthood to old age—in that order. We cannot skip a step or rearrange any of them at will. In the same way, all events in the universe unfold according to their own natural law, and to achieve anything in this world, we must go through all the necessary steps. Not so the Mother; she has absolute freedom."

"And here we are," Samadhi observed, "stuck."

"Well, not so fast, my friend," Medhas responded. "It is not so grim as you imagine. You see, this realm of limitation is the realm of bhukti—worldly enjoyment—as I was telling the king. But it is also the realm of duality, where opposites necessarily define each other. To reach for one is to embrace both. Where there is suffering, there is also enjoyment, and where there is enjoyment, there is also suffering. It cannot be otherwise.

"Moreover, nothing in this relative world is permanent." Medhas recited: "'Salutation be to you, Narayani, who bring change as the moments of ever-passing time, who are the power at the cessation of the universe.'" Now he addressed the king. "Embodied existence leaves you subject to the inescapable processes of birth, growth, maturation, decline, death, and rebirth. Even when the Mother grants heavenly reward, know that also to be impermanent. Because the causes that produce such a reward are finite, so too is the effect. Eventually one is reborn on earth to continue the journey.

"There were two travelers in the night, each far from home. One walked along a crooked road and carried a flaming torch. As he proceeded along the way, the torch lit up the immediate surroundings and revealed one thing after another that claimed his attention and caused him delight. And so he continued unhurriedly toward his home, which lay still unrevealed around some further bend in the road. How different was the other traveler, who was gladdened to see the light of home shining in the distance. The light was just enough to reveal the dim outline of the path lying directly ahead. In his eagerness to reach his destination, he let nothing along the way distract or detain him, for he knew that only at home would he find his true joy."

"Samadhi," the guru said, "you have been given a fleeting glimpse of your divine nature, and although the Mother immediately veiled it again, the impression remains in the form of the single-minded desire for *mukti*—liberation. Nothing in the three worlds can deter your yearning heart."

Anticipating what either disciple might ask next, Medhas continued, "To both of you I say this: It is not a question of whether bhukti or mukti is superior. And most emphatically, it is not a question of one path being right and another wrong. All ways are the Mother's, and that is all you need to keep in mind. The rest is futile chatter.

"To put it a slightly different way, let us consider the distinction between bhakti and *jnana*—devotion and knowledge. Suratha, you will live in the world as a devotee of the Mother in her personal form. As your love increases, you will be drawn ever nearer to her. What joy you will know! And you, Samadhi, are intent on attaining that ultimate knowledge where everything dissolves into absolute oneness. You too are a devotee, but devoted to the impersonal Devi. Your aim is mukti, the liberation that comes from the knowledge of the Devi as the ever-blissful Self. The way to this perfect freedom is to sever all attachments."

No sooner had he said this than the king interjected. "Wouldn't that mean a life of renunciation? How grim! I can't imagine denying the Mother's gracious bounty."

"That may be how you see it, Suratha," Medhas answered, "but this is not your path. *Renunciation* is your word, not mine, and you have it all wrong anyway. Because you still feel attracted to the enjoyments the Mother places before you, it is hard for you to imagine that someone else does not. For you renunciation means resisting or pushing away something desirable. Now tell me, when you are resisting something, where is your attention?"

The king kept silent, but Medhas exclaimed, "On the very object you are trying to resist! Is that freedom from bondage? Of course not! How absurd! What is the point in denying yourself something if it becomes all you can think of? That is not sadhana, but only a pathetic imitation! Nor can we say that liberation is gained through the mere force of will, because such a will only asserts its own desire—the very cause of bondage!" He exploded in laughter at the paradox.

Then, serenely, he explained, "Samadhi has already come to the proper attitude. Through his experiences he has grown dispassionate toward the things of the world. How can there be a question of denial when there is nothing to deny? When the sense of attraction has faded away, it is not a matter of resisting but of simply letting go. Samadhi can tell you: those very things that once delighted him have become like dried blossoms that crumble to dust.

"Renunciation? Use the word if you must, but define it as the conscious choice to direct the mind toward the Divine. You must understand, Suratha, the farther you travel toward the east, the farther away you are from the west. That is only natural. As Samadhi's mind withdraws from the outer world, it becomes ever more free to contemplate the joys of the spirit. When the Devi's essential nature is recognized as one's own true Self, all distinction of worshiped, worshiping, and worshiper vanishes in the ultimate perfection of nondual knowledge. That is supreme bliss.

"Now I shall tell both of you a secret," Medhas confided, leaning forward so that neither one would fail to catch the light in his eyes. "The more you love the Mother, the better you know her; the better you know her, the more you love her. In the end pure devotion and pure knowledge are one and the same.

"But until that realization dawns, there appears to be a difference. In devotion, a trace of ego, of separation, must remain so that the devotee can enjoy the relationship with the divine beloved. In knowledge, the ego melts away, and all sense of separation vanishes. There is complete union."

Smiling, he declared, "It is a difference of tasting honey or becoming honey. But remember, either one is sweet."

CHAPTER 18

LIGHT

"Yesterday," Medhas began when Suratha and Samadhi had taken their usual places, "just a few passages from the hymn to Narayani were enough to settle some unresolved questions. You caught a glimpse of its inner wisdom. This wonderful hymn is a summation of all the teachings that have gone before, but I tell you, in spiritual life there is no summation—only light and more light. As the capacity of your understanding grows, you will find new meanings in the same stories, hymns, and teachings. You will continually see things in a new light."

While he spoke, sunlight flooded the morning with its brilliance. It was not the ordinary brilliance of a beautiful day, but an expansive clarity more easily felt than defined.

"There are special times when the Mother reveals her auspicious beauty," Medhas observed. "Today is such a day. There is something in the air, joyous yet serene. I sense that you feel it too, and will be receptive to what I tell you now."

The disciples settled in contentedly. For now there was no place where they would rather be than at the guru's feet.

"As you recall," Medhas resumed, "after the Devi Durga destroyed all the asuras, the gods bowed to her in thanksgiving and sang their praise. Suratha, for you their hymn is an outpouring of devotion that gladdens your heart and quickens your love for the Mother's personal forms."

The king beamed.

"For you, Samadhi, the hymn celebrates the powers of consciousness, revealed in many different ways. You too are devoted to the Mother, but to her impersonal aspect beyond form. For you she is the sun of knowledge, the ever-blissful Self shining within. She is called the Self, because she is truly the essence of all things. She is being—not being this or that, but pure being in itself. That same being is pure consciousness, the underlying support of all forms of knowing. And she is pure bliss, the essence of all other joys.

"The asuras, whom she conquers, are the strife and impurities that agitate the mind and cause all manner of suffering. Opposed to them, the gods stand as the mind's sattvic qualities. Because of their purity, the gods can approach the Mother, and in her radiant presence they feel joy and elation. That describes your mood today, alive to the light of the beyond that shines through the creation. The purified mind beholds the Mother's glory, and the heart swells with ecstatic praise. For you, that is the essence of the hymn to Narayani."

Suddenly earnest, Medhas said, "We all live in the Mother whether we know it or not. The not knowing is the problem. You see, both knowledge and ignorance are her faces—one sought by the wise, one captivating the foolish. To the wise she is the light of lights, illuminating human awareness. Happy are they who knowingly abide in her presence. But to the foolish she is the dark enchantress, whose shroud of unknowing confounds and stupefies; to them she remains hidden. Cast into the delusion of samsara, they labor under the heavy dullness of attachment and burn with the pangs of desire. No lasting satisfaction comes to the unknowing, whose fleeting pleasures are ever doomed to fade into sorrow."

"Why should this be?" Samadhi asked hastily. "Shouldn't this world be a joyful place if we all live in the Mother?"

Medhas regarded the merchant almost accusingly, as if his teaching had fallen on deaf ears. Samadhi wished he could retract the question, but saving face was his best hope now. "Of course," he stuttered, "I forgot that you said 'whether we know it or not.' As long as we live in duality, we teeter between opposing potentials of happiness and misery, and because either is possible, both happen. As the world is made, our experience can be no other way, can it? Suffering is unavoidable; I understand that." He added, whining, "But why does the Mother create this world in the first place?"

"Why?" Medhas echoed thoughtfully. "After long years of pondering that very question, I shall give you my best answer. Why not?" His features softened, and he added, "It is all her divine sport. To the wise alone is given this secret: it is the Devi who binds and the Devi who sets free."

The guru planted his hands firmly on his knees and leaned back slightly. Closing his eyes, he drew a deep breath while a smile played on his lips. He spoke softly, lovingly. "Let us begin where the hymn begins. The gods' first utterance is, 'O Devi.' Think about how beautiful that is. Everything begins with the Devi. Do you know what *Devi* means?"

"Goddess," the king replied, even though the question was not meant for him.

"It really means 'the shining one,'" Medhas clarified. "Tell me, Samadhi, what is it that shines?"

"Light."

"Yes. And if it did not shine, what would it be?"

"It wouldn't be light."

"It would not. That is because the nature of light is to shine. The Devi is the light of consciousness; this light of consciousness is her very nature. Now when light shines, what does it do?"

"It illumines. It reveals."

"Excellent! The Devi is the power of pure illumination. She shining, everything shines. By her light alone all this appears. This is the truth.

"Next the gods beseech, 'O Devi, who remove the sufferings of those who take refuge in you, be gracious.' They remember the bitter experience of defeat and dispossession at the hands of the asuras and the powerlessness that followed. This describes the ordinary state of human consciousness, perceiving its own smallness and vulnerability. It is natural to seek relief from this afflicted, imperfect condition." Medhas paused to allow the disciples time to associate their own situation with the plight of the gods.

"The first step on the spiritual path," he resumed, "is to recognize that there is a problem. Next comes the glimmer of hope that something can be done about it. The gods declare that the Devi removes the suffering of those who take refuge in her. To take refuge is to turn the mind toward her.

"They pray, 'Be gracious, mother of the entire world.' Repeatedly they ask her to protect them from all evils, 'even as a mother protects her children.' To envision the Devi as Mother is to approach her in the most loving and trusting way possible. Think of a child, helpless and entirely dependent on its mother." Turning toward the king, Medhas said, "The child has unconditional trust, born of love. For you this personal image of the Mother inspires such trust. Know that love dispels all fear.

"Next the gods pray, 'Be gracious, ruler of all. Protect the universe, O Devi, who are the ruler of the moving and the unmoving.'" As soon as he had recited those words, the guru fell into a swoon as if inebriated by some heady meaning still unrevealed to the disciples.

"Samadhi," he whispered, "what Suratha envisions as the compassionate Mother, you revere as the awesome source and sustaining power of all existence. For you to take refuge in the Devi means to direct your awareness to the inner light of consciousness." The guru's face glowed, and he pressed on, "Ah! 'The ruler of the moving and the unmoving.' Do you know what that means?"

Samadhi didn't know, nor did the king. The holy man was speaking from too high a state for them to understand.

"The moving is the universe, which the Mother has set in motion. It is her Shakti, transformed and revealed through every name and form. The unmoving is the Absolute, the ground of all existence. The Mother rules over the relative and the Absolute. She is both, and she is beyond both. She transcends even that final distinction in her inconceivable oneness." Tears trickled down Medhas's cheeks. "She is the ultimate power, and beyond that purity of consciousness there can be nothing else."

While the guru sat enraptured, something stirred vaguely in Suratha's heart. At the same time a question formed in Samadhi's mind but remained unspoken. The silence was too sacred for either the king or the merchant to break.

When at last Medhas spoke, he said, "You are still wondering about devotion in distinction to knowledge. I ask you, is bhakti truly a dualistic attitude? Well, in the sense that there remains a slight distinction between the devotee and the deity, yes. But bhakti is also the link between the worshiper and the worshiped, and the goal of devotion is the union of lover and beloved. When two lovers are separated, think of the unbearable pangs of longing. When they are together, think of their joy. And when they unite, how inexpressible that joy becomes! You see, the ultimate goal of the *bhakta*, the devotee, is the attainment of oneness. That same eradication of duality is the goal of the *jnani*, the knower. The two methods differ, but in the end, it is all the same."

He added, "Samadhi, know that knowledge dispels all fear."

"You've mentioned fear twice now," the merchant observed, recalling what the guru said earlier to the king.

"Yes, and to return to the hymn, notice how the gods say, 'Even as you have destroyed the asuras, protect us always from the fear of enemies.' And again, 'Possessing all power, protect us from fears.' 'Protect us from dread.' 'Protect us in every way.' Even with no immediate threat to their well-being, the gods fear future unhappiness. Is that not how the mind works? Even in good times, there is the fear that well-being will not last. Then the world can appear fraught with danger. Do the gods not speak of it as a place 'where malevolent beings and venomous serpents lurk, where enemies and thieves abound, where forest conflagrations rage'? Now, if you spend your time worrying about all the disasters that could happen, where is your peace of mind?

"There are many different fears, or I should say, fear takes many forms. In the end, fear is something very basic that belongs to the delusion of separation, smallness, and lack that we call the ego. Picture your fears as Shumbha's companions—ugly, misshapen daityas swarming about in your mind, ever trying to assuage the sense of imperfection but never succeeding. Scorning the Devi's illuminating knowledge, they imprison themselves in the darkness of 'I, me, and mine.'

"But even that is her doing. The gods ask, 'Who else confounds this universe in the darkest abyss of attachment?' And to their own question they reply, 'O Devi of unsurpassable strength and boundless might, you are Vishnu's power, the source of all, the supreme maya.' Remember, manifestation is not separate from the light of consciousness, but only a dimming of it. The Mother's maya itself has two aspects. As avidyamaya it is the concealing power that reveals the manifold creation. And as—"

"I'm sorry to interrupt," the merchant broke in, "but you just said, 'the concealing power that reveals.' That sounds like nonsense to me."

"Ah!" Medhas laughed. "Thinking again, are you? One of the Mother's delicious paradoxes! Such oddities belong to the manifest realm, where her deluding power rules. They weave in and out of our thoughts, and now and then we take note. Let me finish what I started to say. From the standpoint of one who is enlightened, manifestation is not separate from the light of consciousness. The Mother's maya has two aspects. As avidyamaya it is the concealing power that reveals the manifold creation, even while veiling her true being. As vidyamaya it is her power to reveal her ultimate oneness.

"The Mother creates this world. That knowledge alone should be enough to overcome at least some fear of it. Nevertheless, fear arises for all the reasons I have already told you. Some fears are fleeting, and we barely notice them. Some vanish when threatening circumstances are removed. Other fears are more deeply ingrained but can be overcome by inquiry and resolve. All these are situational anxieties that come and go, but underlying them is the basic fear that everything is constantly changing. It is not so easily dismissed. When everything is in flux and the foundation of our fragile security is in constant danger of slipping away, human life seems to have no bearings. We are talking about *existential* fear.

"That's about time, isn't it?" the merchant asked.

"Very astute, Samadhi. The foolish cling to the ripeness of life. They despise their graying hair and lament the weight of years. A woman weeps for her fading beauty, a man mourns his lost vitality, while around them loved ones vanish one by one. What do the gods say about this? 'Salutation be to you, Narayani, who bring change as the moments of ever-passing time, who are the power at the cessation of the universe.'

"Even this is the Mother's doing. The Devi herself is the threefold power of time. She who gives birth at the beginning and nourishes in the middle is she who devours in the end. To the wise is given this secret: all this may perish, but she does not. She who devours remains—*between* the moments of ever-passing time. To those who know this secret, self-luminous eternity opens up. The wise fret not. Knowing her as the timeless one beyond all change, they overcome all fear." Joyfully Medhas added, "I shall remind you that one of the Devi's names—a very wonderful name—is Bhavabhayaharini, 'she who destroys the fear of worldly existence.'"

"In spite of what you say, which is beautiful," Samadhi broached, "I have one other fear that won't go away—the fear of my own doubt."

Unperturbed, Medhas looked at him with loving concern. "I am glad you are saying this. Let us consider what the gods say: 'All forms of knowledge are your aspects, O Devi, who have become all things, who abide as intelligence in the hearts of all beings.'

Samadhi didn't see what that had to do with his lingering doubt, not even remotely, and he rephrased the question. "How do I know that I'm not just kidding myself? How do I know if the spiritual experiences I've had—or that anyone else has had—are real? Couldn't they just be imagination?"

"Spoken like a true jnani!" Medhas clapped his hands. His enthusiasm was not the response Samadhi would have predicted, but then again, when had Medhas ever been predictable? "You are well along the path of inquiry, and not only that—you are honest, courageously so, and willing to confront what most deeply troubles you. Truthfulness is indispensable in the pursuit of truth." The guru seemed genuinely happy.

Then he made the sort of dramatic pause reserved for his most profound revelations. "Dear Samadhi," he said, "let me tell you something. The mind naturally manifests itself through thinking and produces what we call *vikalpas*, or thought constructs. Another meaning of vikalpa is imagination, the process of creating something mentally. Imagination is your creative power as an individual. It is often active, is it not?"

Indeed it was, Samadhi admitted.

"As I thought. Now, when the mind is directed inward upon itself, this same imagination plays an important part in what is called *bhavana*, creative contemplation. As such contemplation deepens into a state of undivided attention toward envisioning the spiritual reality, it becomes an intense yearning, you might say a passionate nostalgia of the soul for the source of its being. That source is the Mother. In much the same way, the Devi uses her own imagination, which we call her creative ideation, to give rise to the world. In either instance consciousness is being used to bring about a desired effect, be it the Mother's projection of the universe, or the individual's return to the source.

"So, my dear Samadhi, that which you fear may be autosuggestion is in fact the bringing of your consciousness into alignment with the Mother's. If she can imagine this inconceivably vast universe into existence, then your own imagining surely must count for something too. Your power of imagination may be only a dim reflection compared to the Mother's, *but it is not unreal*. The final proof is that in the end you will not be able to deny the truth of your own experience. What more can I say?"

There was nothing more he needed to say. At long last Samadhi's doubt vanished like mist consumed by sunlight.

Before Medhas had a chance to make his next point, the merchant spoke again. "You used the phrase 'passionate nostalgia of the soul.'"

"I said *nostalgia*, because this is a feeling of intense longing for something familiar. What could be closer to you and more familiar than your very own Self, obscured for so long by the veils of unknowing? The experience of enlightenment is the dawning of recognition. Nostalgia is surely a sign that what is to be known is the Self.

"When it comes to attaining this realization," Medhas said, shifting his emphasis, "we must talk about actual practice. The hymn to Narayani affords insight into various powers of the mind, which can be applied to that end. The gods extol the Devi with this: 'Multiplying your own form into many, you have wrought destruction on the mighty asuras who hate righteousness.' On one level the Devi's shaktis—the Seven Little Mothers along with Chamunda and Shivaduti—are goddesses that a devotee can revere. Endowed with form, they inspire our devotion. Yet they are also our own powers, or specific states of awareness, by which we can defeat the ignorance that the asuras represent. We have talked about those powers before, so I shall be brief this time and try not to repeat myself.

"Kaumari, the shakti of the beautiful young war god, presides over our inner conflicts. She is said to be faultless, because she is the power of the mind to challenge its own ignorance. Her presence is the very seed of spiritual awakening. I remember when the two of you first came to me in distress. You wanted to know how either of you, who should know better, could be so miserable and perplexed. Enough understanding was already there to recognize that there was something amiss with your thinking.

"Maheshvari destroys ignorance. As Lord Shiva's shakti, she rides on Nandi the bull, who symbolizes the dharma. In other words, the power of righteousness is to be the vehicle of your thoughts. How? More specifically, Nandi's four legs represent truth, purity, compassion, and generosity. Cultivate these virtues, these mental powers, at all times. They are essential to the spiritual quest and will take you in the right direction. Practice them unceasingly.

"At first there will be challenges—temptations that would have you turn your back on the dharma. Maybe telling a lie or ignoring a standard of purity, maybe failing to recognize another's need or acting selfishly. Here is where Varahi comes in. She is the power of restraint against all the undesirable impulses that would compromise your efforts."

"In other words," the king interjected, "we must resist evil."

"Not in the way you think," the guru replied. "There is a subtle difference between the words *resistance* and *restraint*. Previously when you brought up the matter of renunciation, we determined that when you resist something, your mind is engaged with that very thing you want to avoid. That is not where you want your attention to be," Medhas chuckled. "Shift your attention away from the object to be avoided and toward the awareness of withdrawing your mind. When the attention is on the mind itself, there is no other object. That is the true meaning of restraint.

"So far you still think of yourselves as mere human beings, but eventually the awareness will dawn that you are something more. Narasimhi—the Mother's half-lion, half-goddess form—reflects your newfound self-image as a physical *and* spiritual being. Do you remember how the toss of her mane scattered the constellations in the heavens? What a beautiful symbol of spiritual aspiration! Reach for the stars, and be resolved never to fall into complacency or lassitude."

"Don't the constellations have an influence over human destiny?" the king inquired, recalling the court astrologers who advised him on the ill-boding of stars.

"So it is believed," Medhas replied. "Thank you for mentioning this, because it brings to mind another meaning of the beautiful image of Narasimhi scattering the constellations. That image symbolizes the Mother's power to override human destiny. She, of course, presides over the law of cause and effect, because all powers are her powers, but her ultimate power transcends all such lesser expressions. In the end, her will alone is supreme."

The seer fell silent at the thought of the Devi's inconceivable grandeur, then said, "After the Mother has willed the universe into manifestation, Vaishnavi represents the power of maintenance. In her we live, and she is our support. We must strive for constant recollectedness of her divine presence, at all times and in all places. We must be established in her holiness.

"The spiritual quest is a constant striving for right understanding, and thousand-eyed Aindri, with her lightning bolt, is the illuminating power of knowledge. She is also the supreme sovereignty. Do you know what that is?" Medhas asked, regarding the king intently. "It is not power over others, but self-mastery. Mastery over the mind makes you autonomous, and Aindri's resplendent sovereignty is the complete freedom of the Devi's own state of being. Shining through our own limited awareness, this shakti awakens us to that possibility for ourselves.

"When the mind becomes established in constant awareness of the divine presence, it is likened to the beneficent Brahmani in her swan-yoked chariot. This vehicle is the power to discern the real from the apparent, the Self from the not-Self. Brahmani represents the mind in a purified state of dispassion. She vanquishes the asuras with the gentle act of sprinkling her holy water. In other words, your own inner purity has the power to dispel anything negative or harmful that might agitate the mind. You may think of Brahmani as gentle, but in her gentleness resides awesome strength."

"Speaking of strength," the merchant asked, "what about Shivaduti? She seems in a class by herself and overwhelmingly fierce."

Medhas gave the question a moment's thought. "She is the Mother's own shakti, the power of all powers—pure, raw power. She is so terrifying to the asuras, because she is the essence of what most threatens them. And not only the asuras. Look how she humbled even the great Lord Shiva! There is a practical message here."

The disciples' inquiring faces invited Medhas to elucidate. "Do you remember when Madhu and Kaitabha battled with Lord Vishnu and grew proud over their strength? In their foolishness they decided to grant him a boon, and the boon he asked was to kill them. That was the folly of their pride, born of Mahamaya's delusion. Later, when the Devi fought against the hosts of Shumbha and Nishumbha, she summoned the Seven Little Mothers. When they gathered around her, Shiva stepped to the center and said, 'Let the asuras quickly be slain for my satisfaction.' Why for *his* satisfaction? He was only an onlooker to the battles. His arrogance was born of delusion. You see, even a god is not immune to the Devi's deluding power. So the Devi, in her wisdom, sent Shiva as her messenger to the asuras in order to break his pride. The lesson for you is this: even a person of high spiritual attainment runs the risk of becoming proud, and this spiritual pride is a most terrible thing. You may think you have become holy and worthy of respect. Then Shivaduti, the Mother's most terrible shakti, appears. Her piercing shrieks will shatter your illusion of false holiness and humble you, for where there is pride there can never be true spiritual attainment, and certainly not enlightenment.

"And speaking of enlightenment, Chamunda is the bridge between relative and absolute consciousness. She destroys the vikalpas, the thought constructs that swarm about in ordinary, unruly human awareness like the demons born from the drops of Raktabija's blood. In ordinary consciousness thoughts arise in rapid succession—perceptions, memories, reasoning, imagination. In this uncontrolled state we become caught up in them and forget the underlying clarity of consciousness itself. Chamunda's gaping mouth with its terrifying teeth devours and swallows up all these vikalpas. Her power of concentrated awareness dissolves the mind into consciousness itself, into what we call the *nirvikalpa* state—an absolute transparency free of all thought.

"In its deepest interpretation the hymn to Narayani is about attaining this ultimate state of awareness through the Mother's grace," Medhas declared. "On the surface, the gods are celebrating the Devi's victory over the asuras. Know this to be the eradication from your own consciousness of everything harmful, agitating, or limiting. To succeed you need only take refuge in her. Make your life a constant act of worship and praise. Turn your mind inward toward the glory of the Self at all times. When the world is revealed in the light of the atman, everything becomes transfigured. How can there be suffering and fear? They dissolve in the radiance of Self-knowledge.

"Knowledge of the Self is not acquired, because the Self always *is*, and its very nature is knowledge. The Self shines eternally, and like the sun behind a passing cloud, it never ceases to shine. Enlightenment is purely a matter of removing the cloud of unknowing. Liberation is simply freedom from ignorance."

Medhas placed his hands on his knees and leaned slightly back. With eyes half closed and a smile lighting his face, he said, "What words of praise can be sung to her who is beyond all praise? The gods say, 'She is eternal, having the world as her form.' The Devi herself, and none other, has become all this, extending far and wide in the form of everything. Heaven, atmosphere, and earth shine with her glory. She is their essence and their sustaining power, the all-pervading Shakti. Feel her strength in the earth beneath you. Know her power in the dark, fragrant soil and the clear water, which together produce nourishment for all creatures.

The Mother is the wide world in whom all prosper. The universe is her cosmic body, born of her shining intelligence, and that intelligence abides in the hearts of all beings. All live in her and she in them, shining through every pair of eyes. To the wise alone is given this secret.

"On his wheel a potter places a lump of clay and fashions a shapely vessel. Yet what is the pot, but the selfsame clay in another form? What has changed? The Devi herself has become all things, all the forms of her creation. Yet what are they, if not she? What is bound and what is free?"

It was a dazzling vision that Medhas proclaimed, spoken by one who *knew*. For him the question was no question at all.

CHAPTER 19

The Promise

Samadhi's astonishment at Medhas's ecstatic revelation stayed undiminished into the following day. Although the merchant had no words for it, he sensed that his mind had broken through to a mode of understanding beyond the usual workings of logic. It was a bold entrance into a luminous realm that was both strange and strangely familiar, neither contradicting reason nor yielding to its constraints. Samadhi could not speak for his companion, King Suratha, but in his own mind no question remained that the holy man's teaching was true, and true in a way that would have been unimaginable only weeks before.

The king, though not sharing the merchant's altered understanding, shared his conviction. He too recognized that his life had changed, that he had changed. Nothing would ever be the same again for either of them.

No longer driven by discontent or despair, each man now tasted the thirst of the soul in his own way and vowed to follow whatever course the guru laid out for him. In view of what had happened in the forest retreat, what other choice was there?

On this fine morning the two made their customary greeting to the guru and sat down, eager as ever to hear his wisdom. Neither knew what to expect, for Medhas had surprised them time and again. This morning would be no different: after the sublime disclosures of recent days, the guru brought them firmly back to earth.

"Since arriving here," he announced, "you have heard me say many things that have changed your understanding. On occasion you have experienced a brief glimpse of something the Mother has chosen to reveal. Though such fleeting moments of grace are overwhelming, you must never believe that they are enough. It is useless to become complacent over what you have received. Instead, you must become established in steady practice. Today we shall talk about practicalities, but first I shall tell you of the Mother's promise.

"After the gods had sung her glories, the Devi Narayani most graciously responded, 'Well pleased am I, O hosts of gods, by your praise. Receive my promise that whenever virtue grows weak and afflictions rise up, I will appear and destroy your enemies. In every age I take form for the welfare of the world.'

"'In every age,'" Medhas emphasized. "That means always. Whenever the mind is beset by troubling thoughts, you need only recall the Mother. Whatever asura, whatever disturbance, stirs within you, that will she swiftly conquer. That is her promise."

"Can you tell us more?" the merchant prompted.

"Of course," the holy man said. "I have not yet finished my story."

> THE GLORIOUS DEVI FORETOLD of future times when she would appear, saying to the gods, "Eons from now, in the seventh age, I shall be born from the womb of Yashoda in the home of the cowherd Nanda. Dwelling there in the Vindhya mountains, I shall be known as Vindhyavasini. Then two great asuras, also named Shumbha and Nishumbha, will arise, and I shall conquer them.
>
> "When the sons of the demon Viprachitti once more throw the world into chaos, I shall reappear in a dreadful form and devour them. Thus my teeth, stained red with their blood, will resemble the seeds of a pomegranate, and I will be known in the world as Raktadantika.

"When no rain has fallen for a hundred years, I shall appear as the hundred-eyed Shatakshi and pour my tears upon the drought-stricken earth. I shall fill the rivers and cause the land to yield food. Then shall I be known as Shakambhari, bearing the bounty of crops from my own body. And after slaying a demon named Durgama, I shall be celebrated in all the world as none other than the great Durga.

"Again I shall take form as the dark blue Bhimadevi in the Himalayas and in this terrifying aspect, to protect the sages, I shall kill malevolent beings.

"Finally, to vanquish a demon named Aruna, I shall appear as a swarm of countless bees. Thus shall I be extolled in the world as Bhramari."

"What does any of that have to do with us?" Samadhi asked, failing to find much import in Medhas's strange narrative. He waited for the guru to disclose the meaning behind the myth.

"These stories are good for all time," Medhas began, "because they express eternal realities about the Devi and her activities in the world. Though one and eternal, the Mother is ever ready to reveal herself in countless ways according to the needs of the moment. That is her promise to the gods and humankind alike.

"Vindhyavasini is none other than Mahamaya, the great deluding power that brought Madhu and Kaitabha to ruin. She confounded them in order that good would prevail. Throughout time she intervenes in human affairs, not only in the mythic past. Five ages hence she will appear as Vindhyavasini to thwart a demon king named Kamsa and to insure the birth of Lord Vishnu in this world as a child named Krishna. Krishna will be a great manifestation of God in human form. But that is a story that has not yet been told. All you need to know is that this fierce, protective power we call Vindhyavasini is ever present.

"Shatakshi and Shakambhari are two separate names for one and the same divine power, the union of heaven and earth that sustains all existence. In and through the Devi alone do we live.

"As Durga, she destroys adversity and overcomes any 'rough going' you may encounter along your life's way. You cannot exist apart from her, because her presence saturates all existence. Be mindful of that.

"As Bhimadevi she is indeed terrifying, but to whom? To the malevolent beings who would do you harm. To the wise she is a reassuring, protective presence. And not only that—she reveals the higher knowledge. Bhimadevi appears in visions as a dark blue goddess with plump, nourishing breasts. She has fierce, glistening teeth. In her four hands she holds a drum to signify creative power, a drinking vessel brimming with the nectar of immortality, a glittering scimitar to cut away illusion, and a severed head to represent the slain ego."

"She sounds a lot like Kali to me," Samadhi observed.

Medhas welcomed the remark because of the point it prompted him to make. "You appear different from moment to moment depending on your mood, your activity, and your manner of dress. Even as your facial expressions, gestures, and poses constantly change, the Mother's self-expression takes on countless aspects, some only slightly different from one another, others greatly dissimilar. Because each of her forms broadens our understanding and reveals particular truths, each is to be revered and contemplated."

"Even Bhramari, the bee goddess?" Samadhi asked in wide-eyed astonishment. "You'll have to explain that one to me, because I have no idea what to think about her, or even why I should." The idea struck him as exceedingly bizarre.

"Even Bhramari." As he said her name, Medhas's face glowed ecstatically. "Glittering, she stands in an impregnable circle of light and holds in her hand a swarm of jewel-like, multicolored bees. She is creative passion, which in its highest expression is bhavana, that profound state of creative contemplation that draws you longingly, irresistibly toward spiritual perfection. Attain this state and you will know how wondrous is this Bhramari aspect of your own consciousness."

Once again Samadhi let the quiet wonder caress him. Even in the least likely places the Devi might suddenly, unexpectedly, reveal her miraculousness.

In a swoon, he heard Medhas take the discourse in a new direction. "You have heard all these teachings from one who is well-versed in sacred knowledge, who knows the truth through experience. That hearing, or *shravana*, is your initial exposure to spiritual knowledge. Shravana itself is a form of knowledge, but only mediate or indirect knowledge, because you are hearing about something from someone else. At first the teachings are little more than words.

"You must reflect on what you have heard. This reflection, or *manana*, brings your own mental action upon a teaching. You are not to accept a teaching at face value. If it is to mean anything, you must subject it to thought, reasoning, and questioning. Yes, even questioning. You are to engage in dialogue with the teacher."

Samadhi, emboldened, said, "That's exactly what we've been doing in our conversations, isn't it?"

"Yes! And through this reflection you test a teaching again and again from every possible angle until you are convinced that it is valid. In this way the mediate knowledge you have received is confirmed and becomes your very own. It reaches the intermediate stage, where it becomes something more than words.

"That is still not enough, though," the guru added excitedly. "There must follow intense meditation, or *nididhyasana*. Here you apply all your power of concentration to the teaching, profoundly and repeatedly, until the intermediate knowledge that you confirmed for yourself becomes immediate knowledge—direct realization."

Samadhi, who had been paying close attention, noted, "So, this practice you describe is all about achieving and then maintaining a certain state of awareness."

"Well put."

"Come to think of it," Samadhi added, "it could hardly be more obvious."

Medhas delighted in his disciple's blossoming wisdom. "We tend to overlook the obvious, do we not? More of Mahamaya's trickery." Growing pensive, he continued, "In the ordinary, embodied state, human awareness is scattered. Look at all the things that constantly clamor for our attention—bodily sensations, perceptions of the external world, the stored impressions and opinions they evoke, emotional reactions, and then the need to understand, to make decisions, and perhaps to act. Under the normal conditions of living, the human mind is rarely still. Do you see why this process of hearing, reflecting, and meditating is so important? Receive, consider, and make your own—there is nothing mysterious or magical about it, yet this practice opens up the way to true and abiding peace. It is so simple."

"In theory," Samadhi remarked.

"In practice, too, if that is what you truly want." Medhas gave this last declaration particular weight. "It only makes sense that before inner peace is possible, you have to make peace with the outer world. The journey to enlightenment begins on the surface, which is the place of greatest limitation. From there it progresses inward toward ever greater freedom."

Once again the merchant flashed that quizzical look that Medhas found so endearing.

"What is it this time?" he asked indulgently.

"You said that the material realm is the place of greatest limitation. What do you mean?"

With mock severity the guru demanded, "Where is your body?"

Samadhi winced. "Here. Right here."

"Where else is it?"

What an odd question, the merchant thought, but not the first of odd questions from the holy man. He replied, "Nowhere else. It's just here."

"Of course! Subject to the limitations of time and space! Your body is restricted to one place at a given moment. If you so choose, you can walk over there." The guru pointed across the clearing. "But you cannot be both here and there at once. And once you have arrived over there, you would still be in the 'now,' and what is 'now' here would have become 'then.'" Medhas tried to suppress a grin, thinking he had made his point rather well in an absurd sort of way. Clearing his throat, he declared, "You cannot move your body suddenly to a distant place or travel back and forth in time at will, because 'here and now' is the limitation of the physical body."

Next he asked, "Where is your mind?"

Samadhi, unsure how to answer, ventured, "Here?"

Medhas burst out laughing. "It is somewhat different with the mind. I can see your body sitting here, but how can I be sure where your mind is? Maybe over there, maybe back selling your textiles, maybe with your greedy wife and treacherous sons, maybe reliving a moment of your childhood, maybe wandering off into tomorrow—or at least how you imagine tomorrow will be."

Samadhi listened solemnly while Suratha barely managed to stifle his amusement.

"What I am saying," Medhas explained, ignoring the king, "is that the mind is not nearly so limited as the body. It has the freedom to travel through time and space in a way that the body does not.

"To return to my original point: in your normal, everyday existence you relate to the exterior world and interact with it. And so the question of your behavior is the place to begin your spiritual journey. Some days ago I outlined the two preliminary steps of yoga. I shall go over them again, this time in greater detail.

"First, there are five ethical precepts concerning your relations with the world: never cause harm to another, always hold fast to truthfulness, refrain from stealing, observe proper sexual conduct, abstain from grasping. These precepts are to be practiced in thought, word, and deed. In your speech and actions, they will help you to achieve peace with the surrounding world. Cultivated mentally, they will bring you inner peace.

"Although these practices require self-control, never think of them as grim, unpleasant tasks. Take noninjury, for example. Think of it as a positive virtue. I cannot imagine you raising your hand to strike anyone, because I know that you are a gentle soul. But what about your speech? Have you always refrained from verbal attacks and consistently restrained a sharp tongue?"

Samadhi shook his head sadly, confirming what Medhas already knew.

"Speak unkindly to no one and of no one, because even a harsh word can wound. Let this principle guide your speech."

"That's not always easy," the merchant countered, remembering some instances that would be best forgotten, but which were certainly gratifying at the time.

"It is *not* always easy," Medhas assured, "but with practice it becomes natural. And remember, even seemingly innocent gossip can bring harmful and horrible consequences." With a penetrating gaze he added, "That is still not enough. You must practice noninjury even in thought. Never entertain thoughts of ill will toward anyone, because those too are acts of violence, however subtle. Even supposing that such thoughts bring no visible harm to someone else, what do they do to *you*?"

"I understand that not injuring, not lying, and not stealing are virtues we should all live by," the merchant commented, "and I understand also that not stealing in thought means not even coveting what belongs to someone else. It's a bit subtler but still fairly obvious. But can you explain what you mean by proper sexual conduct?" The way he asked this clearly revealed his discomfort.

Medhas smiled benignly. "I already taught you the harmful effects of shame. Do you not remember? Now consider this: the Mother herself has assumed all forms in order to experience her creation through the embodied state. In the forms of your earthly mother and earthly father, she enacted the loving union that created the body you now occupy. Why should you feel any embarrassment?

"Without doubt, sex is a powerful force in human affairs, and that is precisely why right attitudes about it are so important. As I have said before, it can be a beautiful expression of intimacy between two people who love each other. It can lead to the creation of new life. Sex is a force to be respected, and because it plays such a vital role in society, there are rules concerning what is deemed proper and improper for each station in life. In some instances, sex is to be celebrated, but certainly not by a monk, who takes a vow of celibacy. And remember, sex misused always turns ugly, and that is why there are stern rules regarding exploitation, coercion, and salacious behavior. Be assured, there is no evil in sex—only in its misuse.

"What I am about to reveal," Medhas confided, "I do not want misunderstood. The sexual impulse and the spiritual impulse are one and the same force, only traveling in opposite directions. Can a river flow in two directions at once? No, and neither can your own stream of conscious thought. It is purely a matter of how you want to direct your awareness—toward the pleasurable sensations of the flesh or toward the indescribably greater joys of the spirit. It is a choice of being engrossed in the extreme limitation of matter for intense but fleeting pleasure or of expanding into the unfettered ecstasy of the Self."

Considering he had said all there was to say on the subject, Medhas moved on. "As for the fifth precept, I used the phrase 'abstain from grasping,' for lack of a better one, but it hardly describes the range of what I want to convey. This principle has to do with not taking hold of anything unnecessarily—anything that would lead to attachment or involvement. That is the basic idea, and it plays out in any number of ways, mentally as well as physically."

"So," the king queried, "if I own two garments and they are sufficient for my needs, I shouldn't go to my friend the merchant and buy ten or twenty more pieces of cloth just because that would make me feel good."

"On the material level, exactly," Medhas laughed, then quickly added, "I didn't mean to make a pun, of course; but seriously, take no more than you need, and use it well. Now, as a king, did you ever receive an emissary in your court who brought you a costly gift from someone who wanted to influence you or win your favor? Did you ever accept such a gift? Was it right to do so? Not according to this principle."

"Those things are done all the time," Suratha protested, a bit too defensively.

"That does not make them right. And I speak not only about matters of state but about any personal exchange, material or otherwise. If accepting a gift or, let us say, a compliment makes you beholden to the giver, that creates a bondage. You become obligated to do something in return, and if you fail to do so you have acted less than honestly. What does that do to *you*?"

"Does that mean we are never to accept the generosity of others?" the merchant asked.

"No, a gift given out of love or an act of selfless kindness should be accepted, because there are no strings attached. But other gifts or so-called acts of kindness must not be accepted unwittingly. You must always remain on guard not to take hold in thought, word, or deed of anything that could create a sense of bondage, obligation, compromise, or mental unrest.

"These ethical precepts will guide you in relating harmoniously to other people, other living creatures, material objects, and your own body—to everything in the objective world."

Medhas broached his second topic. "After you have taken care of the outer business, you need to establish the proper habits and attitudes concerning yourself. Again, there are five.

"First, maintain personal purity. Cleanliness of the body promotes health, well-being, and self-esteem. Watch carefully what you take into the mind through your eyes and ears, for that will color your view of the world. Seek the company of the holy and be sure to practice discernment when among the worldly-minded. Do not judge others, because when your mind is engaged with their faults, what is its own content?

"Second, be content. Cravings for possessions, prestige, power, or pleasure can only disrupt your inner calm and drive you on to profitless action. Look around and see how many people waste so much time and energy in utter foolishness.

"Third—and this is a related point—cultivate simplicity in your thoughts, speech, and actions. Again, look around and see how most people's lives are unnecessarily complicated. So much of their strife is of their own making. It does not have to be that way. If you keep company with the holy, as I have instructed, you will notice their simplicity and clarity of thought. That is a sure sign of closeness to the Divine.

"Fourth, study."

Medhas's deliberately aphoristic utterance provoked the king into recalling long hours spent with demanding tutors in the royal palace. In like manner Samadhi's thoughts traveled back to a humbler setting but to the equally tedious lessons of his schoolmasters.

Medhas feigned innocence. "Did I say something wrong?" Without giving either man a chance to reply, he asked astutely, "Tell me, Suratha, when you were learning to ride a horse, what was that like?"

"I had to practice to acquire the skill. It was intimidating at first—I was only a boy and the horse seemed gigantic—but soon I was riding confidently, and each lesson taught me something new. Looking back, I can say it was enjoyable."

"As your sadhana should be. Study is no more than putting body, mind, and heart to the task of developing skills. Observe the world and your own mind, and you will be surprised at what you learn. Teachers and lessons are everywhere, often where you would least expect to find them. Be open to the knowledge that abides wherever the Devi is present and remember that there is no place where she is not.

"Fifth, the secret to success is devotion. Apply yourself wholeheartedly to these practices and open your heart to the Mother. You cannot fail."

After this exhortation, Medhas smiled sweetly and reiterated, "Hear, reflect, and meditate."

A few moments later Samadhi broke the stillness. "How do we meditate?"

"I was just coming to that. After you have mastered the preliminaries of behavior and attitude, you may begin to sit for meditation—literally. Settle into a comfortable position with the spine held straight. Do this in a quiet place, free of distractions.

"Then, as you sit quietly, observe the breath flowing in and out. You will notice that as the breath grows calmer and calmer, so does the mind."

Medhas thought the merchant looked dubious, so he elaborated. "Did you ever notice that when you are vigorously active or feeling upset, your breathing becomes heavy and irregular? Something is at work here—a case of cause and effect. Agitation disrupts the breath. So, to reverse the process, by regulating the breath you can calm the mind.

"By now your eyes should be closed. You want to withdraw the mind from the objects of the senses. The senses naturally flow outward, because their function is to experience the phenomenal universe. In meditation you want to reverse that—to turn the power of awareness inward and disengage the mind from the outer world.

"Next, hold your attention on the object of meditation. This holding is called *dharana*. The object can be a divine form, such as one of the Mother's manifestations; a mantra, or sacred name; a divine quality; and so on. The point is not to let the attention wander. It *will*—and you will think your mind is as wild as the wind—but do not despair. Every time you become aware of the mind's waywardness, bring your attention gently back. You will have to do this countless times. Just as Raktabija's drops of blood engendered demons beyond number, the thoughts of the unchecked mind proliferate. And just as Chamunda slew the blood-begotten multitudes and finally defeated Raktabija himself, so will your developing power of concentration eventually prevail.

"When the mind is held unwavering, your thought becomes like the unbroken flow of oil poured from one vessel to another. We call this state *dhyana*, or true meditation. Everything that we have called meditation up until now has been only an attempt at meditation. Nevertheless, each stage is essential, and each blends smoothly and naturally into the next.

"When this flow of consciousness results in complete absorption, we call this ultimate stage *samadhi*."

"That's my name!" the merchant interjected with innocent surprise.

"Yes, and your name is the ideal you are to fulfill. Samadhi is the ultimate freedom of oneness with the Devi."

The king wondered if his own name meant something too, but hesitated to appear as guileless as the merchant. Then, recalling Medhas's teaching about modesty in the hearts of the high-born, he brushed aside his residual pride and queried, "Does my name have any spiritual significance?"

"Of course, Suratha. It means 'one whose conduct is beyond reproach.' And that is your ideal."

"And your name?" This time it was Samadhi who questioned the seer.

"Oh," Medhas said casually, "my name means 'insight.' And speaking of insight," he quickly added, "let us look again at the states of dharana, dhyana, and samadhi. A few days ago I told you that in manifesting the world, the Mother first divides her singular consciousness into subject-consciousness and object-consciousness and from that initial seed of duality, the manifold creation systematically emanates. To attain liberation or Self-knowledge you must retrace the steps of creation. In dharana, where you try to hold the mind to the object of contemplation, there is the duality of subject-consciousness, or knower, and object-consciousness, or that which is to be known. When dharana deepens into dhyana, the awareness of knower and known becomes connected by the knowing, which flows like an unbroken stream. Finally, when dhyana deepens into samadhi, the identification of knower and known is complete, and there is only indescribable oneness.

"I have given you a basic outline of spiritual practice. There are many details and techniques that I shall teach you individually. You will keep the teaching private, not even discussing it with each other, because talking about your practice will weaken its effectiveness."

Medhas summarized, "During these many days I have related the stories of how the Devi conquered the asuras. With singleness of mind, reflect on these stories, discover their hidden meanings, and make them your own. I have recited the four great hymns sung by the gods to the all-glorious Devi. Those verses have the power to remove impurities, to produce an auspicious state, and to draw the mind to her presence. The Mother promises that wherever her deeds are recalled with a concentrated mind and proclaimed and heard with devotion, there her presence is abiding. Remembered in distress, she removes fear from every heart. Remembered by the untroubled, she confers still greater serenity of mind. One who is established in her rises above the misfortunes of worldly existence.

"The Devi's victories in battle over the fierce throngs of asuras signify your own psychological and spiritual growth. Know that all her forms are the powers of your own consciousness, ready to conduct you to supreme well-being. Following the blessed way of the Mother, you will be free of all sorrow."

When Medhas said no more, Suratha and Samadhi thought of everything that had transpired since their arrival at the forest retreat. Each disciple traced his journey out of ignorance and suffering to this luminous moment. In the hushed quietude, each one sensed the unknown and indefinable promise that still lay ahead.

ॐ ऐं ॐ

CHAPTER 20

At the Riverbank

"Today I shall finish what I began these many days ago," Medhas declared when Suratha and Samadhi took their now customary places outside his hut. "You have heard of the Devi Durga's victories over multitudes of demons. She confounded the brutish Madhu and Kaitabha with her tamasic power and brought about their defeat. Through her rajasic glory she overcame the mighty Mahishasura and his demonic hordes. Projecting from her lovely sattvic form the full array of her shaktis, she battled the legions of Shumbha and Nishumbha and brought even those two great asuras to destruction. After slaying all the enemies of the gods and restoring the cosmic order, she promised to appear whenever afflictions should arise. Then, blessing the adoring gods, the glorious Devi vanished from sight."

Medhas directed his next words to the king. "Many days ago, from the depths of your despondency you asked me to tell you all there is to know about Mahamaya, who casts humankind into darkest delusion. Existing through all eternity, she brings forth the universe, she herself becoming all this and sustaining it. Then at the end of time, she, the great destroyer, dissolves the creation back into herself. It is she who ensnares us in her play of existence and she alone who sets us free. Such is the nature of her inscrutable play. Though eternal and without form, the Devi takes form again and again for the good of the world and for the delight of her devotees. To those who seek her, she graciously bestows the light of knowledge.

"Take refuge in her, great king, for she is the supreme sovereign. When praised and worshiped, she grants prosperity, good fortune, and all auspiciousness.

"And you, my dear Samadhi, take refuge in her also. To the pure-hearted she confers the supreme bliss of liberation."

Suddenly the holy man appeared altogether more serious than either disciple had ever seen him. "Hear now my final teachings to you. You will take them to heart. You will take them with you to a secluded place at the river's edge and practice without ceasing what I have taught. I have sown the seeds of realization. With your continuing practice, they will flower and bear fruit.

"I am the guru from whom you have heard the truth. Like a flame that is passed from one lamp to another, receive that light that it may illumine your heart. I am ready to grant you the formality of initiation. Henceforth you will be my disciples in the fullest sense. Now, go bathe in the river and put on new garments. Return here with offerings of flawless flowers, red and white. In private I will give each of you a mantra, a name of the Mother. You are to divulge this holy name to no one. The mantra is not different from the deity; it is her embodiment in sound, vibrating with her power. It is sacred. Cherish it in your heart, repeating it silently and unceasingly. Through this practice of *japa*, your mind will become established in divine awareness."

Suratha and Samadhi quickly departed. When they returned, Medhas led the king into the interior of his hut, to the shrine lit by oil lamps. After initiating the king, he did the same for the merchant.

When the guru spoke again, the two disciples listened with new intentness, impressed by the gravity of what had just transpired. Medhas said, "I have spoken of the power of the mantra and explained its use in meditation. Reaching a state of intense concentration is difficult at first, and you will find that ritual worship will be helpful."

Samadhi, ever curious, commented that as much as he had witnessed worship at household shrines and in temples, he had always wondered about the efficacy of ringing bells, waving lights, and offering flowers before an image.

The guru raised his eyebrows and replied, "Ritual worship, or *puja*, begins with external things. You gather flowers, make sandal paste, prepare food offerings, and assemble the necessary implements and items, but all the while you remember that you are performing these actions to please the Mother. All the while these outer actions will be drawing your mind inward toward your chosen deity. I assure you, this method of approaching the Divine has been perfected over a very long time. Of its efficacy you need have no doubt."

Medhas described meticulously every aspect of the ritual and revealed its inner meaning. He spoke of the worshiper's external and internal purification, of consecrating the place of worship, of performing mental worship within the lotus of the heart, and then of enacting it externally before the image with flowers, incense, fire, and libations. In the end, he stressed, even the fruits of worship were to be offered back to the Mother in a spirit of complete selflessness.

"You see, the true essence of worship is devotion—and much more, besides. In your day-to-day existence you experience the outer world through the five senses. Through puja the senses are sanctified and directed back to their source. That is the significance of the offerings. With practice you will understand that ritual bridges the outer world of matter and the inner world of spirit. Puja draws the mind toward divinity and after a while the external ritual may no longer be needed. At that stage you may engage in mental worship alone. Still later you may proceed directly to deep meditation. You see, this sadhana unfolds one step at a time. One who is unawakened beholds an image and supposes that it is nothing more. One who performs ritual by offering oblations into the sacrificial fire sees the deity in the fire. One who is given to contemplation sees the deity in his or her own heart. And one who knows the Self experiences divinity everywhere."

Lowering his voice, Medhas instructed the king, "Take note of what I say. When Mahishasura deposed the gods and seized their sovereignty, the Devi Durga's fiery splendor radiated from their bodies and reunited into her own incomparable form. Each god then stepped forward and presented to her the symbol of his special power and authority. Each one knew that his power was not his, but ultimately hers, for she is the sole power in the universe. Meditate on that scene and acknowledge that all powers are the Mother's and hers alone. Your own efforts are insufficient as long as you wrongly consider them yours. As a man of action, make self-surrender your highest duty to the Mother; as a man of wisdom, you will see that in self-surrender lies true empowerment. Surrender is not a passive act, but one of full-souled passion.

"Throw yourself into this passion of surrender. Worship her who dispels all fear, whose pure knowledge puts to flight the darkness overspreading the heart. Bring your mind to rest in the heart's luminous shrine, there in bliss at the Mother's feet. Meditate upon the faultless form of the all-conquering Durga, the slayer of ignorance, that all attainments may be yours."

After his ardent advice to Suratha, Medhas took Samadhi aside, out of range of the king's hearing, for the knowledge he wished to impart was for the merchant's ears alone.

"You have neither duty nor desire. She to whom the king is devoted as the victorious Durga is none other than the supreme Self—the source, essence, and goal of all beings. In the quiet of your heart, seek that which is ever at the core of your being. Shed the burden of 'I' and 'my,' of body and mind, perception, memory, and opinion. Shed all notions of name and form, time and space, cause and effect. Thinking you were bound, you were bound; but you were never bound. You *are* the infinite Self, the limitless perfection of pure consciousness, ever shining by its own light. Knowing that is liberation."

Medhas led Samadhi back to where the king was waiting and said, "Now that you have received my teaching, consider that it counts for little." The disciples had known the holy man to be provocative before, but this remark was shattering. What could it possibly mean?

"You have come a long way," Medhas declared. "When the two of you first approached me, you thought of yourselves as men of knowledge, though overcome by suffering. I demonstrated that what you understood by knowledge is the lower awareness of the ordinary world. I awakened you to the inkling of a higher knowledge beyond this world. Throughout these many days you have learned in one way or another that as the universal limiting principle of maya, the Devi projects the awareness of difference and plurality and conceals her ineffable oneness. She is Shakti, the veiling brilliance. But now and again she graciously lifts the veil. My teaching, although pointing the way to truth, still belongs to the realm of lower knowledge. The higher, divine knowledge is revealed in the experience of it alone and not by any other means. So, it is not my teaching that will ultimately matter, but the awakening of what is already within you.

"'To the Devi, who abides in all beings in the form of memory, salutation to her, salutation to her, salutation to her again and again.'" The verse Medhas chanted was already familiar to the disciples, but now he revealed it in a new light. "This memory is ultimately the remembrance of your own true nature. What more is there to say?"

Knowing it was his last chance before taking leave, Samadhi could not resist one more question. "How will we know if we're making progress?"

Medhas smiled and assured his two disciples that the signs of spiritual progress are joy, fearlessness, and constant recollectedness of the Divine. "Once you are established in that awareness, there will be no further questions. Now go!" he said and dismissed them lovingly.

After traveling some distance through the trackless wilds of the forest, Suratha and Samadhi arrived at the remote place along the riverbank that Medhas had described. There in the dense shade of a kadamba tree, under its canopy of shiny dark leaves and fragrant orange flowers, they would find little to distract them apart from the wandering of their own minds. After constructing a crude shelter, the disciples settled down to practice the disciplines that Medhas had taught them. They restrained their bodies through diet and fasting and allowed no impurity to enter their minds through the hunger of the senses. They set every faculty to the task of contemplation and immersed themselves day and night in thoughts of the Divine Mother.

Having created an earthen image of her, they devoted themselves steadfastly to worship and meditation and each morning recited a hymn that Medhas had taught them. They contemplated its every word, because by those very words the Mother had revealed herself to humankind:

> *I move through the gods of storm and light, through the gods of the heavens, through all the gods. I uphold the lords of day and night, the sovereign of the atmosphere, the god of fire, and the benevolent celestial guardians.*
>
> *I bear the nectar of immortality. I support the creator of living beings, the protector of the universe and the gracious lord of prosperity. I bestow wealth on those who prepare the sacrifices and offer the oblations with an attentive mind.*
>
> *I am the sovereign in whom all the auspicious gods are united. Shining with consciousness, I am foremost among those worthy of worship. The gods diffuse me in every direction, my presence abiding in many places and revealed in manifold ways.*
>
> *Through me alone all mortals live who see and breathe and hear what is said, not knowing that they abide in me. Hear me as I speak the truth to you.*
>
> *I myself proclaim this, which is pleasing to gods and men alike: I make mighty whomever I wish, I make him devout and open his eyes to right understanding.*
>
> *For the god who puts evil to flight, I draw the bow, that his arrow may strike down the hater of devotion; such is the fervor I stir within that man. Through heaven and earth I extend.*

At the summit of creation, I bring forth the heavens. My creative power flows from amid the waters of the infinite ocean. Thence I spread through all the worlds and touch yonder heaven with my vastness.

I breathe forth like the wind, setting all the worlds in motion. So great have I become in my splendor, shining far beyond heaven and earth.[5]

Three years passed and when Suratha and Samadhi rested in the profound quiet of true meditation, the resplendent Devi revealed herself and declared, "By your worship and austerities you have pleased me well. Whatever is your heart's fondest wish, receive that from me now."

The king, remembering his unfulfilled duty, spoke first. "In honor would I take back my kingdom from my enemies' control and rule justly as your servant throughout my life."

The Devi replied, "So shall it be. In a few days you will reclaim your earthly kingdom, and you will rule wisely and justly for many years. Because you cling to your identity and choose to remain faithful to the dharma and devoted to me, you will reap the rewards of your virtuous actions. After your death you will be reborn on earth to rule again as the lord of the eighth cosmic age. Then you will be called Savarni."

As the afternoon reached the moment of perfect fulfillment and the shadows lengthened in the golden sunlight, the auspicious Devi turned her face to the merchant and said, "Neither duty nor desire binds you, my child. What is the longing of your heart?"

"Gracious Mother," he whispered in words barely audible, "There is but one longing—for the supreme freedom beyond 'I' and 'mine.'"

The Devi replied, "You are bound only by the illusion of bondage, for bondage and liberation belong to the mind alone. See them dissolving now." Her words dissolved into thoughts and the thoughts into meaning beyond thought until everything Samadhi ever was or felt or knew expanded into the light of pure awareness. Samadhi became infinity.

It was all so familiar, so simple. Simple beyond words.

NOTES

1. Brahmastuti (Brahma's Hymn), Devimahatmya 1.73–87.
2. Shakradistuti (Hymn of Indra and the Other Gods), Devimahatmya 4.3–27.
3. Aparajitastuti (Hymn to the Invincible Goddess), Devimahatmya 5.9–82.
4. Narayanistuti (Hymn to Narayani), Devimahatmya 11.3–35.
5. Devisukta (Hymn of the Goddess), Rigveda 10.125.

Glossary

Aditi—one of the most ancient names of the Goddess, found in the Rigveda. It means "boundless" or "undivided," indicating that she is infinite consciousness, infinite freedom, and the inexhaustible source of the universe.

Adyashakti—consciousness as the primal power and supreme reality.

agami karma—karma that is literally "coming up," producing results quickly as a consequence of actions performed in this lifetime, even recently.

Agni—the Vedic god of fire, who acts as the mediator between humans and the gods by conveying sacrifices through his consuming flames.

ahamkara—the ego, the consciousness of individuality which claims perceptions, emotions, and acts of will as its own.

Aindri—Indra's shakti and one of the Seven Little Mothers (along with Brahmani, Maheshvari, Kaumari, Vaishnavi, Varahi, and Narasimhi). She symbolizes sovereignty and the illuminating power of knowledge.

Ambika—an affectionate name for the Devi, meaning "Mother."

Andhaka—a demon killed by Durga. He represents moral blindness.

anuttara—"beyond which there is nothing else," a Tantric term for the ultimate reality.

Aparajita—"the unconquered," a name of the Devi symbolizing her invincibility. She is praised in the third hymn of the Devimahatmya as consciousness abiding in various forms in all beings.

Aranyani—the gentle, elusive forest goddess and protector of wild things.

artha—aim, purpose, or meaning. As one of the four purusharthas or aims of human life, artha is the pursuit of economic security.

Aruna—a demon conquered by Bhramari, the Devi in her bee-form.

ashanti—restlessness, anxiety; the opposite of *shanti*.

ashrama—as used in this book, a place of spiritual retreat.

asura—a demon. In Hindu mythology the struggle between good and evil is often cast as an allegorical war between gods and demons, who symbolize the opposing tendencies within human consciousness.

atman—the true Self, identical with the infinite Brahman, as distinct from the finite self or ego.

avaranashakti—the divine power of self-concealment; the veiling power of ignorance that conceals the boundless unity of absolute consciousness.

avatara—the "descent" or earthly incarnation of a deity.

avidya—ignorance, nescience; the inability to recognize the unity pervading all existence.

avidyamaya—the aspect of maya that binds the soul to worldly existence by producing entangling passions such as anger and greed.

Bhadrakali—a benevolent aspect of Kali.

bhakta—a devotee; one who cultivates love as a spiritual path.

bhakti—devotion; pure love for one's chosen form of the Divine, usually a particular god or goddess.

Bhavabhayaharini—a name of the Divine Mother, meaning "she who removes the fear of worldly existence."

bhavana—a state of creative contemplation that draws the meditator longingly and irresistibly toward spiritual perfection.

Bhimadevi—a particularly terrifying, dark blue form of the Devi. She destroys evildoers but is extremely protective toward the virtuous.

Bhramari—the Devi in her bee-form, representing creative passion.

bhukti—worldly enjoyment or, more broadly, worldly experience.

Bhuktimuktipradayini—an epithet of the Devi, meaning "she who bestows worldly enjoyment and spiritual liberation."

bindu—concentrated shakti as the point of potentiality from which the material universe emanates at the time of creation and into which it collapses at the time of cosmic dissolution.

Brahma—the creator god. He is the first in a triad with Vishnu, the preserver, and Shiva, the dissolver. Together they represent the full range of divine power.

Brahman—the absolute and ultimate reality transcending time and space; pure, unitary being—consciousness-bliss.

brahmana—a member of the highest Hindu caste, which comprises priests and custodians of sacred knowledge.

Brahmani—Brahma's shakti and one of the Seven Little Mothers. She represents the purifying power of knowledge.

buddhi—intellect; the determinative faculty that categorizes and interprets and is responsible for reason and will. It is the highest manifestation of consciousness in the human being.

Chamunda—a fierce, emaciated form of Kali who slew the demons Chanda, Munda, and Raktabija. She represents the power of concentrated awareness and the awakening of spiritual consciousness that transports one across the divide of duality.

Chanda—together with Munda, one of the demon king Shumbha's flattering, scheming servants.

Chandika—"the violent, impetuous one," a frequently used name for the Divine Mother in her wrathful, evil-destroying aspect.

Chikshura—the general of Mahishasura's army of demons.

daitya—a demon. The term is used more or less interchangeably with *asura* and *danava*. All of them are the eternal enemies of the gods. The daityas take their name from their mother, Diti.

Dakshinakali—an auspicious, gentle form of Kali.

danava—a demon. The danavas are the sons of Danu.

Danu—the mother of a race of demons. Her name implies division and separation from spiritual wholeness.

deva—a god; literally a "shining one."

Devi—the supreme Goddess, who manifests in many forms and is known by many names. Among her principal forms are Durga, Kali, Lakshmi, and Sarasvati.

dharana—in yoga, a state of one-pointed concentration where the mind is held steadily on the object of meditation.

dharma—righteousness, virtue, morality, religious duty, truth, the order by which the universe is upheld.

Dhumralochana—the thuggish demon chieftain sent by Shumbha to abduct the Devi from her mountaintop abode.

dhyana—in yoga, a state of intense concentration in which the unbroken flow of consciousness is described as the pouring of oil from one vessel into another.

Diti—the dark opposite of Aditi and mother of a race of demons known as daityas. Her name implies cutting off, division, or restriction.

Durdhara—"the bearer of evil," a demon slain by Durga.

durga—literally "rough going"; spiritual adversity.

Durga—one of the most important aspects of the Great Goddess. Her name means "difficult of access" and suggests that she is an unassailable refuge for her devotees. Usually shown as ten-armed and riding on a lion, Durga is at once the fierce warrior goddess who destroys evil and the fiercely protective, infinitely compassionate mother who bestows her unconditional grace.

Durgama—a demon representing spiritual obstacles, whose destruction gave Durga her name.

Durmukha—the demon of defilement, killed by Durga.

Garuda—a fabulous eagle-like bird, the mount of Vishnu and his shakti, Vaishnavi.

Gauri—"the shining one," a name of the Devi in her gentle, benevolent aspect. She is also known as Parvati, Shiva's wife.

guna—one of the three universal energies: sattva, rajas, and tamas.

guru—a spiritual teacher.

Himalaya—the lord of mountains who gave Durga her lion.

Hiranyakashipu—a wrathful demon king and father of Prahlada, a youth devoted to Vishnu. To protect Prahlada, Vishnu appeared in his man-lion incarnation, Narasimha.

Indra—the king of the Vedic gods and lord of the atmosphere.

Ishvari—a name of the Divine Mother meaning "(female) sovereign." The term is often compounded, as in Maheshvari ("Great Sovereign"), the shakti of Shiva.

Jagadamba—a name of the Devi meaning "Mother of the World."

jagat—"that which moves," a common term for the world, which is the realm of activity.

japa—repetition of a divine name or mantra.

jnana—knowledge, especially spiritual knowledge; the direct experience of the transcendental Absolute.

jnanashakti—the power of knowledge by which divine consciousness plans the manifestation of the created universe.

Kaitabha—together with Madhu, one of two brutish demons overcome by Vishnu with the help of Mahamaya, who confounded them.

Kali—one of the most powerful and complex aspects of the Divine Mother, representing primal energy or the dynamic aspect of reality. Often associated with the terrifying power of death and the relentlessness of all-devouring time, Kali is also adored by her devotees as a loving mother.

kama—1. desire. 2. the pursuit of legitimate pleasure as one of the four purusharthas or aims of human life.

Kamsa—a tyrannical king and cousin of Krishna's mother, Devaki. He was foiled in his attempt to kill the newborn Krishna, because the Devi in the form of Vindhyavasini had taken the infant's place.

karma—1. any mental or physical act. 2. the collective consequences of one's actions in the present and previous lives. Karma determines an individual's character and operates as the law of cause and effect in the continuing cycle of birth, death, and rebirth.

Katyayani—a name of the Divine Mother, associating her with the Katyas, a venerated clan of Vedic sages.

Kaumari—the shakti of the war god Kumara, or Skanda. One of the Seven Little Mothers, she represents the power to challenge ignorance.

kirtana—devotional singing.

Krishna—an avatara of Vishnu and one of the most widely worshiped aspects of God in Hinduism.

kriya—the divine action by which the universe is created, following upon divine will and divine knowledge.

kriyamana karma—karma that is literally "being done" in the present moment and imbued with the power of choice.

kshatriya—a member of the caste of rulers and warriors, whose duty is to uphold the moral order.

Kubera—the Vedic god of wealth.

Kumara—Shiva's son and the god of war, depicted as a chaste and beautiful youth. He is also known as Skanda.

lakshmi—good fortune, prosperity, happiness, wealth, success, beauty, splendor.

Lakshmi—an auspicious aspect of the Divine Mother as the goddess of prosperity and good fortune. She is the consort of Vishnu.

lila—divine play. The concept of lila indicates the freedom, joy, and inexhaustible creativity that pervade and direct the life of the universe, which for the deity is pure sport.

Madhu—together with Kaitabha, one of the two brutish demons vanquished by Vishnu with Mahamaya's help.

Mahadevi—"Great Goddess," a name of the Divine Mother.

Mahamaya—a name of the Devi emphasizing her deluding power, which causes the one infinite consciousness to appear as the manifold universe.

Maheshvara—"Great Lord," a name of Shiva.

Maheshvari—Maheshvara's shakti and one of the Seven Little Mothers. She holds the powers of creation, preservation, and destruction within the eternal cycle of time.

Mahishasura—the buffalo demon who created chaos on a cosmic scale and was slain by Durga.

Mahishasuramardini—"the crusher of the buffalo demon," a name of Durga in her central role as the destroyer of ignorance.

mamatva—"my-ness," the ego's sense of attachment.

manana—the process of reflecting on spiritual teachings.

manas—mind in general; more specifically, the function of consciousness that receives and sorts sensory data.

mantra—a syllable, series of syllables, or verse that embodies divine power, used in ritual and meditation. A mantra given by a guru is a divine name to be repeated as a form of spiritual practice known as japa in order to purify the aspirant's consciousness.

maya—the veiling or deluding power of the Absolute, responsible for the appearance of the relative universe.

Medhas—the seer in the Devimahatmya who becomes the guru of King

Suratha and the merchant Samadhi and imparts to them the knowledge of the Divine Mother.

Meru—a sacred mountain at the center of the world.

moha—delusion; the loss of full and perfect consciousness that causes one to mistake appearance for reality.

moksha—liberation; a synonym for *mukti*.

mukti—release; final liberation from the limitations of body, mind, and worldly bondage through union with the divine reality.

Munda—together with Chanda, one of Shumbha's obsequious servants.

Nanda—the cowherd into whose family the Devi was born as Vindhyavasini. He became the foster father of Krishna.

Nandi—the sacred white bull who is Shiva's mount.

Narasimha—Vishnu's man-lion incarnation, who killed the demon Hiranyakashipu.

Narasimhi—Narasimha's shakti and one of the Seven Little Mothers. She is the fierce power that defends in the face of great evil.

Narayani—the aspect of the Divine Mother praised in the fourth hymn of the Devimahatmya. Her name means "the goal of humanity," and the hymn emphasizes her motherhood, sovereignty, and protective intervention in human affairs.

nididhyasana—meditative concentration on a spiritual teaching, which leads to direct, intuitive understanding.

nirvikalpa—"free of thought-constructs," a term used to describe the ultimate state of pure consciousness.

Nishumbha—the younger brother of the demon king Shumbha. He represents the ego's sense of attachment.

Parivarita—the demon of encircling gloom, an allegorical representation of depression or despondency.

pashu—a tethered animal as a symbol for the bound soul.

Prahlada—the virtuous son of the demon Hiranyakashipu, rescued from his father's wrath by Vishnu in his man-lion form, Narasimha.

prakasha—self-luminous consciousness, another term for the ultimate reality.

prakriti—primal nature or the material principle of the universe, existing as pure, undifferentiated, and unexpressed energy. When activated, prakriti differentiates into the three universal forces (gunas) known as sattva, rajas, and tamas.

pranam—an act of salutation.

prarabdha karma—karma that has already begun to produce results; already activated, it is responsible for the circumstances of one's present lifetime.

Prithivi—the earth, personified as a goddess in the Vedas.

puja—ritual worship. Puja can be simple or elaborate, and although devotional in tone, it is designed to connect the worshiper with the transcendental divine reality.

purushartha—one of the aims of human life. There are four: dharma (virtuous conduct), artha (economic pursuit), kama (legitimate pleasure), and moksha (spiritual liberation).

rajas—one of the three gunas or basic energies of the universe. Rajas is activity, manifesting as restlessness, impurity, urgency, and passion. It is symbolized by the color red.

Raktabija—"he whose seed is blood," a demon with an amazing replicative ability that symbolizes on one level the insatiability of desire and on a deeper level the mental activity that is so difficult to tame.

Raktadantika—a completely red manifestation of the Devi, who is both a fierce destroyer of evil and a beneficent protector of her devotees.

sadhana—spiritual practice; in Tantra, a prescribed path leading to liberation through ritual worship, mantra repetition, meditation, and other disciplines.

samadhi—total absorption in the object of meditation; the unity of consciousness that is the goal of yoga.

Samadhi—the dispossessed merchant in the Devimahatmya, so named because his eventual dispassion leads him, through the Divine Mother's grace, to liberation.

samsara—the ever-repeating cycle of birth, death, and rebirth.

sanchita karma—karma that is stored up but has not yet begun to produce results.

Sarasvati—the goddess of knowledge and creativity and the consort of Brahma. Originally a deified river, she is one of the most ancient Hindu goddesses, understood on a deeper level as the flow of consciousness itself.

sat-chit-ananda—"being-consciousness-bliss," an epithet attempting to describe the indescribable Brahman.

sattva—one of the three gunas or basic energies of the universe. Sattva is repose, manifesting as light, calmness, purity, goodness, and wisdom. It is symbolized by the color white.

Savarni—the ruler of the eighth world-age, yet to come. According to the Devimahatmya, King Suratha will be reborn as Savarni through the Divine Mother's grace.

Savitri—a name of the Divine Mother associated with purity and protection.

Shaiva—1. referring to the theistic tradition that regards Shiva as the supreme being. 2. a follower of the Shaiva religion.

Shakambhari—a very ancient manifestation of the Devi as the earth itself, who brings forth nourishing vegetation out of her own body.

Shakta—1. referring to the tradition that centers on the worship of Shakti, the supreme power and ultimate reality, conceptualized as the Divine Mother. 2. an adherent of the Shakta religion.

shakti—1. power, energy, ability. 2. the individual power of a god, usually represented as his female counterpart.

Shakti—the supreme being according to the Shakta tradition; consciousness in its dynamic, creative aspect, in distinction to Shiva, its changeless aspect as the ground of existence. Shiva and Shakti, seemingly different, are ultimately one—the inseparable unity of consciousness and its power. Shakti assumes all the forms in the universe and is worshiped as the Divine Mother in many manifestations, among them Kali and Durga.

shanti—peace.

Sharvani—the Devi as Shiva's consort in her destructive aspect, presiding over cosmic dissolution.

Shatakshi—"hundred-eyed," a manifestation of the Devi, also called Shakambhari.

Shesha—the seven-headed serpent on whom Vishnu rests, floating on the undifferentiated waters while the universe remains unmanifest.

Shiva—God in his aspect as dissolver. For the Shaivas, he is the supreme reality who embodies compassion and renunciation and grants the liberating knowledge of the individual's identity with the Absolute. For the Shaktas, he is ultimate consciousness, identical to Shakti, the energy of consciousness.

Shivaduti—"she whose messenger is Shiva." The Devi's own fierce shakti, so named because she sent Shiva as her messenger to deliver an ultimatum to Shumbha and Nishumbha.

Shmashanakali—the Kali of the cremation ground, who reduces all created things to ashes.

shravana—the hearing, or initial exposure, to spiritual teaching. It is to be followed by reflection (*manana*) and deep contemplation (*nididhyasana*).

Shri—a name of the Divine Mother, signifying radiance or splendor. An ancient Vedic goddess, Shri was later identified with Lakshmi.

Shumbha—the final demon slain by the Devi, symbolizing the human ego.

Shyama—"the black one," a name of Kali. Shyama is a benevolent aspect, worshiped in household shrines as the dispeller of fear and the granter of boons.

Simhavahini—a name of Durga meaning "she who rides upon a lion."

Skanda—Shiva's son and the god of war, also known as Kumara.

spanda—the inherent vibration of consciousness.

Sugriva—Shumbha's "fine-throated" messenger who delivered a proposal of marriage to the Devi.

sura—a god; the opposite of *asura*, a demon.

Suratha—the deposed king in the Devimahatmya who, together with the merchant Samadhi, becomes a disciple of the seer Medhas and receives wisdom through the Divine Mother's grace.

Surya—the Vedic sun god.

tamas—one of the three gunas or basic energies of the universe. Tamas is inertia, manifesting as darkness, heaviness, dullness, ignorance, error, and negativity. It is symbolized by the color black.

tambura—a musical instrument whose strings produce a steady drone.

Tamra—a demon representing oppression, slain by Durga.

tattva—a cosmic principle or stage of evolution in the manifestation of the universe. The tattvas include various aspects of mind and matter.

Tripurasundari—a name of the Divine Mother indicating that she is the infinite and eternal consciousness beyond the ordinary states of waking, dreaming, and sleep.

turiya—"the fourth"; transcendental consciousness beyond the three ordinary states of waking, dreaming, and sleep.

Udagra—a demon representing arrogance and ostentatious display, destroyed by Durga.

Uddhata—a cruel demon whom Durga bludgeoned to a pulp.

upadhi—limiting adjunct, association, attribute. It denotes any object, quality, or circumstance from which the ego forms a sense of personal identity.

Ushas—the Vedic goddess of the dawn.

Vaishnavi—the shakti of Vishnu and one of the Seven Little Mothers. She represents the powers inherent in his supreme form.

vaishya—a member of the mercantile and agricultural caste.

Varaha—the incarnation of Vishnu in the form of a boar.

Varahi—the shakti of Vishnu in his boar incarnation. One of the Seven Little Mothers, she is the power of conscious restraint.

Varuna—one of the most ancient Vedic gods, the omnipresent supreme deity. His name means "the all-encompassing one."

Vayu—the Vedic god of the wind.

Vedas—the oldest and most authoritative Hindu sacred texts. *Veda* means "knowledge," and it is the knowledge of the divine reality, experienced directly by ancient seers, that is recorded in the concluding portion of the Vedas, known as the Upanishads.

vidya—knowledge, often referring to spiritual knowledge and used interchangeably with *jnana*.

vidyamaya—that aspect of maya that leads toward knowledge and liberation, as opposed to *avidyamaya*, which produces the bondage of ego-consciousness.

vikalpa—a thought construct.

vikshepashakti—the projecting power of consciousness, which sends forth all the names and forms of the manifest universe.

vimarsha—the reflecting capacity of consciousness, which creates the supreme divinity's own sense of "I." Vimarsha is objective consciousness, in which *prakasha*, the pure subjective consciousness, is reflected.

Vindhyavasini—"she who dwells in the Vindhya Mountains," an aspect of the Devi identified with Mahamaya. In her ancient temple at Vindhyachal, along the bank of the Ganga, she is represented as a black, bird-headed goddess standing on a lion.

Vipracitti—the progenitor of a class of demons who threw the world into unrest.

Vishnu—God in his aspect as preserver. For members of the Vaishnava sect, he is the supreme god, who incarnates in every age as the guardian of dharma to deliver humanity from ignorance and evil. Rama and Krishna are his two most widely venerated avataras.

Vishnumaya—an epithet of the Devi identifying her as the supreme being's inscrutable power.

vishva—the universe in its totality.

Vrikshamadhyanivasini—"she who dwells in the midst of a tree," a very ancient form of the Devi whose representations go back 4500 years.

Vritra—a demon who withheld life-giving water from the earth until his strongholds, the clouds, were breached by Indra's thunderbolt. Shaktas attribute Vritra's defeat to Indra's shakti, Aindri.

vritti—activity, movement. In yoga, a vritti is a thought wave through which knowledge of the objective world becomes possible. Vrittis can be either positive thoughts that lead toward truth or restless, distracting, and negative thoughts that deepen ignorance and bondage.

Yama—the Vedic god of death.

Yashoda—the wife of the cowherd Nanda, Krishna's foster mother and the earthly mother of Vindhyavasini.

Guide to the Story

CHAPTER 1: King Suratha's arrival at the forest retreat—the merchant Samadhi's arrival—meeting the seer Medhas—Medhas's teaching: nothing in this world is as it seems to be

CHAPTER 2: Ashrama life and more teaching—the story of Madhu and Kaitabha, with Brahma's hymn—Medhas's discourse on nonduality, duality, and cosmic evolution

CHAPTER 3: Durga's appearance and the destruction of Mahishasura's forces—the king's response and Medhas's teaching about Durga

CHAPTER 4: Suratha's crisis

CHAPTER 5: Durga's victory over Mahishasura—the eight fetters—the king's humbling—the meaning of Mahishasura's defeat

CHAPTER 6: Indra's hymn and its meaning

CHAPTER 7: Conversation on karma: destiny or free will?—the king's further humbling

CHAPTER 8: Hymn to Aparajita—divine immanence—Suratha and Samadhi's experience of nature

CHAPTER 9: The divine presence in the natural and human world

CHAPTER 10: A magical evening and more teaching on divine immanence

CHAPTER 11: Monkey trapping—Samadhi's tale of dispossession and wandering

CHAPTER 12: Samadhi's awakening insight and doubt—Shumbha's attempt to win the Devi—truth and falsehood—continuing attempts to seize the Goddess—the story's meaning

CHAPTER 13: Kali's appearance on the battlefield—Kali's nature—the Seven Little Mothers—the powers of consciousness

CHAPTER 14: The demon Raktabija—going deep into the workings of the mind—Suratha's fear and Samadhi's shame

CHAPTER 15: Samadhi's intimation of mortality—the impermanence of the world—the slaying of Nishumbha—attachment and personal identity

CHAPTER 16: Medhas in ecstasy—the slaying of Shumbha—the death of ego and the self-luminosity of consciousness

CHAPTER 17: Suratha's and Samadhi's temperaments—Hymn to Narayani—the aims of life—liberation—knowledge versus devotion

CHAPTER 18: The light of consciousness—the powers of consciousness—Samadhi's doubt dispelled

CHAPTER 19: The disciples' sojourn nears its end—the Devi's prediction of future manifestations—further insights on the powers of consciousness—the eight limbs of yoga

CHAPTER 20: Initiation of the disciples—Medhas's final instructions—Suratha's and Samadhi's practice—the Devi's hymn—Suratha's attainment—Samadhi's enlightenment

Guide to the Teachings